The Career of JOHN COTTON:
Puritanism and the American Experience

THE CAREER OF
JOHN COTTON

*Puritanism
and the American Experience*

BY LARZER ZIFF

Princeton, New Jersey
Princeton University Press
1962

Copyright © 1962 by Princeton University Press

L. C. CARD 62-7415

ALL RIGHTS RESERVED

*

Printed in the United States of America
by Princeton University Press, Princeton, New Jersey

*

LARZER ZIFF, a native of Holyoke, Massachusetts, attended Middlebury College, and received his M.A. in English from the University of Chicago in 1950; he received his Ph.D., also from Chicago, in 1955. From 1952 to 1956 he lectured in Humanities at Chicago, and became Director of the Academic Program at University College of the University of Chicago. In 1956 he joined the Department of English at the University of California, Berkeley, where he is now an associate professor. He has edited and annotated various works of Thoreau, Franklin, and Hawthorne, as well as contributing to scholarly journals.

for LINDA ZIFF

⚔ PREFACE ⚕

Since 1702 when Cotton Mather began the series of lives of divines in his *Magnalia Christi Americana* with an essay canonizing his grandfather, John Cotton, no extended study of the career of that eminent New England pioneer has been published. While men of less note in his generation have received intelligent examination, Cotton, the acknowledged leader in the acknowledged leading class, has remained a relatively obscure figure. The reason for this condition may be located in the works of Moses Coit Tyler, who fixed in words what has come to be the conventional attitude toward John Cotton. When we open Cotton's books, Tyler said: "At once, the immensity of his contemporaneous influence becomes a riddle to us. In the writings of his great associates . . . at least some threads of immortal light, some lingering movements of a once glorious energy, some half-blurred foot-prints of a departed genius, may still be traced by us, after these two centuries. . . . The same can hardly be said of the writings of John Cotton. These are indeed clear and cogent in reasoning; the language is well enough; but that is all. There are almost no remarkable merits in thought or style. One wanders through these vast tracts and jungles of Puritanic discourse—exposition, exhortation, logic-chopping, theological hair-splitting—and is unrewarded by a single passage of eminent force or beauty."[1] While saying this, Tyler appreciated Cotton's importance in the young colony of Massachusetts Bay and characterized it thus: "He wielded with strong and brilliant mastership the fierce theocracy of New England. Laymen and clergymen alike recognized his supremacy, and rejoiced in it. He was the unmitred pope of a pope-hating commonwealth."[2]

[1] Moses Coit Tyler, *A History of American Literature* (New York, 1890), I, 215-16.
[2] *Ibid.*, p. 212.

[vii]

If we accept Tyler's assumptions, neither half of the paradox of John Cotton is escapable: he was a man of wide influence in his widely influential community, but he has left hardly a trace of the reasons for his stature. While other men may have enjoyed lesser reputations in their day, at least they seem at one point or another in their lives to have performed deeds or recorded ideas which have penetrated the wall of time, and they offer us meaningful contact with the shaping past. But John Cotton, for all his greatness, is immured in the seventeenth century.

The very riddle Tyler develops, however, is the main purpose for the following consideration of the career of John Cotton. The England of Elizabeth and the Stuarts defined John Cotton's course for him and the New England of Winthrop and Williams shaped it and, in turn, was shaped because his path led thither. So thoroughly was his progress the result of the immediate realities he perceived that, unlike many of his lesser contemporaries and some few of his greater ones, he clung to his time and receded into the past with it. To trace the course of his career, then, is to see his time afresh.

John Cotton will escape us again, however, if we neglect to examine seriously what he seriously believed, for the institutions and habits of his society were certainly the result of these beliefs. I therefore maintain a constant cross reference between the great events in which Cotton took part and the ideas of the nature of God and man which he held. Moreover, since he was an influential actor in important events—the migration to America, the Antinomian controversy, the toleration controversy, and others—I have again traced the circumstances of these familiar occurrences. This look at frequently reviewed events is justified by the insight Cotton's sense of their meaning gives us. What we look back upon as familiar is frequently novel when we look forward to it with the awareness of a participant. For example, abundant material exists for the study of the Antinomian controversy, but this material has been interpreted for us, in the main, by historians who regarded the theological basis and the theological terminology of the disputes as fortuitous matters. However valid or invalid their view may be, I have, nevertheless, in this matter as in others, attempted to see the situation from the outlook of John Cotton and to explain it by explaining the range of possibilities present to him. The limitations of my method are self-evident, but the merits will serve, I trust, to complement and supplement the more general histories of the period. No one is so well qualified to reveal what the American experience meant to the Puritan movement as John Cotton, provided we can appreciate the realities which caused him to articulate his perception in "logic-chopping" and "theological hair-splitting."

I have not, then, considered a documented life of John Cotton to be its own excuse for being, because the result, I fear, will be a further compounding of the riddle spelled out by Moses Coit Tyler. Therefore, although I give the life of John Cotton the most detailed attention it has yet received, I am reluctant to represent this work as a biography. Certain details which would appear in a documented life (such as his property holdings, the provisions of his will, or a specific meeting he had at a specific place with a specific person) are not included here, while more space than would be justified in a documented life is devoted to John Cotton's sense of the world in which he lived. If I may be somewhat nice about terms, I choose rather to characterize this study as one of the career of John Cotton, meaning the course his life ran, than of the life itself. That career, in turn, can best be summarized as a movement through Puritanism and the American experience, and I have, therefore, put these terms in the subtitle. I trust, nevertheless, that the parts of the sheer record of John Cotton's life which I have gathered together present an integrated unit, and I have been especially careful to fill in the details of his English career since they are not so familiar to students of the period as are the facts of his American career, facts which can be gathered from such well known sources as John Winthrop's *Journal*.

The core of this study is the considerable body of the works of John Cotton, and the interested reader is directed to the Bibliographical Note at the end for a discussion of the discrepancies between the dates of composition and the dates of publication of certain of them, together with a brief consideration of the sources not cited in the chapter notes.

ACKNOWLEDGMENTS

Whatever the shortcomings of the present work, I am confident that it is improved over earlier versions because of the advice given me by Professors Carl Bridenbaugh and Robert E. Streeter. Each read a different stage of the manuscript, and each worked manfully to tame the rhetoric and validate the scholarship. I am greatly indebted to them.

I have benefitted also from the advice and encouragement given by Dr. John E. Pomfret and Professors Walter Blair, James D. Hart, Robert McNulty, and Roy Harvey Pearce.

Grants from the trustees of the Henry E. Huntington Library and from President Clark Kerr of the University of California contributed time and facilities for the preparation of this work. I wish to thank them as well as to thank the staffs of the Henry E. Huntington Library, the Library of the Massachusetts Historical Society, and the Rare Book Room of the Boston Public Library.

ᶜᴿ CONTENTS ℘

The Career of JOHN COTTON:

Puritanism and the American Experience

CHAPTER ONE

EDUCATION FOR PURITANISM
(1584-1612)

RECUSANT AND PURITAN were confusing yet common terms in the vocabulary of the Elizabethan, terms which were defined daily in deeds as well as in words. They indicated the two extremes of opposition to the established church, and during the first quarter-century of Elizabeth's reign, that church was more easily characterized in terms of what it was not—neither Roman Catholic nor Puritan—than in terms of what it was.

A recusant was a Roman Catholic who refused to attend the services of the Church of England or conform with its laws in any way. John Cotton, born in Derby in December of 1584, was too young to understand the denotation of the word when he was three and one half years old, but his betters taught him the connotations in July of 1588, for in that month the Earl of Shrewsbury succeeded in his long effort to capture the famous Derbyshire recusant, John Fitzherbert. Acting on information supplied by Fitzherbert's son, Thomas, who was thereby guaranteed the estate of his criminal father, Shrewsbury paid a surprise visit to the family seat, Padley Hall, and took not only his prey but also two Catholic Priests, Nicholas Garlick and Robert Ludlam. In the Derby gaol, the priests found a third colleague, Richard Sympson, who, in awe of the law which declared all priests with a foreign ordination to be guilty of high treason, had promised to recant by attending the services of the established church. Buoyed by the presence of his fellow priests, however, Sympson changed his mind and decided to visit the gallows with them.

Consequently, on the twenty-fifth of July, the three priests were drawn on hurdles to the place of execution, and when

Sympson, the first in line, appeared to hesitate at the ladder, Garlick stepped before him, kissed the ladder, and was hanged first. The other two deaths followed quickly, Ludlam just having time to utter, *"Venite, benedicti Dei,"* before he was thrown from his perch to hang suspended. If little John Cotton missed the lesson at the place of execution in his native town, he had ample opportunity to learn it by playing in his neighborhood during the next few days, for the three bodies were drawn and quartered, and the heads and quarters set up on poles in various places throughout Derby.[1] Young Cotton's house was but a block in one direction from the market place and town hall, and but a block in another direction from the River Derwent. Market places and bridges were choice locations for such displays.

The term, Puritan, however, was more difficult for a growing boy to appreciate, for being one was not necessarily a capital crime—indeed, the last Archbishop, Edmund Grindal, was a Puritan—and a boy's parents hardly bothered to lower their voices when they identified one or another of their fellow townsmen as Puritans. Yet, on the other hand, Puritanism could bring loss of living, imprisonment, banishment, or death, so that the term, while a useful and used one, was complex and in need of a great deal of qualification.

John Cotton's education in the meaning of Puritanism proceeded together with his education in Latin and the skills which would gain a lad admittance to Cambridge. The son of a struggling lawyer whose scanty income suffered from his benevolent habit of settling differences outside of court, John was the second of four children. His sister Mary had been born fifteen months before him, and his brothers Roland and Thomas were, respectively, three and one half and nine

---

[1] William Page (ed.), *The Victoria History of the County of Derby* (London, 1907), II, 24-26; Richard Challoner, *Memoirs of Missionary Priests* (London, 1924), pp. 129-33.

and one half years younger than he.[2] When Thomas was born in May 1594, John had already completed nearly two years of schooling under the tutelage of Richard Johnson in the Derby Grammar School, which claimed a twelfth-century origin but had been refounded in 1554.[3] Master Johnson had received his A.B. and A.M. degrees from Trinity College, Cambridge,[4] and he prepared pupil Cotton not only for his university but for his college. The tutor was also an ordained priest in the established church, a usual position for a grammar school master, for the main end of university training was the production of a learned clergy, and, accordingly, the learned clergy were the best preparers of young men for the university.

The term Puritan may not have defined itself in so many words during the course of a curriculum which was conducted mainly in Latin and concerned principally with the authors who had the "very Roman eloquence joined with the wisdom."[5] But what school failed to supply in this respect, street, parish, and home provided fully. John's family were sober and orthodox members of St. Alkmund's Church, the fourth in size of Derby's five churches. Vicar Thomas Swetnam was an Oxford man who, although he conformed with the demands of the officials of his church, in all probability regarded the degree of reformation in that church as incomplete. His son, Joseph, was to go to Cambridge rather than Oxford, a sign, though far from a certain one, that the father's tendencies were reform; Joseph was later to become a prominent Presbyterian minister in Derby.[6] Joseph Swetnam's

[2] H. G. Somerby, "The Cotton Family," *The Heraldic Journal* (Boston, April 1868), No. XXII, 49-58.

[3] *Victoria Derby*, II, 208-23.

[4] John and J. A. Venn (eds.), *Alumni Cantabrigiensis* (Cambridge, 1922), Part I; II, 480, 530.

[5] Quoted from Strype in David Masson, *The Life of John Milton* (London, 1881), I, 76.

[6] A. G. Matthews, *Calamy Revised* (Oxford, 1934), p. 471.

son, Samuel, however, was to die fighting for the Royalists at the age of sixteen.[7] Presbyterian but Royalist, this was the pattern of what the more radical reformers of the future were to refer to as the old nonconformity.

Conformity, on the other hand, meant acceptance of the royal supremacy in matters ecclesiastical as well as civil, acceptance of all forms prescribed in the Book of Common Prayer, and acceptance of the Thirty-Nine Articles as in agreement with the Bible. The second point was the stickler for most dissenters. Ever since the Marian exiles had returned in 1558 to find a far more conservative protestantism than that which they had enjoyed under Edward, even though it was to the lukewarmness of the Edwardian variety that they attributed God's punitive permission of Mary, there had been agitation against the more "romish" of the rites of Elizabeth's church.[8] Kneeling at the sacrament, employing the ring in marriage, dressing the clergy in ceremonial robes, all smacked of antichrist. But the generation of reformers trained on the continent under Calvin, Beza, Bucer, and Zwingli tilted at these in vain. Elizabeth and her policy makers sensed that the objectionable rites were only the facade which the reformers wished to shatter in order to get to more important ground: the amelioration of ecclesiastical incomes through the eradication of plural livings and the machinery of simony which they believed to be inevitably connected with an episcopal system; the extirpation of the illiterate ministry; and the promoting of widespread preaching to a people whose opportunity to hear their ministry expound the word unbound by ritualistic formulas was severely limited. Once across this ground, the reformers, Elizabeth suspected, would attempt the inner sanctum of the establishment—the hierarchical system of bishops—in order to replace it with a synodical ministerial

[7] J. Charles Cox, *Notes on the Churches of Derbyshire* (Chesterfield, 1877), III, 112.

[8] M. M. Knappen, *Tudor Puritanism* (Chicago, 1939), pp. 103 ff.

organization. Consequently, the Queen defended the facade and the reformers shattered their lances. John Knox was refused readmission to the kingdom, and church officers like Edmund Grindal, Archbishop though he was for a brief period, were sequestered for refusing to maintain severe restrictions on the amount of preaching allowed.

The Puritans of John Cotton's boyhood were the heirs of these defeated reformers. As the establishment grew in strength, aided by time, the greatest of all allies to an institution based on tradition, so the reformers regrouped slowly after the death of the continentally trained generation. They no longer had the naive and relatively uniform platform of their predecessors but existed in every stage of disagreement with the establishment, from a simple reservation about vestures to complete opposition to government by bishops. The label Puritan could be applied to a man of even the palest tint of reform, as Bishop Hacket complained when he observed that even "the good Office of Preaching, perform'd often by a Bishop, was call'd Puritanism by some."[9] As a result, the term was nearly meaningless, for young John Cotton could hear of men deprived of their livings for being Puritan, yet observed that others equally Puritan—perhaps Vicar Swetnam of St. Alkmund's—did not suffer for their practice. He could hear that down at Cambridge they were weeding out the Puritans and blocking them from appointments to livings, while at the same time the Queen had allowed Sir Walter Mildmay to found the Puritan college called Emmanuel, and all the advanced lads in the Derby Grammar School had heard that plans were underway for another Puritan foundation, Sidney Sussex College.

What saved the term from total irresponsibility was the fact that its implication was always one of some degree of difference with the establishment and that that difference was always one of dissatisfaction with the insufficient extent

[9] John Hacket, *Scrinia Reserate* (London, 1693), II, 39.

of reform since Mary's day. To be sure, the namecalling was wildly meaningless at times; indeed, even Archbishop Whitgift with all his insistence on conformity was attempting to reform the irresponsible ordination of immature, ignorant, and unplaced persons and was himself open to the charge. Nevertheless, the citizen who felt all the more snug in his holdings when he fancied "menaces" outside could, after the defeat of the Armada, titillate himself with the prospect of a poorly defined and badly organized group of reformers who had to be kept down lest they unseat the hierarchy and set up chaos in its place. Every year brought greater numbers and better organization to this group so that by 1594, the year in which Whitgift's protégé, Richard Hooker, produced a long awaited philosophy for the establishment and bishops could look with satisfaction on an adult generation which had experienced no other church discipline than that which Hooker had so ably defended, there was also a fairly regular flow of illicit Puritan propaganda and a strengthening alliance between various nonconformists and the common law lawyers who were irked at the presumptions of the ecclesiastical courts.

Every man in Derby knew, for instance, that his Bishop, William Overton, had in recent years been saluted by the most illegal of all illegal Puritan propagandists, Martin Marprelate, as a famous dunce. Whereas Martin was here unfair, as he frequently was, nevertheless the Bishop was considered by many to have earned the title by association since he did seem to ordain ministers without much attention to their preparation for their offices, and he was an adept pluralist. Bishop Overton also saw to it that the amount of preaching in his diocese was as firmly restricted as his superiors demanded, and less than a fifth of the Derbyshire clergy were licensed to preach.[10]

[10] William Pierce (ed.), *The Marprelate Tracts* (London, 1911), p. 90, 156n-157n.

As John Cotton, twelve years of age in 1597, neared the end of his schooling under Schoolmaster Johnson and looked forward to Cambridge, the world he was about to enter loomed as the arena in which many of the stirring religious battles of his day were taking place. It was at the very Trinity which Cotton was about to enter that Archbishop Whitgift, then Master, had rehearsed the anti-Puritan role he was to play as primate and, in 1570, led the attack on Thomas Cartwright which resulted in the latter's being removed from the Lady Margaret Professorship of Divinity and going abroad. Cartwright, expounding the Book of Acts, had pointed out that "Peter's supremacie in this place [the first vicar of Christ] was no greater then is the speaker in the lower house or proclaimer in the convocation." With Peter thus comfortably located as a Presbyterian moderator, he went on to deduce that no prelates should exist save those with purely spiritual functions, that deacons should care for the poor, that church government should be in the hands of local presbyteries, that each parish should choose its own minister, and that no one should seek or receive church office at the hands of a bishop.[11] This was Cartwright's first attack in his long losing battle with the establishment, a battle which was to serve as an effective rallying point for the Puritans some decades later. But in 1570 they were too poorly formed to give their champion succour.

In 1595, two years before John Cotton arrived at Trinity, another Lady Margaret Professor of Divinity had come a cropper at Cambridge. Peter Baro had lectured in a "Lutheran" manner, casting grave doubt upon the doctrine of predestination as it was expounded by John Calvin. As zealous an opponent of Calvin's church polity as he was, Archbishop Whitgift was an equally ardent upholder of

<hr>

[11] A. F. Scott Pearson, *Thomas Cartwright and Elizabethan Puritanism* (Cambridge, 1925), p. 26; John Strype, *The Life and Acts of John Whitgift* (Oxford, 1822), II, 16-20.

Calvin's theology, and, together with Humphrey Tyndall, Master of Queen's, and William Whitaker, Master of St. John's, he made matters sufficiently uncomfortable to cause Baro to leave the University, and indicted William Barret, Baro's most outspoken adherent. Then, for good measure, the three churchmen adopted a number of resolutions strongly affirming the central position which the Calvinist theology enjoyed both in church and university, naming the set of propositions the Lambeth Articles.[12]

The year before Cotton's arrival at Trinity, Hugh Huddleston, a fellow at that college, had raised the old quibble against the Queen which all nonconformists were busily trying to forget had ever been initiated by John Knox, who, in his ire at Queen Mary a half century earlier, had failed to foresee the succession. "It is hereticall," said Fellow Huddleston, "or heresie for a woman to governe the state, for that weare to make the woman above the man." He was promptly committed to safe custody in Cambridge Castle.[13]

These were three of the many landmarks of modern Cambridge history by which the thirteen-year-old boy from Derby could locate himself as he entered upon his studies. The most immediately instructive was that offered by Professor Baro's experience, for it contributed a new dimension to the gathering definition of Puritanism. The boy learned that as vehement as the establishment was against the church polity of John Calvin, his Christian doctrine had so successfully filled the need for a systematic theology, a need created by the expulsion of the Catholics and the discounting of the works of Aquinas and the schoolmen, that it was accepted doctrine. Bishops as well as nonconformists were

[12] James B. Mullinger, *The University of Cambridge from the Royal Injunctions of 1535 to the Accession of Charles the First* (Cambridge, 1884), pp. 347 ff.

[13] James Heywood & Thomas Wright (eds.), *Cambridge University Transactions During the Puritan Controversies of the 16th and 17th Centuries* (London, 1854), II, 148-51.

Calvinists, and a man's doctrine was no accurate reflection of the degree of his conformity. This knowledge Cotton added to his growing stock of information on the various degrees of nonconformity. In matters of doctrine, all Puritans were Calvinists, but the proposition could not be converted.

The statutes of Cambridge in 1597 were such that any boy who upon entrance planned to continue through to his Bachelor of Divinity degree had to look forward to twelve years of connection with his university.[14] For the first four years, he would pursue the quadrennium of undergraduateship: first year, rhetoric; second and third, logic; fourth, philosophy. He carried on these studies through readings and conferences with his tutor in his college and attendance at lectures in the university. His proficiency was further measured by four set Latin disputations in which he had to take part, twice as a respondent and twice as an opponent.[15] The successful conclusion of this program was the Bachelor of Arts degree, and if the student wished to advance further he had now to enter upon the "triennium of bachelorship": further responsions and opponencies together now with a declamation; continued study in the subjects begun as an undergraduate; and mastery of Greek, Astronomy, and Perspective. Most of the young men who continued after completing their undergraduateship did so as fellows; at the turn of the century the interpretation of the statutes was loosening so that those bachelors who could not obtain fellowships and yet wanted to continue for their Master's were given some means of maintaining a tangential connection with the University in order to provide a show of the necessary residence while, in fact, they were employed elsewhere. Such an interpretation was not formalized until 1608, however,

[14] Masson, pp. 111 ff.
[15] Detailed accounts of the content and form of these disputations are to be found in William T. Costello, S.J., *The Scholastic Curriculum at Early Seventeenth-Century Cambridge* (Cambridge, 1958).

when residence after the Bachelor's Degree was declared optional.

John Cotton was one of the last students to continue under the old interpretation of the statutes; after taking his Master's in 1606 he then entered upon his "regency," continuing his university activities for another five years as he was sworn to do: now concentrating heavily on Hebrew, Theology, and disputation, and now permitted to preach in the University. When these five years were up he was free to leave the University, although the Bachelor of Divinity degree would not be granted until seven years after the Master's was taken, or, in other words, until two years after his final period of compulsory residence.

To certain sharp-minded contemporaries, such a curriculum seemed hopelessly old-fashioned and eminently unsuited to prepare a young Englishman to be of the greatest service to himself and society. Even as Drake circumnavigated the world, young Cambridge scholars were learning their geography from Strabo, Pliny, and Pomponius Mela. Mathematics was too mechanical an art to be taken seriously at the University and the scientific masters were Plato and Ptolemy.[16] Indeed, John Cotton's thoughts were always to reflect the obsolescence of a great part of his education. For example, he used a medieval psychology: "The mind of man, as Philosophers have observed, is somewhat assimilated into the nature of the Object which it studieth, and is conversant about: as Mariners who are conversant about winds, and seas, and storms are more boysterous. Shepherds and Herds-men more brutish, Forresters more wild, Butchers more bloody." His end in citing this particular bit of psychology was to caution against the study of natural science as one's principal object in life: "The study of these natural things," he said, "is not available to the attainment of true happiness; For how should that which is restlesse (and as *Solomons* word is;

_____
[16] Mullinger, p. 402.

full of labour) procure us setled rest and tranquillity which accompanieth true happinesse?"[17]

Although medieval lore and antique philosophy were interwoven in such assertions, nevertheless the Cambridge man of the early seventeenth century had an abortive sense of the need for objective proof as well as for authority in such matters, even if the authority were scripture. For example, this is the fashion in which Cotton refuted Copernicus: "If the earth moved swiftly, when a man throweth a stone, the same way the earth moveth, he might easily overtake the stone before it fell: or (it may be) standing still, the earth speedily moving forward would carry him so far, as to be under the stone when it should fall."[18] Although Ecclesiastes and the Psalms are the source of the anti-Copernican principle, observed data can be adduced to support it, and Cotton felt the need for adducing these data. Indeed, in the knotty matter of the origin of fresh water rivers he even abandoned his classical sources and speculated on his own with a bold mixture of reasons which tended at times to reject the valid in antique sources together with the invalid propositions which prompted his distrust of the ancients on physical matters. Fresh water, he asserted, comes from the sea:

"*Aristotles* reason to the contrary, that water coveteth to run to the lowest place: And if the water should have this vicissitude, of course from the Fountaines to the Sea, from the Sea to the Fountains; then the same place should be higher and lower then it selfe; will not hold. For some parts of the Sea are lower than the Fountaines, and into them the Fountaines send forth their streams to run; other parts of the Sea are as high, or higher then the Fountaines, especially in great storms, when the waves seem to ascend up to heaven, *Psalm* 107. 26. And they by secret channels another way send forth Springs of water to feed the Fountaines.

[17] John Cotton, *A Briefe Exposition with Practicall Observations upon the Whole Book of Ecclesiastes* (London, 1654), p. 13.
[18] *Ibid.*, p. 14.

[13]

"*Plato's Barathrum* in the hollow *Ca*verns of the earth, which he maketh to be the originall of Fountaines, is hence also refuted, unlesse he derive the supplying of that Barathrum from the Sea. . . .

"The earth, through which the Sea waters passe to the Fountaines, doth percolate and strain the Salt out of them; else, as the sea waters are salt, so would also the Fountaine waters be."[19]

This is one way in which the Cambridge of the first decade of the seventeenth century left her imprint on her sons. Bound to the a priori precepts of their ancient and medieval texts, they nevertheless felt the need for speculation and empirical verification. But, in the last analysis, the hold of the past was greater. John Cotton, for example, delivered his remarks on the relation of salt to fresh water to a community which was in great need of an efficient process of taking the salt from the sea so that the commodity would not have to be imported. But neither Cotton nor his colleagues ever extended their remarks into speculation on how this might be done. To clear the Book of Ecclesiastes of ambiguity he could border on the empirical, but true happiness was reserved for the man who then contemplated the eternal words of God rather than the man who allowed the natural world to impress its fluctuating character on him.

Cambridge University, in John Cotton's day, was not enlisted in the cause of scientific or learned research; it was the nursery of ministers, and criticisms of its lack of modernity were, for the majority of its members, singularly irrelevant. Moreover, as quaintly remote from the daily activities of life as its curriculum may have seemed, Cambridge had two great extracurricular lessons to teach John Cotton, and these formed a far greater determining influence on his character than did any of his scientific texts.

[19] *Ibid.*, p. 18.

The first lesson was political and was a continuing part of his awareness of nonconformity: its origins, degrees, and practical manipulation. The Master of Trinity was Thomas Neville, friend of Whitgift and loyal to the establishment, but Cambridge's colleges presented a veritable rainbow of theological hues filling the space within and glowing beyond the borders of the Church of England. At Pembroke Hall, Lancelot Andrewes, who had inspired the students with his lectures when he was catechist, had been Master since 1589, yet episcopalian though he was he consistently refused preferment under Elizabeth because the bishoprics offered him involved alienation of a portion of his income. Robert Goad presided over King's. He was so stout a Calvinist as to have taken the lead in opposing the doctrine of Baro, and he had tutored George Abbot during the future archbishop's brief flirtation with nonconformity. Robert Some, Master of Peterhouse, was also an assiduous Calvinist, who, when he was a fellow at Queen's, had taken the pulpit in defense of Cartwright, had been, nevertheless, made Master by the influence of Whitgift, and, notwithstanding, included Whitgift as a covert target in his attack on Barret and Baro. Humphrey Tyndall, President of Queen's, was a well known Puritan, quick to react against anything which smacked of Roman Catholicism and equally quick to patronize promising young nonconformists like John Preston. Yet at St. Catherine's, the Master, John Overall, was so far opposed to both his Calvinistic but episcopalian brethren on the one hand, and his Puritan colleagues on the other, that he had courageously defended Baro when the storm was unleashed against him.

Located at Trinity, somewhere near the center band of the theological rainbow, John Cotton was learning that ecclesiastical questions were not matters of black and white but that the sensible man tempered his show of doctrine with expedience. The great example Elizabeth set her subjects was that of the proper management of doctrine to suit immediate ends, and although this policy, in the long run, built up a national frustration which exploded eventually into civil war, few sensible men in the year 1600 considered compromises, even in religious matters, to be hypocritical or sinful. Indeed, the Puritans themselves were the most adept at negotiations, and for every Cartwright whose convictions broke into inexpedient demonstrations, there were numerous Tyndalls and Somes who had learned how to temper their practices while maintaining their principles. Even the man whom Cambridge recognized as her greatest theologian and who was considered, by his enemies as well as his admirers, to be England's most influential religious thinker, a man whose works ranked next after Calvin's in the annals of the English reformation, even this man, William Perkins, fellow of Christ's, learned public compromise. After being reprimanded in 1587 for his too vehement lecturing against kneeling at the sacrament and facing east, he had worded his Puritan messages more carefully and gone on to become Cambridge's great preacher. Puritan theoretician that he was, he kept himself above political commitments and never took a public stand against clerical subscription to the Three Articles which, of course, included the swearing of allegiance to the ceremonies against which he so vigorously inveighed in theory. The behavior of countless others followed Perkins's, and they were regarded as admirable men, living their lives prudently and honestly. Within the church black and white issues were few; the Puritan of legend who divided his universe into those two categories had not yet appeared. He needed his William Laud to harden him into such a position even as William Laud needed him. The Elizabethan Puritan saw a far richer spectrum of possible conduct.

The political lesson John Cotton learned, then, was how to disagree and yet conform; how to oppose and yet be with; how to practice what one believed and yet retain favor. He was well equipped in both station and talent to receive the lesson. The son of a struggling lawyer, he matriculated in 1598 as a sizar, the lowest of all the classes of paying students. He was expected to share a bed and do menial tasks such as waiting on table and running errands. If the humble learn compromise sooner than the proud, thirteen-year-old John was likely to be an apt student.

Cambridge, like all such institutions well before and ever since 1600, had a large group of students who considered the wisdom of life to be contained in the classic undergraduate statement of misadvice, "It's not what you know but who you know." Because of the prevalence of this philosophy, a needy student had grave doubts as to whether he would ever secure a decent clerical living once his studies were completed. The dilemma was satirized by the students of St. John's College during Cotton's last year of undergraduateship when they put on a play in which the hero, Studioso, the poor but unconnected Cambridge scholar, is passed over for a living by the bishop in favor of Immerito, who, while awaiting audience with the bishop, cautions his father thus: "Well father . . . when thou haue gotten me the gratuito of the liuing, thou wilt likewise disburse a little money to the bishops poser, for there are certaine questions I make scruple to be posed on."[20] Immerito is also keenly aware of the fact that he must not betray the least shade of Puritanism, and, accordingly, when the bishop's examiner comes to question him on his utterance in order to certify that he has a fit delivery for the pulpit, Immerito prudently confines himself to pronouncing, "If any man or woman, can tell any tidings of a Horse with foure feete, two eares, that did straye about the seuenth houre. . . ."[21] He wins the position, and the qualified but poor Studioso returns to the university. A member of the bishop's household sums up the poor scholar's

[20] *The Return from Parnassus, or The Scourge of Simony* (London, 1879), p. 25.
[21] *Ibid.*, p. 38.

[17]

shortcomings thus: "He is one that cannot make a good legge, one that cannot eat a messe of broth cleanly, one that cannot ride a horse without spur-galling: one that cannot salute a woman, and looke on her directly."[22] The poor lawyer's son from Derby was surely such a person, but surely also he was spared this portrait of himself, for neither did such scholars attend plays.

John Cotton's second great extracurricular lesson was religious. Schoolmaster Johnson, Vicar Swetnam, and his parents had combined to send him to Cambridge as a pious lad, but questions of man's relation to God were as yet matters of rote learning. Preaching in Derbyshire was severely restricted by Bishop Overton, and thus the keenest weapon the clergy had in their assault on man's spiritual condition was blunted. But at Cambridge, young Cotton was not only exposed to a superabundance of preaching but was able to hear the greatest pulpit men the Church of England had developed, Lancelot Andrewes and William Perkins.

The preaching of William Perkins[23] especially disturbed the adolescent Cotton, for the fellow of Christ's, through instilling in him a deep discontent with his spiritual condition, demanded so arduous a response that the undergraduate felt powerless to act. Cotton had finally resolved to avoid the issue entirely by absenting himself from the meeting whenever Perkins lectured, but the doctrine of the man attracted as strongly as it repelled so that it was with a shameful joy that John Cotton in his last year of undergraduateship heard the bells sound for Perkins's funeral and sighed at his escape from a major spiritual crisis.[24] But Perkins's preaching

[22] *Ibid.*, p. 33.

[23] For an incisive modern summary of Perkins's theology, see: Harry C. Porter, *Reformation and Reaction in Tudor Cambridge* (Cambridge, 1958).

[24] John Norton, *Abel Being Dead Yet Speaketh* (London, 1658), p. 12. The principal facts in this chapter about Cotton himself are taken from Norton; Cotton Mather's *Magnalia Christi Americana* (Hartford, 1855);

did not fail of its intent. Though the great theologian was not present at the harvest, he had successfully harrowed the soul of young John Cotton and prepared it for the milder cultivation of Richard Sibbes.

The doctrine Perkins taught Cotton, more effectively than the young auditor realized at the time, was derived from Calvin and based on the generally received proposition that Adam was the representative of all mankind so that his fall resulted in all men being born sinful. Consequently, man's nature is in itself ample reason for his damnation. God, however, offered man salvation under the covenant of works which provides eternal life to him who gives perfect obedience to the conditions of the law, an incisive abridgment of which is contained in the Decalogue. The impossibility of man's fulfilling the conditions of so rigorous a covenant is no valid criticism of its effectiveness, Perkins warned, for the law has a threefold use: to lay open sin and make it known; "Accidentarily to effect and augment sinne, by reason of the flesh, the which causeth man to decline from that which is commaunded, and euer to incline to that which is prohibited;"[25] and to damn for the least disobedience without any hope of pardon. Perkins acknowledged that the reign of law was one of threats and terror, from which, however, only one sanctuary existed: "The continuance of [the] . . . law is perpetuall; vnlesse a sinner repent: and the very first act of repentance so freeth him, that he shall no more bee vnder the law, but vnder grace."[26] Perkins concluded his interpretation of the law by emphasizing its use even for those under a covenant of grace ("It guideth them to *new obedience*

and Samuel Whiting's "Concerning the Life of the Famous Mr. Cotton, Teacher to the Church at Boston, in New-England," *Chronicles of the First Planters of the Colony of Massachusetts Bay*, ed. by Alexander Young (Boston, 1846), pp. 420-44.

[25] William Perkins, "A Golden Chaine," *Works* (London, 1626-31), I, 69.

[26] *Ibid.*, I, 70, as is the next citation.

in the whole course of their life, which obedience is acceptable to God by Christ"), and then turned to the new covenant.

The covenant of grace Perkins defined as "that whereby God freely promising Christ, and his benefits, exacts again of man, that he would by faith receiue Christ, & repent of his sins." Under this covenant, man does not promise anything, but receives a free gift just as if the heir to a will were asked to perform nothing for the late testator. Man's progress toward salvation through God's promise of grace is marked by four degrees, the first of which, effectual calling, is a summoning by the Maker to become engrafted to Christ and to partake of the offices He exercised on man's behalf. The usual way for man to receive this summons, Perkins asserted, is through diligent listening to the word of God preached, for the spirit more frequently operates through the word spoken livingly than through set formulas. Hence the nonconformist's insistence on more extensive preaching, and hence his answer to the question of where the true church was when there was no church but that of Rome: it existed wherever a group of true believers gathered to hear the word preached, and no matter how corrupt the times there always existed some such groups. Although the usual order of natural philosophy, Perkins said, is first the perception of a truth through experience and afterward the assent to it, in the practice of faith matters are reversed: "For first, wee must consent to the word of God, resisting all doubt and diffidence, & afterward wil an experience & feeling of comfort follow. . . . They therefore doe very ill, who are still in a doubt of their saluation, because as yet, they feele not in themselues, especiall motions of Gods spirit."[27]

The second degree in salvation is justification, whereby those who are called and believe are, in spite of their sinful natures, accounted just in God's eyes, their sins being remitted and Christ's righteousness being imputed to them. The third

[27] *Ibid.*, I, 80.

degree, sanctification, is the bit-by-bit strengthening of their holiness and righteousness which enables them to observe such edicts as the ten commandments with greater ease although, to be sure, not perfectly, for no man is capable of such obedience. However, those who are called, justified, and sanctified are saints—saved in spite of their human fallibility and consequent inability to yield perfect obedience to the strictures of the Old Testament. Those who are not thus elected, the reprobate, remain under the covenant of works and are, consequently, damned. Glorification, the fourth degree, is the perfect transforming of the elected person into the image of the Son of God and takes place after death.

Perkins's teaching was emphatic against those who agreed that some were elected to salvation and a much greater number to damnation, but who insisted that those who were damned were damned because God foresaw that they would be wicked. These interpreters were obviously attempting to soften the decrees of God by avoiding a direct statement that most of mankind were ticketed to hell regardless of anything they could do. The Lord did not need the apologies of men, Perkins insisted, and he reiterated that there was absolutely nothing man could do to affect his status as a saint or a sinner: "God . . . did vpon his meere pleasure elect some, & reiect others eternally, not mooued or vrged thereunto by any thing whatsoeuer out of himselfe."[28]

The familiar doctrine of Calvinism as interpreted and urged home by Perkins profoundly stirred the adolescent Cotton. The tremendous emphasis Perkins placed on grace as a free gift and on man's helplessness in the face of it meant that all the assumptions the young man had made about his salvation, assumptions based on his growing knowledge of the Bible, his belief in the trinity, and his zeal for a reformed church, were foundations laid on shifting sands. He was not saved, according to the preacher, until he had *felt* God moving in

[28] *Ibid.*, I, 109.

[21]

him, and that feeling would not come, if it came at all, until he had undergone an intense period of soul searching. If he were to follow Perkins he would have to set a watch upon himself to detect the faintest signs of the Holy Spirit moving in him, and he would dare not call the watch in for a moment's respite, because, unless these signs were noted, his eternal future was one with damnation. All he had done, all he had lived in and for during his brief life, was for naught. He was completely passive in his relation to his God; he could but watch and yearn.

Such a lesson ran violently counter to a young man's dependence on his maturing self. After four years at Trinity, John Cotton knew he had been successful, that he could count upon a fellowship, that his learning, especially in rhetoric and the tongues, was remarkable. To be sure, Perkins, scholar that he was, by no means urged the abandonment of studies—the clergy must be learned, for it was the chosen instrument through which the Lord spoke His converting word—but Perkins did undermine Cotton's hard-earned confidence in himself. This was the last thing the self-made young man from Derby could afford to part with, so he rejoiced with shame-flushed face when the Cambridge breeze carried the sound of the bell tolling for Perkins.

In 1602, the year of Perkins's death and Cotton's A.B., Thomas Neville, Master of Trinity, was busily engaged in extensive architectural revisions and enlargements at the college. Master Neville was drawing deeply upon the financial resources of the college as well as making generous visits to his own purse, and the strained financial circumstances of the college severely restricted the funds available for fellowships.[29] Fortunately for his son, Attorney Cotton's practice in Derby was now flourishing, so that he could provide the Cambridge scholar with fuller maintenance; indeed, remembering his father's increased income after he had entered college, John

[29] G. M. Trevelyan, *Trinity College* (Cambridge, 1946), pp. 21 ff.

later observed, "God kept me in the University."[30] Nevertheless, the eighteen-year-old bachelor sought a fellowship, for
he had many years of Cambridge learning yet to undergo and
a fellowship was as important a sinecure for prestige as it was
for maintenance. He therefore accepted a fellowship at
Emmanuel, and moved his belongings to that godly institution
which had been founded in the year of his birth when Sir
Walter Mildmay and Queen Elizabeth were said to have
had their famous exchange of words. "Sir Walter," said the
sovereign, "I hear you have erected a puritan foundation."
"No, madam," replied the knight who had just returned from
seeing work begun on Emmanuel, "far be it from me to
countenance any thing contrary to your established laws; but
I have set an acorn, which, when it becomes an oak, God alone
knows what will be the fruit thereof."[31]

In 1602, Sir Walter's acorn was a sturdy sapling, thanks
to the ready watering of Puritan merchants delighted that
Mildmay's influence with the Queen had enabled him to make
such a planting, and to the careful nurturing of its first Master,
Laurence Chaderton. The son of a Roman Catholic, Chaderton
had become interested in Puritan principles while he was
an undergraduate at Christ's, 1564-1567. Hearing of this,
his disapproving father had sent him a letter which had become
legendary as the grand archetype of the sort of message many
radical young men at Cambridge could expect to receive
from home: "If you will renounce the new sect which you
have joined you may expect all the happiness which the care
of an indulgent father can secure you; otherwise I enclose
in this letter a shilling to buy a wallet with. Go and beg for
your living. Farewell!"[32] Young Laurence persisted in his

[30] Norton, p. 11.
[31] Thomas Fuller, *The History of the University of Cambridge* (London,
1840), p. 205.
[32] William Dillingham, *Laurence Chaderton, D.D.*, trans. by Evelyn S.
Shuckburgh (Cambridge, 1884), p. 4.

[23]

Puritan principles and supported himself by securing a fellowship at Christ's and then by becoming afternoon lecturer at St. Clement's. In 1576, he married Cecelia Culverwell, daughter of the Queen's wine merchant and sister of two Puritan ministers. Just as Cecelia's father was able to manage Puritanism and favor at court, so Chaderton had the experience to administer a Puritan foundation at Cambridge and yet avoid reprisal. He was reluctant, however, to add the fame of being Master of the most Puritan college in the history of the kingdom to his already large local reputation as a preacher and a student of the classical tongues, and it was not until Mildmay, his former schoolmate at Christ's, told him, "If you won't be master, I certainly am not going to be founder of a college,"[33] that he consented to head Emmanuel.

Chaderton's skill at steering Emmanuel on a Puritan course while avoiding the shoals of hierarchical reprisal became an object of widespread admiration in reformed circles and a topic of bewildered dismay in others. "All other colledges in Cambridge do strictly observe, according to the laws and ordinances of the Church of Englande, the form of public prayer prescribed in the Communion Booke [noted one contemporary]. In Em. Colledge they do follow a private course of publick prayer, after their own fashion, both Sondaies, Holy daies and workie days." On the vexed question of ecclesiastical vestments, the same observer noted that, "They of Em. Colledge have not worn that attier, either at the ordinary divine service, or celebration of the Lord's Supper, since it was first erected."[34] And as for the ritual connected with the sacrament, the shocking report from Emmanuel was that "they receive that holy Sacrament sittinge upon forms about the Communion table, and doe pull the loafe one from the other, after the minister hath begon. And soe the cupp, one drinking as it were to another, like good fellows, without any

[33] *Ibid.*, p. 7.
[34] Baker Mss., quoted by Mullinger, p. 313n.

particular application of the saide words, more than once for all."[35] Even the academic cap and gown were sadly disregarded at Emmanuel, and scandalized conformists learned that Friday supper was served at the college, and that from a college kitchen which faced east although the unconsecrated college chapel did not.

John Cotton knew full well the commitment he was making when he accepted the Emmanuel fellowship. If there were any doubt before 1603, it was now dissipated. He was a Puritan. But the term was hardly more descriptive in detail when he entered Emmanuel than it had been when as a boy in his early teens he had heard the tales of the conformists' skirmishes with the reformers. For Cotton, becoming a Puritan meant committing himself to a number of church practices not thus far acceptable to the establishment, and yet, he felt, more adequately representative of the true Christian forms (the practices of the apostolic church) which the pioneers of Protestantism had attempted to establish. While he was ready to maintain a brisk defense of these practices as they were performed at Emmanuel, he was also capable of compromising on them should he see sound reason to. And he was uncertain as to the limits of his reforming zeal. When the day on which he received his divinity degree arrived, would he subscribe to the Three Articles even though they pledged his solemn allegiance to practices which he had come to Emmanuel to avoid? Probably so; even Perkins had not spoken against subscription. How far was he willing to carry his preference for a non-episcopalian ecclesiastical system? Perhaps no farther than it was safe to do in the political climate. Even Chaderton was reported to have said, "Those who dislike the government of the Church by bishops will substitute something far less beneficial both to Church and State."[36] Although he was now ready to be called and to call

---

[35] *Ibid.*, p. 314n.   [36] Dillingham, p. 10.

himself Puritan, he was still an Elizabethan, and in his view the possible consequences of his commitment were many and various.

A fellow who declared himself for certain church practices was automatically putting his views on public, or at least semipublic display, whereas a man could change his doctrine of man's relationship to God without the same exposure. Nevertheless, Cotton's explicit Puritanism began with the former, seemingly less cautious, change. Following the Emmanuel model of ecclesiastical behavior was a calculated political risk, but an Elizabethan at Cambridge knew what was involved in the calculation. Accepting the experiential Calvinism of Perkins was a far more agonizing decision. Even though the Emmanuel practice was a logical outgrowth of the doctrine which held that the true apostolic succession resided in the true preaching of the word, and that all church officers should be preachers, following such a practice without a commitment to Perkins's interpretation of religious experience was not illogical. For one could have more confidence in the Lord's relating His decree of election or reprobation to a foreknowledge of the man's merit than did Perkins and still insist upon less ritualistic procedure in the church. Accepting Perkins's interpretation did not leave so much room for compromise as did accepting Puritan polity, and while less risky politically was far more agonizing personally. Matters of this world, Cotton knew, will never be ordered perfectly although a great margin for visible improvement exists. But the question of salvation was not subject to compromise, recantation, and alteration. It was of the most awful seriousness and he hesitated even as he embarked on his fellowship at Emmanuel to adopt the doctrine of most of his puritanic colleagues.

John Cotton resided at Emmanuel College for ten years, from 1603 to 1612. In 1606, he received his M.A. degree and continued on his regency, being ordained at Lincoln in

1610, and in 1613, after he had left the University, receiving his Bachelor of Divinity degree. His years as a graduate student brought him increasing recognition as a scholar and preacher. When the time arrived for him to keep his Divinity Act by reading a thesis he had composed in Latin and responding to an opponent, no less a person than William Chappell was chosen to oppose him. That opponent, a fellow at Christ's, was recognized as the greatest disputant in the University, a rigorous scholar and an incipient enemy to Calvinists, but Cotton maintained his thesis to the satisfaction of the president and the increase of his reputation.[37] As Cotton advanced in years at Emmanuel he was entrusted with various responsibilities in addition to tutoring: as dean, he supervised the conduct and studies of his juniors, maintained discipline among them, presided over their formal disputations, and presented them for graduation; as lecturer, he gave formal academic discourses as did the professors; as catechist, he conducted oral examinations on the fundamentals of Christianity and delivered lectures on these points. His learning in the curriculum was profound and his knowledge of the tongues, like that of Master Chaderton, was phenomenal. The poser in Hebrew who had tested his fitness to enter into his fellowship at Emmanuel could not impede the promptness of his answers, though the text for examination was Isaiah 3, which, said another Cambridge man, "hath more hard words in it, then any place of the Bible within so short a compass."[38]

It was in the pulpit, however, that John Cotton achieved his first glory—recognition as the successor if not the superior in fame to the late William Playfere, Lady Margaret Professor of Divinity. Cotton's preaching chores had increased steadily as his years of residence passed until, in 1609, he was so promising as to be chosen to deliver the funeral oration at

[37] Norton, p. 15. This is the same William Chappell who went on to astound King James with his ability in disputation, to tutor John Milton, and to become a recipient of Laud's favors.

[38] Norton, p. 10.

the ceremonies for Robert Some, the rigid Calvinist who had been Master of Peterhouse. The sermon was "so accurately performed in respect of Invention, Elegancy, Purity of Style, Ornaments of Rhetorick, Elocution, and Oratorious beauty of the whole, as that he was henceforth looked on as another *Xenophon,* or *Musa Attica* throughout the University."[39] His triumph at Master Some's funeral assured him of a large and expectant audience whenever he next exercised his pulpit talents, but, murmured the devouter of his fellow Puritans, such ornamented sermonizing revealed a deplorable Athenian itch after novelty and gave precedence to the Muses over Moses, to Plato over Paul. The main end of the sermon, the saving preaching of the word, was defeated by ornate rhetoric and the citation of abstruse philosophy. The true preacher confined himself to words of wisdom and did not fall prey to the fascination of the wisdom of words.

The newly famous John Cotton was well aware of this viewpoint. Besides being wary of the troublesome experiences Perkins's preaching was designed to lead him into, he had shied away from those lectures because of the plainness of the style.[40] The way of life Perkins seemed to have been holding would, if he accepted it, not only have interfered with his studies, it would also have discredited a good part of the rhetoric which he was coming to relish. But in 1609, just as his fame was taking flight and a prosperous academic, if not ecclesiastical, future glowed before him, cold doubt took hold. Surely he had prospered in the affairs of this world, but how much closer did this bring him to an assurance of his prosperity in the invisible world? Even though Perkins and his Emmanuel colleagues may not have been literally correct in their description of the degrees of conversion, surely he should

[39] *Ibid.,* p. 13.
[40] For a thorough discussion of the scholastic bases of such problems, see Wilbur S. Howell, *Logic and Rhetoric in England, 1500-1700* (Princeton, 1956).

have received some inner signs of his acceptance into the covenant of grace. Once achieved, his outward gains seemed less sweet, for they were not matched by any change in his inner disposition. Did this mean that his greater acceptance among the silly undergraduates was a vain snare of the devil keeping him from salvation?

No young man believes he will die, but at twenty-five that fact becomes terrifyingly impressive, especially if questions of life and death are the very substance of his daily activities. So as the index of John Cotton's fame rose, his spiritual barometer sank until, in desperation, he all but succeeded in convincing himself of the most horrible fact known in his world—he would die in sin never to live again; he was not a saint; he was damned.

In this despairing condition he carried on his duties, continuing to preach the popular way, for it seemed obvious that if he could do nothing to affect God's disposition toward him then he should best continue in his accustomed round. But he could not resign himself to his condition, call in the watchman of his soul from the task of announcing the arrival of the Holy Spirit, and pursue a *carpe diem* course of pleasure in the only life he was ever to live. Part of his inability to do this was, of course, the result of the fact that, no matter how wildly he despaired, hope always glimmered; the wages of the eleventh hour worker were equal to those of the laborer who had been at his task from the first. But even without the glimmer of this very faint hope, Cotton, as countless others in his condition, was checked from hedonism by the very philosophy which had led him into his despondent state. The commitment of faith which convinced him that he was damned was so profound it was not to be replaced by a giddy fatalism when its findings were reported. This would mean that the very cause of despair, faith in a specific relationship of God to man, would be denied by its effect, a reckless living for the day. This, on the face of it, was an impossibility, although countless spectators from without Calvinism were confident that the connection existed and puzzled that there was no widespread evidence of it.[41] It stood to reason, they argued, that if one accepted the doctrine of predestination and were equally convinced of his reprobate condition, then no censure would be strong enough to check his consequent immoral acts. But the condition of John Cotton in 1609 was the condition of the castaway confident that he would drown, not of the apprentice rid of his master.

The immediate cause of John Cotton's depression in 1609 and the immediate cure of it were both the work of one man, Richard Sibbes. A fellow of St. John's, Sibbes had received his M.A. in 1602, shortly before Cotton had received his A.B., had been converted to Puritan principles by the lecturer at St. Andrew's in Cambridge, Paul Baynes, was made college preacher in 1609 and lecturer at Holy Trinity in Cambridge in 1610. Sibbes's preaching, far less popular than Cotton's, served as a double reproach to the latter, for Sibbes spoke convincingly against negative righteousness and did so in the plain style. Those who lived civil, sober, honest lives and appeared blameless before men were, Sibbes explained, only negatively righteous. True righteousness, of course, could be purchased only through an application of Christ's sacrifice and was the possession of only the justified saint.

For three years Cotton continued in a state of uncertainty, preaching in his elaborate style to a wide audience and desperately searching for a sign that the Lord had chosen him as one predestined to live in glory. During these same three years, Sibbes continued his preaching in another part of the town, speaking to far fewer than did Cotton, and doing so in an unadorned style. The Emmanuel preacher attended

[41] Richard Bancroft, the future Archbishop, was reported to have complained at the Hampton Court Conference that the doctrine of predestination was a desperate doctrine and had made many people libertines. Those historians who have shared his belief have been equally hard pressed to produce significant examples of Calvinistic libertines.

frequently. The crucial message Sibbes had for him was one
which he repeated over and over to himself: "It is a sin for
a child of God to be too much discouraged and cast down
in affections." But can it be sinful in a man to be sensible
of his desperate condition? questioned the unregenerate
listener. How can I know when I am "too" cast down? Sibbes's
simple reply was, "Grief, sorrow, and humility are good;
but discouragement is evil."[42] Finally, after three years of
waiting, two of them spent after his ordination as a priest
in the established church, Cotton's watch was rewarded. He
felt the Spirit quickening his heart and illuminating his
consciousness; he perceived a growing strength in himself,
an ability to be moved feelingly by the contemplation of
Christ's passion; and he knew that he had been called to
salvation.

The conversion of John Cotton committed his loyalty to
the person and doctrine of Richard Sibbes, and Sibbes's
doctrine differed in a significant way from that of Perkins.
Sibbes was not a powerful theologian; he was, rather,
a spiritual counselor, what his colleagues called a "physician
of the soul."[43] His great aim was to bring the saved to a
recognition of their estate and his special talent was for
alleviating the pains of those who, like Cotton, were under-
going the agonies of doubt. As a result, he tended to disregard
or skirt about the doctrine of reprobation which the system
of Perkins logically deduced and uncompromisingly insisted
upon with a vigor equal to that devoted to the doctrine of
salvation. Sibbes's rhetoric assumed that the listener had been
elected from eternity; his specialty was bringing his listener
to this awareness by fanning his faint hopes. The possibility
that the listener may have been damned formed no part of

[42] Richard Sibbes, "Discouragement's Recovery," *Works*, ed. by Alexander
B. Grosart (Edinburgh, 1864), VII, 52.
[43] The most popular and representative of his works is *The Bruised
Reede and Smoaking Flax* (London, 1638).

Sibbes's public outlook, for he conceived of his task as being the consolation of weak Christians. As a result, he appeared to be preaching what Perkins had so vigorously castigated as false, a doctrine of universal calling.

John Cotton was developing into a theologian as well as a preacher and he would have to face some of the problems which Sibbes disregarded, but his immediate reaction in 1612 was one of unmitigated devotion to the man whose preaching had brought about this awareness of his salvation, the man who had been the chosen instrument of the Spirit's call to him. He was now convinced that the plain style was the saving style, and he realized that he must abandon his elegant oratory. But as the time approached for him to preach at St. Mary's and he received indications that the usual anticipatory crowd would be on hand to hear his display, he had to strive manfully to put down his doubts.

However, he went through with his plan and soon realized his worst fears. Many of his listeners pulled their caps about their ears, astonished undergraduates looked in amazement at the fellows who had enthusiastically herded them to the church, and the hum of approval, the preacher's version of applause, did not break the silence after his conclusion. Disconsolately, Cotton returned to his room, painfully aware that if he had gained a stronger foothold in the kingdom of heaven it was not without paying a price in the kingdom of man.

But that same afternoon the near miracle occurred which confirmed John Cotton in his Puritanism forever. For there came a knocking at his door and in strode the talented, witty, and proficient expounder of Aristotle, John Preston, fellow of Queen's, to announce that the sermon delivered in St. Mary's that day had brought home to him the corruption of his nature and the uncertainty of his salvation.[44] In his own words, Preston asked Cotton the question asked of Peter

[44] Norton, p. 14.

by the first converts, the agonizing question asked of Sibbes by Cotton himself: "What shall I do to be saved?"

No stronger reinforcement of spirit could have been provided. The Pope of Rome claimed to be the direct descendant of the apostles, and the Church of England was now anxiously asserting that its Archbishops had a valid claim to the chain of ordinations which extended back to Peter. But the apostles had spread their influence through the preaching of the word; he, Cotton, had experienced the same feeling as the hearers of Peter when he had heard God in the words of Sibbes, just as Sibbes could testify that he had heard God in Baynes's preaching, and Baynes, in turn, could make testimony of a similar experience. Now John Preston turned to Cotton's sermon as a manifestation of the Spirit. This was the true apostolic succession. No recognition by bishops could equal it.

As John Cotton from 1602 moved more steadily toward Puritanism in both polity and doctrine, so the Puritans were tightening their organization and assuming the aspect of a political party with a specific platform and powerful allegiances. As vexing as was Elizabeth's policy, and as stern as was Whitgift, the Puritans, nevertheless, had been relatively unmolested under their reigns and were, consequently, loosely knit. But when James came to the throne in the spring of 1603, and Richard Bancroft succeeded Whitgift in the following year, the hammer and the anvil of oppression which would shape the Puritans into a strongly united party had come into being. The platform of the Puritan party was the list of requests made of James in the Millenary Petition, and the tactics of the party were to capture parish after parish and maintain a reformed service in them, shielding the practicers from episcopal punishment by a variety of complex legal and ecclesiastical devices designed to maintain a placid surface. The battle was moving into the parishes. The harder Bancroft struck with his insistence upon *ex animo* oaths, and upon the acceptance of canons which proclaimed the fact of the divine origin of the Church of England, the ceremonies of the Prayer Book, and government by hierarchy, the stiffer became the resistance. Small numbers of Puritans, called Brownists or separatists, were even fleeing to the continent, maintaining that the Church of England was thoroughly antichristian and there was no salvation within it, but these were condemned by the vast majority of the Puritans who believed that the establishment was not hopelessly corrupt and that reformation from within was needed.[45]

By August 1604, Emmanuel and Sidney Sussex Colleges had to cease their public flaunting of the established order of service. At Hampton Court in January of that year, Master Chaderton had been one of the four representatives of the Puritan party who had appeared to oppose the nine representatives of the establishment but who had found their chief opponent in the moderator, King James. The King had concluded the conference by promising to make the Puritan party behave, "Or else I will harrie them out of this land, or else do worse, only hang them, that's all."[46] Nor was this the sum; Chaderton brought word back to Emmanuel that Bancroft, at the conference, had revealed a deep distrust of Calvinistic doctrine and that the anti-Calvinist party would gain headway among the bishops once Whitgift died.

Some respite was provided when George Abbot, episcopalian but Calvinist, succeeded Bancroft in 1610, but the anti-Puritan rigor of Bancroft had touched a responsive chord in many of the younger clergymen of the establishment who were shocked at the liberty the Puritans appeared to enjoy

[45] This very important distinction between separating and non-separating Puritanism is now a commonplace as a result, mainly, of Champlin Burrage's immensely influential *The Early English Dissenters in the Light of Recent Research (1550-1641)* (Cambridge, 1912), 2 vols. What the American consequences of the distinction were, however, is a more clouded matter as will be seen in the following pages.

[46] Daniel Neal, *The History of the Puritans* (London, 1837), I, 403n.

under Whitgift. This group was now rising to power under Abbot. The University was an obvious area of close scrutiny by the bishops, but reports kept coming into Emmanuel that the political battle was being joined in parish after parish, that certain bishops were content to wink at reformed practices, and that others could not enforce conformity without losing a goodly number of their clergy. In 1612, John Cotton, a thorough Puritan, received his call to arms from the proprietors of St. Botolph's Church in Lincolnshire. He accepted, and at the age of twenty-eight left the cloisters to test in deed the principles, political and religious, which had been forming his character at Cambridge since he had arrived fifteen years before as a poor boy from Derby.

❧ CHAPTER TWO ❧

THE FIRST BOSTON
(1612-1633)

IN THE YEAR of John Cotton's birth, 1584, the Mayor of Boston in Lincolnshire wrote in a pathetic strain to Lord Burghley. His city, a center of prosperity in the medieval period, famous for its fairs, its guilds, and its friars, had been in the trough of a depression during Elizabeth's reign. The once great international port at the mouth of the Wash, complained the Mayor, had that year seen the departure of nought save 260 quarters of barley-malt. And, indeed, four years later the town which had sent a proud fleet as its contribution to the prosecution of the Hundred Years War contributed only six pounds and a handful of men to the defense against the Spanish Armada.[1]

Boston's break with its glorious medieval past, a break which caused its contraction even as the majority of English towns during Elizabeth's reign radiantly expanded, was marked by a growing Puritanism. When some twenty of the Lincolnshire clergy petitioned Archbishop Whitgift in 1583, pleading against the establishment's insistence upon the proper clerical garb and the use of the ring in marriage, the Reverend Mr. Worship, Vicar of St. Botolph's Church in Boston, was among the group. The town of Boston as a corporation controlled the living which Mr. Worship held, and so far were its members from disagreeing with their vicar that in 1590 they consented to his destroying the rood screen in the church.[2]

Vicar Worship's successor was Thomas Wooll, who was, in August 1604, presented before the Bishop of Lincoln "for not wearinge the surplice nor signinge with the signe of the

[1] A. M. Cook, *Boston (Botolph's Town)*, (Boston, 1934), pp. 59 ff.
[2] *Ibid.*

[36]

crosse in baptisme." To make matters worse, since the visitation at which his misdemeanors had been recorded, "notice hath bene given to the courte that the surplis hathe bene tendred him and he in scorne thereof (as yt seemeth) maketh it his cushion to sitt on." In the following January, Vicar Wooll's case was discharged by the bishop's court "vpon certificat of conformitie," without the oath of subscription to the Three Articles being exacted of him.[3] William Chaderton, the Bishop of Lincoln, was happy to have succeeded in exacting this degree of conformity from Wooll and others, for he realized that if he urged subscription too strongly he would find his already undermanned diocese virtually vacant. Vicar Wooll, after all, was but one of 137 nonconformists detected by his visitors that year.

After twelve years of service at Boston, Thomas Wooll retired to the rectory at Skirbeck, but in keeping with the corporation's desire to replace him with an equally dedicated nonconformist, he did not officially send a resignation to the bishop until the town had chosen his successor. For a few months after his retirement, his former assistant, Benjamin Alexander, filled the vicariate. Mr. Alexander had also come to the bishop's attention when he was curate at Torksey, where, it was reported, he did not annually read the Canons of 1604, and where he omitted reading the litany on Wednesdays and Fridays and was seldom seen in his surplice on the sabbath.[4]

In July of 1612, Wooll headed a delegation of five from this nonconformist town on a visit to his alma mater, Cambridge, there to find a new vicar. Some debate took place among the members of the committee, but without too great difference they came to the conclusion that they should offer the post to the twenty-eight-year-old scholar who was represented to

---

[3] C. W. Foster (ed.), *The State of the Church in the Reigns of Elizabeth and James I as Illustrated by Documents Relating to the Diocese of Lincoln,* "Lincoln Record Society," XXXII (Horncastle, 1926), pp. cxvi, 369.

[4] *Ibid.,* p. lxxviii.

them as the best preacher in the University. Both Richard Sibbes and Paul Baynes spoke warmly for him, and his Emmanuel training seemed to assure his continuing the tradition of his immediate predecessors. Having issued the invitation, they returned home, where they confirmed their selection of John Cotton as Vicar of St. Botolph's in a council meeting held on 12 July.

Once he had accepted the position at St. Botolph's, John Cotton had grave misgivings as to the wisdom of his leaving the University. The King seemed bent on enforcing uniformity, and although he had been exaggerating in his threat to harry the Puritans out of the land, nevertheless, the path of nonconformity was bound to be more difficult to follow in the parish than it had been at the college. Cotton was not quick to adapt to new circumstances—he had taken every bit of his fifteen years at Cambridge to arrive at his present position—and he was uncertain, even then, as to just what his position would be in a crisis. Certainly he had had no experience in the pacifying of bishops or the manipulation of their aides, which seemed to be part of the job of any Puritan minister. Moreover, although those who controlled his living were, in the main, nonconformists, there certainly existed in Boston a goodly number who would insist upon more orthodox procedures and who would serve as constant spies for the authorities. And what of his ardent supporters? Would they find his pace acceptable or would they urge a quicker or a slower reformation? Finally, he had to fight down his vanity, for the audience to which he would now preach was not capable, he feared, of appreciating his best efforts.[5]

[5] Years later, in a sermon to his St. Botolph's congregation, Cotton drew upon his own experience when he remarked: "It is wonder to see, when Scholars are admitted into the Ministry in their young times, how they despise the people, think themselves unmeet to condescend to Peasants, but they will rather exercise their Gifts in the University, and so fall into the condemnation of Satan." *A Practical Commentary or An Exposition . . . upon the First Epistle Generall of John* (London, 1656), p. 96.

With these misgivings in mind, Cotton was presented with an opportunity to escape his commitment when William Barlow, Bishop of Lincoln, criticized the town for choosing him and informed him that he seemed too young a man to be set over so turbulent a parish.[6] The vicar-elect was inclined to agree and prepared to retire again to his college, but his more practical adherents were skilled in the ways of insinuating a Puritan cleric.

They knew their bishop well. William Barlow had been the chaplain of Elizabeth chosen to attend Essex at his death and to preach at Paul's Cross the following Sunday under explicit instructions to publish the news that at his death the Earl had made full acknowledgment of his guilt and professed repentance for his treason. This nasty task having been well accomplished, Barlow grew in the favor of the court and was, in 1604, called upon by King James to do some more discreet reporting. This time he was to represent to the public in print what had gone on in the Hampton Court conference at which he had appeared as one of the establishment's spokesmen. His representation of that conference, the only authorized eyewitness account, was greeted with outraged protests by the Puritans, who complained that their cause had been severely distorted, but Barlow grew greater in favor and, in 1608, was rewarded with the bishopric of Lincoln. His ambitions, however, could not be realized if he remained far from London, so, although he established his residence in the diocese, he lived for the most part at his prebendal house at Westminster, the better to keep an eye on the counters he had staked in the game of power.

The demonstrable fact that Barlow and many bishops like him did find their chief inspiration at court rather than in the diocese supplied impressive evidence for the Puritan charges of absenteeism, pluralism, secularism and simony,

[6] Unless otherwise noted, matters of fact about Cotton are taken from Norton, Whiting, and Mather.

just as the bishops' near constant attendance on the King also gave the Puritans more than occasional opportunity to proceed in nonconformity undisturbed, or to bribe the subordinate left in charge. So John Cotton did not, after all, retire from Boston at the bishop's remarks but learned a lesson in diocesan politics from the practical aldermen of Boston. A contemporary reported: "Understanding that one Simon Biby was to be spoken with, which was near the Bishop, they presently charmed him; and so the business went on smooth, and Mr. Cotton was a learned man with the Bishop, and he was admitted into the place, after their manner in those days." The same reporter sardonically noted in his margin, opposite the name of the charmable Simon Biby, "Which some call *Simony and Bribery*."[7] On this sharply expediential note, John Cotton, M.A., entered upon his duties as vicar.

As he had done at Cambridge, so at Boston the new curate began with a policy of cautious observation. When he was instituted into his benefice he was required to swear to the Three Articles, so that he had, for the time at least, agreed that "the Booke of Common prayer, and of ordering of Bishops, Priests and Deacons, containeth in it nothing contrary to the word of God, and that it may lawfully be so vsed, and that hee himselfe will vse the forme in the saide Booke prescribed in publike Prayer, and Administration of the Sacraments, and none other."[8] He had practiced nonconformity at Emmanuel until 1608 and then, together with the rest of the College, had conformed, and it was the latter procedure he now followed at Boston. Within a year of his settlement he had made the two acquisitions which the Puritans regarded as eminently desirable although not absolutely necessary for a promising young minister. The first was a Bachelor of Divinity degree which he received at Cambridge after

[7] Whiting, p. 423.
[8] *Constitutions & Canons Ecclesiastical*, *1604* (Oxford, 1923), Canon XXXVI.

returning to preach the required sermon and participate in the Divinity Act. The second was a wife, Elizabeth Horrocks, whom he had met through Paul Baynes, and who came from a family of nonconformists, the most distinguished of whom was her brother James, a Lancashire minister.

A concern more immediate and more profound than ecclesiastical polity to the young vicar was that of doctrine, for pressing as matters of vestures, rings, and signs were, nevertheless, they were concerned merely with the best forms in which to clothe the church of God, and that church existed wherever true believers heard the word. To the preaching of the word, then, John Cotton bent his greatest energies and, although he now used the plain style, the vast majority of the parishioners at St. Botolph's had full reason to concur in the choice of the corporation. Other towns suffered from restricted preaching or poor preachers, but at Boston there was a "feast of preaching." So great was the demand to hear Cotton that he added a Thursday lecture to his Sunday sermon, a practice which was to become a happily accepted feature of life in New England.

Richard Sibbes, Paul Baynes's disciple, had converted Cotton, and it was in this tradition rather than in that of William Perkins that he taught. Preaching to parishioners whose attendance was required by law and who had equal right under that law to the sacraments, he could not but view with distrust a doctrine which insisted so thoroughly upon the majority of his listeners being regarded as reprobates. Although he was completely committed to Calvinism and avoided the slightest indication that obedience and faith could bring salvation, Cotton did argue that reprobation was conditional: "Upon the presupposall of the carelesse or wilfull disobedience of the word, either in refusing the meanes of grace in Christ, or abusing other talents and helps of the knowledge of God in nature, God rejecteth or reprobateth them . . . for their sinnes, to the glorifying of his power,

[41]

justice and wrath."[9] The epitome of this doctrine of reprobation was that men were damned not by Adam's fall alone, although in that fall, certainly, all men had fallen and because of it were born into sin. Rather, although born fallen, man was damned because of "voluntarily falling from the meanes, either of grace in the second *Adam,* or of the knowledge of God in nature, by some acts of carelesse or wilfull disobedience."[10]

Cotton, then, told his Lincolnshire listeners that God's grace was given absolutely to those who were elect and neither good works nor self-produced faith could obtain it, but that reprobation was conditional on man's misbehavior during his life and was decreed by God in His foreknowledge of such misbehavior. The absoluteness of the decree of election and the conditions associated with the decree of reprobation did not very logically square with one another in a consistent doctrine, and one William Twisse, an erstwhile disciple of Perkins's, hearing of this some years later, sat down to refute it. But by that time, 1646, Cotton was in another land and of another mind, preaching a more consistent doctrine and willing to accept Twisse's rebuke in silence.

In the second decade of the seventeenth century, however, harmony and not logic was the Vicar's immediate objective, while the saving of souls was his ultimate goal, and the Christian doctrine he preached seemed, as far as he could tell, to be achieving his ends. The growing Arminianism of the country was supported by a vocal group within Boston, and the way to check them, Cotton believed, was not to insist so rigorously upon the absoluteness of God's decree that in reaction they would deny predestination entirely. Arminians, he believed, refused "the excellent and heavenly benefit of the sound and comfortable doctrine of Election, by reason

[9] William Twisse, *A Treatise of Mr Cottons Clearing Certaine Doubts Concerning Predestination, Together with an Examination Thereof* (London, 1646), p. 43.
[10] *Ibid.,* p. 54.

of some hard saying which they observed in the usuall manner of handling the . . . decree of Reprobation."[11] By softening God's seeming arbitrariness in damning men through pointing out that original sin alone did not make a man a reprobate but that he also during his lifetime behaved wickedly, Cotton disarmed the Arminians, he thought, and yet did not grant them their basic claim that man could work his own salvation and was not passively awaiting God's grace. The results in Boston were gratifying. The Arminian party diminished in numbers, at least ceased its volubility, and lecture days were well attended by citizens from throughout the countryside. One such neighbor who came to town to hear the Vicar as often as she could was Mrs. Anne Hutchinson.

For twenty years at St. Botolph's, regardless of disputes on polity and trouble with officials, John Cotton maintained a solid reputation as a great and learned preacher, whose influence spread to a number of various groups. One such group came under his sway as the result of the rise of John Preston, who, in 1614, became a political power in Queen's College; in 1615, debated an academic point with a brilliance which much took the King; and, in 1622, succeeded Chaderton as Master of Emmanuel when the venerable Puritan resigned deliberately to assure the succession of so able a foe to the Arminians. In the same year that he became Master of Emmanuel, Preston also succeeded John Donne as preacher at Lincoln's Inn. Throughout his resplendent career Preston remembered Cotton, affording him, from time to time, a needed friend in power, and sending him a steady flow of Cambridge students who lived and studied with him. At Cambridge they said that Mr. Cotton was "Dr. Preston's seasoning vessel."[12] The students whom Preston sent for seasoning were to hold positions of influence during Cromwell's reign and did not forget their mentor; one of them, Thomas Hill, rose to the mastership of Trinity, where with

_____

[11] *Ibid.*, p. 135.   [12] Mather, I, 260.

parliamentary backing he held harsh sway over a group of recalcitrant undergraduates. To this group of disciples was added a band of young Germans who, as Protestant fortunes waned in their homeland, found it necessary to come to England for their training. So well attended were the tutorial lectures Cotton held at his home that the press of people finally became unmanageable. To the Thursday afternoon and Sunday morning public lectures he added public lectures on Wednesday and Thursday mornings, and on Sunday afternoon. No parish preacher taught so frequently or at such length; none could claim so devoted a following.

Others besides students and parishioners felt the appeal of Cotton's lectures. In the 1620's a group of noblemen were busy about Boston in a project to drain the fens, and they too heard and admired the famous Puritan. Royalists though they were, they were also staunch Protestants, jealous of the political favors the bishops were receiving from their king and impatient with the many ceremonies of the establishment. Edward Sackville, Earl of Dorset, the man who was to refuse to carry the Prince to safety at the Battle of Edgehill, for he would not be thought a coward "for any King's son in Christendom," pledged his aid to Cotton should his influence ever be needed. Dudley Carleton, Viscount Dorchester, and Robert Bertie, Earl Lindsey, were also admirers and well-wishers of the Boston preacher, as were the members of the greatest family in the neighborhood, the Clintons, who held the Earldom of Lincoln and were stout Puritans whose seat was a sanctuary for silenced ministers. When the Lincolnshire vicar, Samuel Skelton, lost his living, the Clintons took him in, and as the year 1630 approached, their home at Tattersall became a center of Puritan meetings and a base from which issued forth many, like Skelton, who were on their way to the new world.

A third group keenly aware of Cotton's activities at Boston were the members of the Puritan party throughout the kingdom. From conservative Archbishop Usher to zealous young Roger Williams, they sought correspondence or interviews with him, and Cotton's name was among the most respected in a lengthening list of clergymen who were destined to serve in crucial public positions: some as leaders of a rebellion; others as founders of new commonwealths.

Finally, the episcopal hierarchy became increasingly and painfully aware of Cotton's growing stature. For two years after his institution at St. Botolph's, Cotton proceeded in accordance with his subscription, bending all of his efforts to preaching his Christian doctrine and opposing Arminianism. The registrar at the bishop's visitation of 1614 was able to note that the young vicar was "a man of great parts for his learning, eloquent and well spoken," adding cautiously that although there seemed to be a large number of communicants there did not appear to be any great forwardness in having children confirmed[13]—the Puritans, of course, viewed confirmation as a distasteful vestige of Roman Catholicism. But Cotton was left to preach as he would, for the establishment was far from a codified position on doctrine and the bishop who had replaced Barlow in 1613, Richard Neile, was as busy in London as had been his predecessor. Indeed, in the same year that his visitors were noting Cotton's conduct at Boston, Bishop Neile's zeal to ingratiate himself with his monarch misled him into affirming in a speech in Lords that the Commons' position on impositions struck at the root of prerogative and that the lower house was sure to be seditious and undutiful should the Lords consent to meet with them on the matter. His vilification was greeted with powerful indignation and with suggestions in Commons that the profits of his bishopric be confiscated for the next seven years, that he be banished, or that his head be set upon Tower Hill. After frantic negotiation with the Lords, the matter was settled by Bishop Neile's tearful protestation of good will towards

[13] Cook, p. 65.

Commons, but the lower house desisted from planning Neile's utter ruin only when the King threatened dissolution.[14] Such was the position of Cotton's bishop, a man who had attained his diocese through urging the Essex divorce against the sentiments of the greater part of the nation and in particular opposition to such conscientious prelates as Archbishop Abbot and Lancelot Andrewes.

By 1615, John Cotton was salaried at 100 pounds per annum, respected in his parish and known especially as a teacher and scholar. Although he was in an active political arena, the alert intervention of the town's politicians shielded him from a great deal of the petty turmoil so that, with the responsibility of the immense amount of study required to prepare for the private lessons and public lectures which he gave each week, his days were filled in a manner not so unlike his Cambridge days as he had anticipated. Of course, with a parish came responsibility for cases of conscience, for the guidance of children and women as well as of men, but this was one of the reasons a minister married, and Elizabeth Cotton proved helpful with the problems of the women while his studies in the Bible and in pastoral writings supplied the archetypes he needed for the religious solution of all personal problems. In short, life in Boston was very pleasant for a thirty-year-old minister whose tastes had been shaped almost exclusively by the academy, whose habit of mind was cautious observation and hesitancy before decision, whose character was shy and patient. But life in England was uneasy for a man who could not square his practice with his beliefs.

Over the years from 1612 to 1615, John Cotton weighed his convictions and his conduct. On the one hand, his ordination by and subserviency to the bishops were based on a succession which eventually led to Rome and to antichrist, but, on the other hand, surely there were true godly men

[14] Samuel R. Gardiner, *History of England from the Accession of James I to the Outbreak of the Civil War (1603-1642)* (London, 1883), II, 174, 243-44.

in his church who had chosen him, and where there were such was there not a holy community in spite of the parish system? Besides, the example set by the separatists was not one to be repeated. This group, in denying themselves communion with the Church of England, had committed the grievous sin of schism from a church which did have true believers in it. His parishioners well remembered the nearly one hundred people from Scrooby who had been arrested on ships in the Wash in 1607 as they attempted to flee illegally to Holland and who were imprisoned and tried in Boston. Eventually, they did get to Holland, but surely they were gravely mistaken if they believed abandonment of the church was the way to bring about their salvation or the church's reformation.

Yet to conform seemed repellent. He was increasingly certain that he would be guilty of hypocrisy if he continued to maintain an allegiance to the Book of Common Prayer, the Preface of which claimed that all ceremonies contained therein did serve "to a decent Order and godly Discipline, and [are] such as be apt to stir up the dull mind of man to the remembrance of his duty to God, by some notable and special signification, whereby he might be edified."[15] For Matthew, 28:20, seemed clearly to limit all church power to the commandments of Christ "which made it appear . . . utterly unlawful, for any Church-power to enjoyn the observation of indifferent Ceremonies which Christ had not commanded."[16]

The crossroads at which Cotton thus stood had been visited by many Puritans before him. Some had chosen the path which led back to complete acceptance of the principles of the hierarchy, others the path to prison, and still others the path to exile. There was now no Emmanuel College to provide a shield behind which he could stand. As experienced

---

[15] *The Book of Common Prayer* (London, 1853), p. 5.
[16] John Cotton, *The Way of Congregational Churches Cleared* (London, 1648), p. 19.

as Boston was in maintaining nonconformist vicars, to make a break with conformity was a radical move and he teetered on the brink of decision.

When his decision on the matter was crystallized, he pictured his reasons for acting as loose syllogisms, the major premise drawn from the Bible, the minor from experience, and the conclusion, therefore, appearing sound. The second verse of the second chapter of Canticles reads, "As a lily among the thorns, So is my love among the daughters." For Cotton, the lily clearly signified the community of those who had been elected to salvation; the thorns, those with whom the elect held external fellowship. Therefore, he argued, the true believers at St. Botolph's need not, on the one hand, separate, but must, on the other, devise some means of maintaining their identity within the larger congregation. The lily is to be distinguished from the thorns, not torn from them. Cotton argued: "It is not straight no Church, that is commingled . . . with notorious wicked ones: the Church may be Christs love, yea, and a fragrant and pure flower in his sight and nostrils, and yet live amongst bryars and thornes."[17]

Paul, in his first epistle to the Corinthians, enjoined, "Let all things be done decently and in order." Surely, Cotton reasoned, it is neither decent nor in order for church officers to have commanded his allegiance to ceremonies which were not prescribed by Christ. And he went so far as to reason that in disobeying he was not only aiding his parishioners but instructing his opponents, for "By yielding Obedience to these things, we should offend their [the church governors'] Consciences in edifying them unto Sin, and provoke the Lord to be offended with them and us."[18]

[17] John Cotton, *A Brief Exposition of the Whole Book of Canticles* (London, 1648), p. 62.

[18] John Cotton, *Some Treasure Fetched out of Rubbish* (London, 1660), p. 8.

The power of church governors, Cotton concluded, came far short of the authority of civil magistrates, for the latter may "in civil matters make binding Laws for any thing expedient to publick weal, which Subjects are ready to submit unto."[19] But expediential ecclesiastical matters could not be legislated by bishops and must be left to the conscience of each minister.

Accordingly, in 1615, John Cotton, with cautious firmness rather than enthusiastic zeal, set about distinguishing the lily from the thorns. He accomplished this, in keeping with his reasoning, not by withdrawing from a parish church which, of necessity, included all persons in the area howsoever scandalous, but by identifying the elect and withdrawing into a tighter inner group with them, a group which avoided the offensive ceremonies and which was truly qualified to receive the sacrament. This group, a prosperous portion of the community, entered into a covenant with the Lord and with one another "to follow after the Lord in the purity of his Worship."[20] They became, in effect, a congregation within the congregation.

The outsiders in the congregation were outraged at the action of the covenanters and at the encouragement and leadership they seemed to be receiving. Protests were soon registered at the bishop's court in Lincoln and Cotton was suspended. His political adherents urged him to appeal to a higher court, choosing Alderman Thomas Leverett to carry the appeal. This representative went about his task with customary magisterial efficiency. He located a proctor of the court susceptible to aldermanic charms and with "pious subtlety," as an observer noted, persuaded him to have the vicar treated as if he were a conformable man.

The pattern was now established and St. Botolph's parish flourished. John Cotton preached his peculiar doctrine of

---

[19] *Ibid.*, p. 3.   [20] *Way Cleared*, p. 20.

absolute grace and conditional reprobation, administered the
rites of the church in a reformed manner with special attention
to the inner group of true believers, and followed a prodigious
schedule of teaching and preaching. The church wardens
gladly cooperated with him in making a series of badly needed
repairs to the frame of the church and in maintaining a church
furnished with all the requirements of the ecclesiastical
authorities. At the same time, the members of the corporation
were alert to any threat to their vicar's well-being and
protected him from interference, while the hierarchy uninten-
tionally lent its support by continuing to appoint bishops
whose main interests lay out of the diocese. In 1617, George
Monteigne replaced Neile as Bishop of Lincoln, the latter
being translated to the richer diocese of Durham shortly after
the banquet he held for King James. The new bishop elicited
nothing but contempt from the Puritans; their most magnificent spokesman, John Milton, some years later characterized
him as a man with a "many-benefice-gaping mouth" and a
"canary-sucking and swan-eating palat."[21] Monteigne it was
who eventually came to join forces with William Laud and
who with him was blamed for the evils in the church with
as great a frequency as Buckingham was held accountable for
the evils in the state.

In 1618, as much in appeasement of the "thorns" in St.
Botolph's as in aid to Cotton, the corporation appointed
Edward Wright as mayor's chaplain. Wright could preside
over the parts of the ceremony to which Cotton objected
so that the Vicar could feel easier in his conscience and have
more time for concentrating on his sermons. An interesting
shuffle took place of a Sunday on the steps of St. Botolph's
as the Puritan members waited until the Apostle's Creed, at
which their orthodox fellow members would stand, was
completed under the direction of Chaplain Wright and then

[21] John Milton, "Of Reformation in England," *Works* (New York,
1931), III, 19.

filed in to hear Cotton's sermon while the Anglicans passed on their way out.[22]

As Cotton neared the close of a decade of service, however, trouble flared with unusual violence for Boston. One night in April 1621, shortly before the time appointed for the celebrated Anglican minister, Robert Sanderson, to preach the bishop's visitation sermon at St. Botolph's, a party broke into the church, shattered the stained glass windows, tore down the ornaments, and destroyed the statuary. About the same time it was noticed that the cross on the King's arms atop the mace carried before the mayor every Thursday and Sunday as he made his way to church had been cut away. This, said the chafing minority in Boston, was sedition, and they saw to it that the royal authorities were notified and a civil commission was issued to look into the mutilation of the mace. Bishop Monteigne, alerted now by a civil matter, suspended Cotton for nonconformity.

An investigation having been duly made, the commissioners reported to the crown that the act had been committed by persons unknown and that the mayor had caused the mutilated mace to be carried before him only so long as the goldsmith had been away from town, but that upon the artisan's return the mace had been repaired. The suspicions of the government were not allayed, however, because their original informant, David Lewis, claimed that during the course of the commissioners' examination the witnesses had been tampered with. Lewis reported that "When Mr. Srjeant Bawtree did examine div'se of the examinates to any materiall pointe, Mr. Irby would answeare before ye examinate and say, 'Thou knowest nothing of this businesse,' and yf any examinate did answeare any thing which he tooke to be materiall, he would then say, 'Hould thy peace, ffoole,' so yt

---

[22] Conjectures as to how Cotton manipulated the church routine to suit himself may be found in Nicholas Hoppin, "The Rev. John Cotton A.M.," *The Church Monthly*, IV, V (1862, 1863), pp. 40-54, 161-67.

Mr. Srjeant Bawtree found fault with him for soe doing."[23]
Lewis further complained that all of the witnesses were with
the mayor before and after giving testimony.

Accordingly, the authorities ordered a second examination,
to be conducted this time by the King's solicitor-general rather
than by local magistrates acting as commissioners. Again a
complete vindication of all known persons resulted: the deed
had been done by persons unknown; it had been rectified as
soon as a goldsmith was available. During the course of this
second commission, the testimony of Thomas Cony, town
clerk and brother-in-law of Cotton, cleared the Vicar of any
involvement: "Mr. Cotton said in this examinants hearing
that they might as well refuse the kings coyne because crosses
were on it, as forbidd the crosses and therefore this examinant
is p'suaded that Mr. Cotton never did conyv at the cutting
of thos crosses."[24]

Doubtless, Cony spoke the truth. A mild and scholarly
man such as Cotton was not directly involved. He limited
his opposition to idolatrous practices to an ingenious use of
his chaplain to perform offensive ceremonies and to a covenant
with an inner circle. But his ideas had consequences in the
actions of his less controlled followers. How could he square
his own sober and pacific intentions with their seeming results?
Was this not the chaos at which Puritanism really aimed
and into which it would lead England if not checked? Bishop
Monteigne wanted to see the suspended vicar.

John Davenant, President of Queen's College, Cambridge,
was invited by Monteigne to join him in the examination of
Cotton. At one time, Monteigne had been considered as the
most likely successor to Tyndall as President, and it was
common rumor that he had been foiled in his ambitions by
John Preston, who had moved very quickly after Tyndall's

---

[23] G. B. Blenkin, "Boston, England, and John Cotton in 1621," *The
Historical and Genealogical Register*, No. CX (Boston, April-June, 1874),
XXVIII, 127.

[24] *Ibid.*, pp. 136-37.

death to secure the necessary court favor for Davenant so that Monteigne hardly had time to digest the news of the vacancy before the forces for Davenant's election were set in motion. Monteigne had recovered from his pique at this turn of affairs, consoled by his appointment to a bishopric, and in inviting his former rival to join in the examination of Cotton he was inviting a man who while conformist enough to receive a bishopric later that year was also friendly toward John Preston and his friends. Monteigne was not inclined to be severe now that the civil commission had found nothing to report, for he had his eyes more than ever fastened on the bishopric of London which had just become vacant.

Davenant and Monteigne, impressed by Cotton's learning and his mildness, debated matters of polity with him, and, satisfied that he was not a firebrand but a scholar with scruples, promised to restore him if he would conform at the taking of the eucharist by kneeling just one time, or, in lieu of this single act, show good reason why he would not. Whichever he did, he might resume his ministry. Cotton, predictably enough, chose the latter alternative and sent Bishop Monteigne the following syllogism:

> Cultus non institutus, non est acceptus:
> Genuflexio in perceptione Eucharistiae est
>   cultus non institutus;
> Ergo, non est acceptus.[25]

Monteigne was free to receive such a reply either as an affront to his generosity or as literal satisfaction of his requirement. He chose the latter alternative, in part because other scenes were calling him.

One of George Monteigne's first official acts as Bishop of London was to serve on the board which consecrated John Williams as Bishop of Lincoln. The existence of the board was an ominous rebuff to the Puritans, for it represented

[25] *The Way Cleared*, p. 19.

the successful forcing into retirement of George Abbot, Archbishop of Canterbury and opponent of the Arminian party within the hierarchy. His accidental killing of a man while hunting was the event which his foes used successfully to block his exercising his powers and Monteigne was one of the group, headed by Laud, who were to exercise them for him. However, the new Bishop of Lincoln, John Williams, was an ardent opponent of the Laud-Monteigne group which not only was intent upon removing him from a controlling voice in the church, but had also alienated the King from him and effected the exchange of his once great secular power for a bishopric. As the establishment tightened its insistence on conformity and became more and more openly Arminian in its doctrine, therefore, Williams in reaction ruled Lincoln in a more and more tolerant manner, although he was hardly a Puritan.

From London in 1622 there issued forth instructions that preachers should adhere strictly to their biblical texts and not become absorbed in applications of the passage to modern times, and that afternoon services should be confined to some part of the catechism or Creed, Ten Commandments, or Lord's Prayer. Two years later, all books dealing with religious subjects were required to receive proper licensing before they could be published. In 1625, William Laud recorded a note in his diary of even more serious consequences for all Puritans: "I exhibited a schedule, in which were wrote the names of many Churchmen, marked with the letters O [Orthodox] and P [Puritan]. The Duke of Buckingham had commanded to digest their names in that method; that (as himself said) he might deliver them to King Charles."[26] This was the way the new King would take to educate himself in church matters. At his coronation in January 1626, Charles made a point of omitting Williams, who should have attended

[26] *The Autobiography of Dr. William Laud* (Oxford, 1839), p. 34.

in his capacity as Dean of Westminster, and of substituting Laud.

During these years in Lincoln, Williams contemptuously disregarded the new powers' rage for conformity and ruled his diocese with a gentle hand and with greater interest in what occurred in the parish than his immediate predecessors had evinced. His Puritan critics pointed out that, besides being a Bishop and the Dean of Westminster, he had a canonry in Lincoln Cathedral and a rectory in Walgrave, so that he was a diocese within himself. However, they were not anxious to alienate his tolerance of them, even though some of them perceived that his moderation was as much the result of a negative reaction on his part as of a positive conviction. As he busied himself in diocesan matters, Williams, who shared his former patron James's high but not particularly critical regard for learning, took a great interest in Vicar Cotton. Here was a man who, unlike most Puritans, did not appear to be a zealot but preached a more gentle species of Calvinism and pursued his nonconformity quietly. Such a man would prove an instructive correspondent, a man with whom debate could be held on church polity for the sake of the truth of the matter as much as for the sake of enforcing conformity. Besides, if the unexpected should happen and the tide should turn against Laud, Cotton might be a useful subordinate in a return to power.

Just as John Cotton had stiffened in his resistance to conformity under uninterested and secular-minded bishops, so he loosened under Williams's interest and tolerance. By 1624, in a letter to Williams which began, "As your Lordship hath dealt honourably and frankly with me, so might I justly be esteemed impiously ungrateful if I should deal otherwise than ingenuously and honestly with your Lordship," he was willing to confess that his ideas on whether or not ceremonies could be commanded by church governors were still in flux.[27]

[27] Blenkin, pp. 137-39.

He wrote: "I have thus far gained (what by conference, what by study, what by seeking unto God) *as of late to see the weakness of some of these grounds* against kneeling which before I esteemed too strong for me to dissolve. The experience or the failing of my judgement (in some of these things) maketh me the more suspect it in other arguments and grounds of a like nature. Besides I shall never forget what your Lordship gravely and wisely once said to me— 'The ceremonies I doubted of were nowhere expressly *forbidden* in Scripture: the arguments brought against them were but by *consequence* deduced from Scripture: deduction of consequences was a work of the judgment: other men's judgment (so many, so learned, so godly) why should I not conceive? did as infallibly deduce just consequences to *allow* these things as mine own to *doubt* of them.' "

He went on to lament the shallowness of his judgment, which he had become cognisant of when it was set at difference with that of "centuries of godly men." These doubts he cited as evidence of how little Williams's tolerance of his practices had stiffened him into a "private conceit" or established his parish as an attractive nuisance for all of its neighbors. He continued: "The truth is, the ceremonies of the ring in marriage, and standing at the creed, are usually performed by myself; and all the other ceremonies of surplices, cross in Baptism, kneeling at the Communion, are frequently used by my fellow-minister in our church, and that without disturbance of the people." His parishioners, he said, were diligent in their attendance on services, and as for those who did not kneel at the communion, they had told him, and he was willing to believe it, that so great was the throng of communicants that "they can hardly stand (much less kneel), one by another." Cotton concluded by entreating Williams for further time for "better consideration of such doubts as yet remain behind," promising satisfaction should he find his scruples weak.

Convinced of the Vicar's sincerity, Williams allowed him to proceed untroubled. Cynics could suggest that Cotton's use of the ring in marriage was the result of his having decided that a wedding was really a civil ceremony anyway, so that the rites of marriage did not much matter one way or another, and as for standing at the Creed, this part of the service came just before the sermon and the Vicar could have stood as he was making his way to the pulpit preparatory to his delivery rather than out of respect to the ordinance of the church. The other ceremonies, the cynics could continue, were still not observed by him, and his readiness to believe that those who did not kneel refrained because of the press of people was simply incredible.

His admirers could counter that Cotton was an unworldly man, a scholar rather than a politician. The greater part of his time was given to preparing for and delivering lessons, and he was, indeed, an abstracted observer of what actually went on about him, trusting in those he believed were elect and accepting their explanations. Certainly, the mutilations of 1621 had taken him by surprise. What he told Williams, then, was doubtless sincere and a true reflection of his perception of the situation although it may not have been accurately descriptive of what was taking place in Boston.

Cotton himself was far from hypocritical, but as a veteran of Elizabethan university politics he had learned that when he had a superior inclined to sympathy, the wisest procedure was to agree with him as far as was conscientiously possible, and then to disagree in an humble tone, professing always a willingness to cooperate. The latter profession was sincere; the zealot was generally born out of persecution by a narrow-minded superior so that he was hardened in his "private conceit." His nonconformist brother could be equally committed to the zealot's doctrine and just as anxious to see the apostolic church reborn in England, but his experience with sympathetic or negligent superiors taught him that the reed withstood the storm better than the oak. However, as James's reign proceeded, and especially after it gave way to that of Charles, fewer and fewer members of the Puritan party could accept the lesson taught by their Elizabethan predecessors. Especially since Laud's star had risen, the church was insisting upon a close approximation of Roman Catholic ceremonies and was becoming more outspoken against Calvinism, so that not even the link of doctrine remained to unite Puritan and bishop. But thanks to his manipulating aldermen, his superiors (at first grossly negligent, at last sympathetic), and especially to his own obvious sincerity, learning and modesty, John Cotton's parish and fame had flourished. If his pupils were asked to single out the one of the many factors which most contributed to his success, they would not have hesitated in naming his piety. Church polity was of importance to their teacher, of course, but the first and foremost task of the minister was preaching the word of salvation and Cotton did this with such forthright piety that even his ecclesiastical enemies were taken by his dignity. "He was of admirable candor, of unparalleled meekness, of rare wisdom, very loving even to those that differed in judgment from him,"[28] observed a colleague; and Cotton's grandson, remembering the many anecdotes of his meekness and patience, said of his mildness under attack, "He would not set the *beacon* of his great soul on *fire* at the landing of . . . a little cockboat."[29]

So the fame of Boston spread in Puritan circles. As one after another of the nonconformist ministers were summoned to the High Court, silenced, or forced into hiding, the feat of the Vicar of Boston became increasingly sensational. Samuel Ward, the Puritan incumbent at Ipswich, remarked with facetious wonder, "Of all men in the world I envy Mr. Cotton, of Boston, most; for he doth nothing in way of

[28] Whiting, p. 425.   [29] Mather, I, 277.

conformity, and yet hath his liberty, and I do everything that way, and cannot enjoy mine."[30]

For those who lacked Cotton's temper and his success, a new alternative opened at the close of the 1620's. Heretofore the only choices seemed to be the precarious underground or exiled existence of nonconformists, or a break with the church and a setting up elsewhere as a separatist. The new solution was colonization, the establishment of a plantation in America, one which, if rightly managed, could become a holy commonwealth on earth. The Earl of Lincoln's home at Tattersall became a center for Puritans concerned with colonization, and the third Earl's chaplain, Samuel Skelton, was established in 1629 as the first minister in Massachusetts when he joined John Endicott's company in Salem.[31]

John Cotton watched the increase in plans for colonization with mixed feelings. When he had been asked to write a preface to his friend Arthur Hildersam's *Lectures upon the Forth of Iohn*, he had thought it the better policy to single out Hildersam's zeal against the separatists (rather than his nonconformity) in order to recommend the work to the licensers, and had said, "That one Letter of his to a Gentlewoman against the separation which without his consent, a separatist printed and refuted, hath so strongly and clearly conuinced the iniquity of that way, that I could not but acknowledge in it both the wisedome of God, and the weakenesse of the separatist."[32]

With such views on separation, he was disturbed at the news that reached him from the emigrants at Naumkeag (later Salem) in Massachusetts in 1629. From his conferences at Tattersall with Skelton as well as those at Sempringham

---

[30] Whiting, p. 427.

[31] The unfortunately small amount of information which exists in print on this influential founder of Massachusetts church polity may be found in Sidney Perley, *The History of Salem, Massachusetts* (Salem, 1924), I, 156-57.

[32] Arthur Hildersam, *Lectures Upon the Forth of Iohn* (London, 1629), p. [vii].

before Skelton had been ejected from his living, Cotton gathered that the emigrants were of his way, unconformable with certain of the practices of the Church of England but still members of it. Now, however, word reached him that the colonists would not commune with any who did not enter into covenant with them regardless of the new arrival's standing in the Church of England. He wrote in alarm to Skelton, pastor of the Naumkeag Church, admonishing him for what seemed to be his acquiescence in the ways of his separated neighbors at Plymouth and warning him that the anti-episcopal faction at home did not regard this as mere reformation.[33]

The following year, 1630, Cotton consented to journey down to Southampton, there to deliver the farewell sermon to the most considerable body (both in quality and quantity) of colonists yet to leave for America. Included in the group were John Winthrop, who was to be the new governor, and Lady Arbella Johnson, daughter of the third Earl of Lincoln, in honor of whom the transporting ship had been christened *Arbella*. Cotton conceived his task as preacher on that occasion to be twofold: to assure the colonists that their removal from England was just and holy; and to admonish them to remain steadfast in their holiness once they were established in the new world. The text he chose was II Samuel 7:10: "Moreover I will appoint a place for my people Israell, and I will plant them, that they may dwell in a place of their owne, and move no more."[34]

For such a removal as was being undertaken, Cotton presented three groups of reasons under the headings of procurement of good things, avoidance of evil things, and special providences of God concurring. As he spelled each

[33] Robert Baillie, *A Dissuasive from the Errours of our Time* (London, 1645), pp. 15, 65.

[34] The sermon, "God's Promise to His Plantation," appears as No. 53 in the series, *Old South Leaflets*.

reason out, he provided nonseparating Puritanism with a guiding colonial doctrine. The good things which were legitimate motives for emigration, he said, were the gaining of knowledge (as Sheba had travelled to meet Solomon); the better earning of one's daily bread ("Daily bread may be sought from farre," said the Book of Proverbs); the planting of a new city ("when the hive of the Common wealth is so full that Tradesmen cannot live one by another, in this case it is lawfull to remove"); the employing of one's God given talents more efficiently (Joseph was a better counselor than shepherd and was sent by God to Egypt); and the gaining of liberty of ordinances (as Englishmen were wont to do on the continent even before Mary began her persecutions). In citing "liberty of ordinances," Cotton's wording was very careful; he meant freedom to enjoy God's statutes, not freedom *from* any particular church. Official ears were doubtless listening, but they had no cause for offense. The religious motive was listed last in a group designed to bring prosperity to the homeland and was ambiguous as to its relation to the existing situation in the church.

Cotton went on to say that colonization was further justified if the colonists thereby succeeded in avoiding any of the three evils: widespread sin in their homeland (the example was taken from the recent troubles in the Palatinate with no allusion made to conditions in England); the miseries of debt (but not the paying of debts incurred); and persecution (as the Apostles were moved). In addition, God might tell any person or persons to migrate by a special address to their spirits, but, Cotton made clear, there were ample external checks on God's message so that it could not be confused with personal enthusiasm.

Having spelled out his theory of colonization to the passengers of the *Arbella*, Cotton proceeded to urge that they cling to the true religion, and, with fresh memory of the people of Naumkeag who appeared to have gone too far in

[61]

their degree of separation from the home church, he cautioned: "Forget not the wombe that bare you and the brest that gave you sucke. Even ducklings hatched under an henne, though they take the water, yet will still have recourse to the wing that hatched them: how much more should chickens of the same feather, and yolke?" England was the "Ierusalem at home," of which the colonists needed to be ever mindful.

Only as he closed his sermon did Cotton mention the Indians whose conversion was cited in original Puritan travel propaganda as a main if not the chief cause of colonization. He had given a rationale rooted in scriptures and Christian history and yet more ambiguous and capable of more expeditious application. Mentioning now the "poore Natives," he urged the colonists not to offend them but to enter into an exchange with them, and "as you partake in their land, so make them partakers of your precious faith: as you reape their temporalls, so feede them with your spiritualls." The conversion of the heathen, according to Cotton, was not the reason for the plantation but was the price and profit the Puritans would bestow upon the Indians in exchange for sharing the land. The practical mixture of religious doctrine and common sense concluded with a typical combination of temporalls and spiritualls: "Neglect not walls, and bulwarkes, and fortifications, for your owne defence; but ever let the name of the Lord be your strong Tower; and the word of his Promise the Rocke of your refuge."

A month after the departure of the fleet, Cotton again had occasion to concern himself with the tendency of exiled Puritans to become more separatist once away from the homeland. In April, he wrote to Hugh Goodyear at Leyden, one of the few Puritan ministers who had chosen to ally his congregation with the Dutch Reformed Church, differing from that body only in the use of English. One subject of Cotton's letter was the behavior of separatists in Holland, and, he wrote: "What deteyneth yᵉ Separatists from ioyning with you, I desire to know at your leasure. Unfeigned fellowship with Christ would easily admit, yea gladly seeke fellowship with his members, y^t walke before him in ye simplicity and purity of his Ordinaunces."[35]

As in his sermon to Winthrop's group and his letter to Skelton, Cotton was emphasizing his belief that Puritanism should seek the reform of distasteful ordinances within the established church and should not attempt a radically new or separate polity. Goodyear's group belonged to a Dutch classis very much like what Presbyterian Puritans hoped to establish in England, but Cotton did not see this as any obstacle to fellowship for a sincere reformed believer. He was far from being a Barrowist or Brownist and seeing the Church of England as rotten from top to bottom, in need of so radical a reformation that setting up apart from it was a justifiable solution. He was, therefore, disturbed by Skelton's tendency and the tendency of some English congregations on the continent to stay aloof from an established Protestant church. But reform ideas had radical institutional consequences as he had learned when the stained glass shattered in 1621 and as he was going to have to learn again in America.[36]

[35] D. Plooij, *The Pilgrim Fathers from A Dutch Point of View* (New York, 1932), p. 87.

[36] Frances Rose-Troup, in *John White the Patriarch of Dorchester and the Founder of Massachusetts* (New York, 1930), details the way in which White, too, tried unsuccessfully to see that the intellectual distinction between nonconforming Puritanism and separatism had institutional consequences in America so that the allegiance of the exiles to the home church would be one of practice as well as profession. But, she notes (p. 80), the Massachusetts Bay "emigrants were gradually drawn towards the Pilgrim Fathers to such an extent, that the line of demarcation became impossible to trace." Within ten years, John White became "dissatisfied with the trend of religious opinion" in Massachusetts, and the patriarch of the nonconformist migration "ceased to take active part in the affairs of the Colony of Massachusetts." With one exception, to be considered in the following pages, no modern historian of the period concerned with theories of polity as they revealed themselves in institutional and social patterns is able to maintain a sharp distinction between separatist and nonconformist practices once England was left behind. The distinction so well established by Champlin Burrage and so well elaborated for American Puritanism

At the time when Cotton wrote to Goodyear, Boston seemed to be the last public home of nonconformity in England. How long it would continue as such was a question which was more than vexing. Laud had that year succeeded in being elected Chancellor of Oxford, a post which had no great significance in itself, but one to which his appointment was vigorously opposed by such as Bishop Williams who controlled the votes of Lincoln, Balliol, Brasenose, and Oriel Colleges. The campaign against Laud had been forceful, and his election seemed to be the final blow to any successful organized resistance to him from within the existing structure of church and state. Now Bishop of London, Laud was the assured successor to the sequestered Abbot and already exercised almost all of the Archbishop's powers. How long could Cotton place Bishop Williams, the aldermen of Boston, or his own rhetoric between himself and the quasi-Archbishop? The restive minority in Boston now was assured of sympathetic attention from the High Court.

Such concerns were quickly cut short, however, for within the year in which he saw off the New England colonists both Cotton and his wife became gravely ill of malaria ("tertian ague"), a disease which posed a periodic and mortal threat to Lincolnshire, which in its fens provided a lush breeding place for the infecting mosquitoes. Theophilus Clinton, fourth Earl of Lincoln, a staunch Puritan who was to stand with his party even to agreeing to sit as one of the few aristocrats in Cromwell's parliament, offered his manor as a hospital to Cotton and his wife, and for the better part of a year they rested there and fought their chills and fevers. Cotton slowly recovered, but the malaria killed his wife,

---

by Perry Miller in *Orthodoxy in Massachusetts* (Cambridge, 1933) was essentially one of profession rather than practice. Cotton's early distress at the polity of the exiles, Dutch and American, is the first indication his career gives of the practical breakdown of a distinction which was all-important in England. It is only the beginning.

Elizabeth, and the Vicar was left without a family; to his great sorrow he had, in eighteen years of marriage, never become a father.

Recuperating at the Earl's seat, Cotton was at one of the English centers of information about the Massachusetts colony and he now began to regard it as a possible refuge should the threatening persecutions come. After burying his wife he resolved to travel in order to restore his health. In his visits to his Puritan friends about the land, he had brought home to him again and again the peculiarly fortunate position he and the people of Boston enjoyed and the growing danger of the times. During his absence, the chaplain presided in safety, for Anthony Tuckney, his late wife's cousin, who had succeeded Edward Wright in 1629 and who was as yet conformist (although when the rebellion came he was to turn Puritan and go on to fame as a theologian and professor at Cambridge), was presiding in a way to satisfy the High Court. But could Cotton resume his activities unmolested?

The question was temporarily postponed, for on 6 April 1632 John Cotton, in the tradition of the Puritan ministry, remarried, this time taking to wife a widow, Sarah Hawkridge Story, who brought a daughter with her. But he was not to enjoy his remarried state in Boston. News came to him, travelling faster through Puritan informants than through the formal channels designed to communicate it, that letters were out to summon him to answer to the High Court for his practices. The man to be answered was William Laud; no one could appear in his place; and only one set of answers would be deemed acceptable. The immediate solution was clear and inescapable. He must disappear, as many had done before him, into the well-organized Puritan underground, and, in whatever time concealment could purchase, consider his next move. When the High Court's messenger arrived in Boston, therefore, he failed to find the Vicar, and in the early fall, Sarah Cotton, married less than a year, began to receive letters from her husband assuring her of his safety and cautioning that it was not yet safe to join him, "For if you should now travel this way, I fear you will be watched and dogged at the heels."[37]

Cotton's first intention upon going into hiding was to look to his friends in power for relief, but he was quickly informed that the days of their influence in ecclesiastical matters had passed. The Earl of Dorset bitterly remarked that if Cotton had been guilty of drunkenness, uncleanness, or any such lesser fault, pardon was available, but that the only solution for nonconformists was to "fly for your safety."[38] But John Cotton was unsure of the prudence or righteousness of such a move. To him as to his contemporaries, flight meant Protestant Europe, Holland principally, where a precarious existence could be eked out in service to English congregations at a distance which would make possible secret visits to England and a prompt return should the Puritans move against Laud. Flight was what the apostles undertook when harried. It was a far different matter than colonization. One did not go to America merely to fly for safety, but also to establish a new home. The text from II Samuel on which he had preached to the colonists were the Lord's words on appointing a place for His children and concluded, "they may dwell in a place of their owne, and *move no more.*"

America, then, was not immediately in Cotton's mind as he considered his next move. The question he was debating was whether or not to cross over to Holland. Although a few ministers had gone to America, none of the outstanding Puritan clergymen had made such a move, for to make it was to remove one's self from the scene of action, and although the Lord had doubtless appointed the westward movement of the Gospel, He had also marked England for a great reformation which was due to take place soon. As precarious as remaining in England might be, it was perhaps the more satisfactory choice. Friends might do something yet; many

[37] Whiting, p. 432.   [38] Mather, I, 263.

a silenced minister had managed to be reinstituted or to find another patron.

On his southward journey to London, where he could hope either to find a hiding place as permanent as he might need, or an opportunity to cross over into Holland, Cotton visited John Dod, the venerable mentor of many a younger Puritan, a man who had a great reputation as a pastoral advisor and a trainer of the godly. Dod was insistent that Cotton fly, pointing out that soon the better sort in his congregation would doubtless be uneasy in England also and would follow him. Cotton was bothered, however, by the significance of the flight. Was he not known as the most successful of the practicing nonconformists, and should he now, like a coward, abandon his parish, thereby filling his friends with misgivings about their allegiances? But, he was reminded, flight is an announcement that a sincere profession of faith is more desirable than all the comforts which are thereby abandoned, and Dod said, summing up the argument which convinced Cotton, "I am old Peter, and therefore must stand still, and bear the brunt; but you, being young Peter, may go whether you will, and ought being persecuted in one city, to flee unto another."[39]

Southward from Northamptonshire, then, Cotton continued and by October 1632 was in hiding in London. There he became aware of two important reactions to his decision to flee Laud. The first came from his old friends and allies about Cambridge. Preston and Sibbes had steadfastly held to a Puritan Christian doctrine and were eager to see the church make a number of sweeping reforms in polity. But, they said, the ceremonies with which Cotton refused to comply, while they were distasteful, were, after all, matters indifferent, and need not cause an outward show of nonconformity. In admitting they were indifferent, back in 1615, Cotton had also held that it was therefore a sin that they were made

[39] Mather, I, 263 and Cotton's letter of 3 October 1634 to friends in England in which he cites Peter's case (Whiting, p. 432).

compulsory, whereas his Cambridge friends refused to agree
that they were sufficient cause for an open break. To his
London hiding place now came two eager upholders of this
position, anxious to convince John Cotton, whose learning
they appreciated and whose presence in England they felt
was essential to the party: Thomas Goodwin was Vicar of
Trinity Church in Cambridge and one of the most promising
of the protégés of Sibbes and Preston; John Davenport was
the minister of St. Stephen's, Coleman Street, a living he had
obtained by forswearing any Puritan inclinations in 1624.
Both men were wavering in their positions, and went to Cotton
determined to be convinced if they failed to convince.

Precisely that occurred. The crux of the difference was
Cotton's insistence that conformity with the rites of the church
was against the commandment which forbade graven images,
and that, his conscience being so convinced, he would sin
against it if he complied with the ceremonies. Again, he
revealed his mild and equable temper, listening as well as
urging, no more zealous in his demeanor that he had been
when he had argued the same points with Williams and had
confessed doubts. The results of his convincing Goodwin and
Davenport were farther reaching than anyone present could
have conjectured. Goodwin was to find it difficult to continue
in his conforming ways, and, after a year of trying, in 1634
he resigned his living in favor of Sibbes and fled to Holland,
returning to England to become leader of the ministerial
party which blocked Presbyterian control in Cromwell's day,
and (consciously or not) kept the door open for the left
wing of the Puritan movement. Davenport was, within the
year, to resign his living, go to Holland, and thence, in 1637,
to New England, where he helped to found the strong and
influential colony of New Haven. Both men, from the date
of their London meeting with Cotton, were his steadfast
friends. Davenport summed up his impression of Cotton at
that time when he wrote: "The reason of our desire to confer
with him rather then any other touching these weighty points,

was our former knowledge of his approved Godliness, excellent learning, sound judgment, eminent gravity, candor, and sweet temper of Spirit, whereby he could placidly bear those that differed from him in their apprehensions, All which and much more we found, and glorified God, in him, and for him."[40]

The second important reaction to Cotton's decision to avoid confronting the authorities by fleeing was that he was made aware that a considerable number of people, in Lincolnshire especially, were taking his action as the signal that true religion was no longer tenable in England and were prepared to follow him. This meant that, whether he willed it or not, his flight might not be temporary but could result in swelling a colony, so that to Holland he now added the Barbados and New England as possible refuges to be considered.

Holland was finally ruled out largely as the result of Thomas Hooker's experience there. This former colleague of Cotton's at Emmanuel had fled his bond to appear before the High Commission in 1630 and had gone to the Lowlands, where he had served congregations in Delft and Rotterdam. From the latter place, he had written Cotton, "The state of these provinces, to my weak eye, seems wonderfully ticklish and miserable . . . the power of godliness, for ought I can see or hear, they know not; and if it were thoroughly pressed, I fear least it will be fiercely opposed."[41] Now Hooker appeared in London to testify to the fact that Holland was an unsatisfactory home and to indicate that he was listening with a sympathetic ear to the pleas of his former parishioners from Chelmsford, now settled in New England, who were urging him to join them. Lincolnshire interests had always been strong in the Massachusetts Bay group and when word reached Winthrop's company that Cotton was in hiding, letters were sent pressing him to join them.

Consequently, on 7 May 1633, John Cotton wrote to

[40] Norton, p. 33.   [41] Mather, I, 340.

Bishop Williams to inform him that "the Lord, who began a year or two ago to suspend, after a sort, my ministry from that place by a long and sore sickness, the dregs whereof still hang about me, doth now put a further necessity upon me wholly to lay down my ministry there, and freely to resign my place into your Lordship's hands."[42] He thanked Williams for his mildness and the wisdom of his admonitions, assuring him that, as he had promised to do, he had studied the great churchmen recommended by the Bishop ("in comparison of whom, what am I, poor spark?"), but that if he conformed it would only be from respectful courtesy to his Bishop and reverence for the recommended writers. This was not enough, for the apostles required great faith in these matters and "howsoever I do highly prize and much prefer other men's judgment and learning and wisdom and piety, yet in things pertaining to God and his worship, still I must, as I ought, live by mine own faith, not theirs." He concluded by commending his vicarage and his congregation into Williams's hands, asking that the Bishop see that a vicar acceptable to the corporation replace him. His letter was, evidently, received kindly, for the members were allowed to name Anthony Tuckney his successor, as they desired.

Thus, what began as a journey into the underground to provide time to consider a possible course of action ended in the Downs early on a June morning in 1633. While pursuivants searched the known haunts of Puritans and a watch was set on all ports, the forty-eight-year-old Cotton, his wife, and her daughter, were rowed out to the *Griffin*, and, as their predecessors on that watery road had phrased it, took passage away not from the Church of England but from the corruptions in it.

[42] Printed in Whiting, pp. 434-37.

℃ CHAPTER THREE ℘

THE SECOND BOSTON
(1633-1636)

MR. JOHN WHITE, since the second year of King James's reign rector of Trinity Church in Dorchester, had pursued a course of compromise with the church authorities. In 1621, his interest in the spiritual and material welfare of the men who sailed from his area to fish and trade on the other side of the Atlantic took a practical form. With interested ship owners who believed they would find a profit in it, he formed an unincorporated stock company, the Dorchester Adventurers, the purpose of which was to found a settlement for sailors and traders on the coast of New England where they could have shelter when not at sea, where they could farm and hunt for sustenance and trade, and where, thus established, they would be receptive to religious influences.[1]

The first such plantation, founded at Cape Ann in 1622, was a fiasco. The ships were faulty, the men were mutinous, and the sale of fish, which had been counted upon to supply funds, was unsatisfactory because of a drastic drop in prices. Most of the adventurers became discouraged in the face of this failure, but Mr. White did not despair, for by 1627— the year in which Archbishop Abbot was suspended by a commission headed by Bishop Laud—he saw his New England project as a refuge for other than between-season mariners.

There were nonconformists in London and most of the eastern counties who expressed great interest in White's plan to erect a new colony on the old foundations, and they entered into a combination with him. Sir Henry Roswell and Sir John Young, Knights, and Thomas Southcote, John

---

[1] The facts of the founding of Massachusetts are documented in Frances Rose-Troup, *The Massachusetts Bay Company and its Predecessors* (New York, 1930).

Humphrey, John Endicott, and Simon Whitcomb, Gentlemen, obtained an enlarged grant of land from the Council of New England through the aid of Puritan sympathizers at court, under the claim that they would bring the clear sunshine of the Gospel to the benighted Indians. John Endicott was put in charge of the new company's first expedition, and when, in 1628, he arrived at Naumkeag the addition of his group to the remainder of the first company's settlers brought the number to around sixty persons.

Interest in the new project of the Dorchester Adventurers grew, but since it grew among those who were disaffected with the rule in church and state, something more than distance was desired to provide security from easy interference by the authorities. What was needed was the power of self-government which incorporation and the charter consequent upon it could ensure. Accordingly, the enlarged company petitioned for and obtained from the crown a charter of incorporation in 1629. Under this charter, new colonists were sent out, John Endicott was named head of the settlement, and power over the entire corporation remained with the London patentees.

Adverse policies toward nonconformity, however, kept abreast of the adventurers' schemes. With fines, imprisonment, and recall of the charter a distinct possibility for most of the English adventurers, more drastic action was required: the charter and governor of the corporation had to be removed to New England in order to prevent the chain of self-government within the corporation from being severed by the authorities in England. This done, the settlement and the corporation would be essentially one, and it would be a round trip of over 6,000 miles for anyone sent to bring back the charter. Accordingly, those corporation officers who were unable to migrate resigned; John Winthrop was chosen governor, and a deputy governor and assistants were elected. The charter was put aboard the *Arbella* with these leaders, and John Cotton came down to Southampton to preach their farewell sermon. On 12 June, 1630, the *Arbella* sighted Salem and came to anchor inside Baker's Island. Winthrop was soon ashore and home rule came to Massachusetts.

Within a year of Winthrop's settlement, the chief problem of civil concern, enfranchisement, was settled. Until 8 May 1631, the condition of freeman was enjoyed by the incorporators and any whom they chose to recognize as a freeman, but on that day it was ordered that "no man shall be admitted to the freedom of this body politic, but such as are members of some of the churches within the limits of the same."[2] By 1633, the number of freemen was slightly more than three hundred, more than two thirds of them having been admitted following the institution of the religious qualification.[3] Whereas the requirement of church membership assured the young commonwealth that its government would be of the godly, by the godly, and for the godly, the civil and ecclesiastical spheres were separate. Samuel Skelton and Francis Higginson, pastor and teacher of the church at Salem, had served as assistants to Endicott prior to Winthrop's settlement, but after that time both clergy and magistrates deemed it wiser that the clergy have no official capacity in the civil government and that no magistrates serve as ruling elders in the congregations.

The employments of the colonists were dictated by their physical situation. They brought with them cattle and swine which they tended with anxious care as a secure source of

[2] *Records of the Governor and Company of Massachusetts Bay*, ed. by Nathaniel B. Shurtleff (Boston, 1853), 1, 87. The spelling of citations from these records has been modernized.

[3] Unless otherwise indicated, all facts of New England history set forth here are documented in John G. Palfrey, *History of New England* (Boston, 1892), Vol. 1; Herbert L. Osgood, *The American Colonies in the Seventeenth Century* (New York, 1904), Vol. 1; and Charles M. Andrews, *The Colonial Period of American History* (New Haven, 1934-1936), Vols. 1 and 11. There is substantial agreement among these three works on the facts set forth here although noticeable difference among them, and between them and this work, on their interpretation.

meat. The land was worked mostly for crops of Indian corn, and every man, whether he were minister, cobbler, or merchant, was also a farmer. Hunting, fishing, and trading with the Indians were relied upon not only for material supply but for products which could be exchanged for articles of convenience and luxury. Immigrants arrived in steady numbers and house-building, land-fencing, and road-clearing were constant activities. For even the wealthiest, a day in the Massachusetts Bay settlement was a day of toil.

Within three years after Winthrop's arrival, Salem had lost its position as chief town to Boston, so named in honor of the home of some of the settlers, the famous beacon of nonconformity in old England.[4] The largest weekly market was held in Boston as were most of the periodic meetings of the Court. Besides Boston and Salem, the dwellings which were dotted around the mouth of the Bay clustered into the towns of Dorchester, Watertown, Charlestown, Roxbury, and Saugus. Some of these were already crowded and, in anticipation of a continuing surge of migration, the Court was jealously guarding unassigned tracts, fixing prices which, an observer noted some fifty years later, might have bought a whole province in 1680.

The church polity, unlike the civil polity, did not linger for the arrival of the charter before taking pronounced form. On 2 February 1629, the company in London made a contract with two clergymen, Samuel Skelton and Francis Higginson: "To do their endeavour in their places of the ministry, as well in preaching, catechising, as also in teaching or causing to be taught the Company's servants and their children, as also the salvages and their children, whereby to their uttermost to further the main end of this plantation, being, by the

---

[4] The report by Mather, Hubbard, and others that the town was named Boston as an honor to John Cotton cannot be supported by primary evidence, and is apparently contradicted by the name's having come into use more than a year before Cotton's settlement.

assistance of Almighty God, the conversion of the salvages."[5]

Although the Salem company which Endicott headed had been formed from dissenters who professed as great repugnance to the idea of total separation from the Church of England as they did to the idea of conformity with all of the established church's "corrupt" ordinances, Endicott had need to draw upon the nine-year experience his separated Plymouth neighbors (some forty-five miles away) had had with the American soil. Especially in the spring thaw of 1629, he had need of Samuel Fuller, deacon of the church at Plymouth and skilled in medicine, to check the infectious fever which was wasting his party. On 11 May, Endicott wrote to Governor William Bradford of Plymouth, telling him: "Gods people are all marked with one and ye same marke, and sealed with one and ye same seale, and have for ye maine, one & ye same harte, guided by one and ye same spirite of truth; and wher this is, ther can be no discorde, nay, here must needs be sweete harmonie. . . . I acknowledge my selfe much bound to you for your kind love and care in sending Mr. Fuller among us, and rejoyce much yt I am by him satisfied touching your judgments of ye outward forme of Gods worshipe. It is, as farr as I can yet gather, no other then is warrented by ye evidence of truth, and ye same which I have proffessed and maintained ever since ye Lord in mercie revealed him selfe unto me; being farr from ye commone report that hath been spread of you touching that perticuler."[6] The distinction between separatist and nonconformist upon which John Cotton was insisting within the range of the attentive ears of the bishops was becoming one of profession rather than practice on the stony shores of New England.

Governor Bradford was further cheered by the letter he

[5] "The Company's Agreement with the Ministers," in Young's *Chronicles of Massachusetts*, p. 211.

[6] William Bradford, *History of Plymouth Plantation* (Boston, 1899), pp. 315-16.

received from Salem, dated 30 July 1629.[7] It was from Charles Gott, a Salem settler, and described how the Salem church was founded. The resemblance to the Plymouth church was remarkable. The Salem men had not, as had the Plymouth men, come to America with the experience of having practiced together as a reformed congregation. They were not, as a seventeenth-century historian put it, "like *rasa tabula* fit to receive any impression, that could be delineated out of the word of God, or vouched to be according to the pattern in the mount, as they judged;"[8] still, they were inexperienced in practical matters, and the result was that advice from Plymouth was welcomed. The Salem church differed in six essential features from the established church of which it claimed to be a part: it was a local church and refused communion with members of other churches which were not so reformed; it admitted to membership only persons who evidenced signs of conversion to the extent of regeneration; it was united by a covenant; it chose its own officers; it ordained its own officers; and the officers were pastor, teacher, and ruling elders. News of the first of these features had been the occasion of Cotton's worried letter to Skelton about the distrust with which English nonconformists viewed his proximity to separation.

Governor Winthrop, when he landed in 1630, was not invited to communicate at Salem church. Since he had as yet no reformed church allegiance, he had to profess himself a converted believer and subscribe to a church covenant before he would be acceptable. Faced with the accepted fact of a covenanted local church, Winthrop presented no objections and within a month after his arrival entered into a similar body which accepted the right hand of fellowship from

[7] *Ibid.*, pp. 261 ff.
[8] William Hubbard, "A General History of New England from the Discovery to MDCLXXX," *Collections of the Massachusetts Historical Society*, Second Series (Cambridge, 1815), V-VI, 117.

Plymouth as well as Salem. On the same day that Winthrop's church was covenanted at Charlestown, another was settled at Watertown, and there the minister, George Phillips, informed Samuel Fuller that "if they will have him stand minister by that calling which he received from the prelates in England, he will leave them."[9] He never had occasion to carry out his threat. By 1633, seven churches had been formed in Massachusetts Bay, each with its own peculiarities but all maintaining, insofar as clergymen were available, the six essential features of the Salem church.

This was reformation at a gallop which outstripped the pace John Cotton had set himself or had planned for the hypothetical day when he would be rid of episcopal interference. It had been hurried on at this rate by men who departed from their blueprint when they discovered themselves in a wilderness free to do as they pleased so long as they did not choke off their sources of supply, spiritual and temporal, from England. This meant, in effect, so long as they maintained the profession and semblance of remaining within the Church of England. The original nonconformist theory by which they proceeded had been in existence for years,[10] but the remoteness of their situation and the influence of the separatists at Plymouth caused them rapidly to outstrip their theoretical models.

The polity which resulted from this mixture of influences —old nonconforming theory, frontier isolation, Plymouth example—was to become, in the nineteenth century, a source of uneasiness for anxious descendants and pious historians. To them, it appeared that the Bay settlers had been either bald hypocrites, professing allegiance to the Church of England while in earshot of Canterbury but practicing separation once on their own, or intellectual weaklings, easily seduced from

[9] Joseph B. Felt, *The Ecclesiastical History of New England* (Boston, 1855), pp. 135-36.
[10] See Burrage, I, 281-311.

their original intention by their social inferiors at Plymouth. So the matter stood when Perry Miller made his valuable contribution, demonstrating that nonconformity and separatism were not synonymous and that the Bay settlers had their own ecclesiastical theory derived from sources different from those of Plymouth. Bearing in mind these distinct sources, Miller explained that "neither Plymouth nor Massachusetts would have to persuade the others to become Congregationalist," and that it could be predicted "that their relations would be rather a matter of putting their heads together over a common program they had approached from slightly different but important angles."[11]

In his study, however, Miller places a premium on the influence of pre-existing nonconforming theory almost to the exclusion of the effects of Plymouth and of distance from England. The fact that John Winthrop had accepted the ecclesiastical formula which he found in practice at his arrival and turned his efforts to solidifying civil foundations seems to support this emphasis. But on 4 September 1633, John Gallop piloted the *Griffin* into Boston Harbor by way of a newly discovered channel past Lovell's Island.[12] On that ship was John Cotton, the man who was to coin the term "Congregationalism" and who was recognized as a pre-eminent expert on the theory and practice of nonconformity within the Church of England. Yet he was to be made very uneasy at the extent to which the Bay churches had responded to Plymouth in their isolated condition.[13] What would he do in the face of the accomplished fact?

[11] Perry Miller, *Orthodoxy in Massachusetts* (Cambridge, 1933), p. 128.
[12] John Winthrop, *Journal 1630-1649*, ed. by James K. Hosmer (New York, 1908), I, 105.
[13] All scholars who have approached the period since 1933 owe a great debt to *Orthodoxy in Massachusetts*, yet their findings reveal that Plymouth played a more important role than Miller assigns it. For example, C. M. Andrews finds *Orthodoxy in Massachusetts* (I, 379n.) "altogether admirable and conclusive" in showing that the Salem settlers "did not contract their

The answer was predictable to any who knew the preacher. John Cotton upon landing on the shores of the wilderness at the age of forty-eight would do what John Cotton upon arriving at Trinity at the age of thirteen or what John Cotton upon settling at Boston at the age of twenty-eight had done. He would keep his silence and observe, neither approvingly nor disapprovingly to all outward appearance. He would bide

---

church polity by a species of contagion from the Separatists at Plymouth." Yet in his text (1, 378), he states categorically that Deacon Fuller "brought pressure to bear on Skelton and Higginson and in conjunction with them erected at Salem . . . a church shaped after the Separatist model."

George L. Haskins, concerned with the legal consequences of ecclesiastical theory, *Law and Authority in Early Massachusetts* (New York, 1960), says of the Bay settlers that (p. 19) "Separatism in civil as well as ecclesiastical affairs was one of the direct consequences of their efforts to put their doctrines into effect." At another point, he reports that his findings indicate that (pp. 194-95) "However much the Separatist and non-Separatist Puritan sects differed as to the necessity of breaking the ties with the Church of England, their agreement on matters other than the issue of separation was always substantial. The influence of Separatist ideas upon the Massachusetts colonists was therefore not merely a result of the proximity of Plymouth but was also a part of the common heritage which the two groups had brought with them from England. Nevertheless, the substantive similarity of the details of the Plymouth marriage laws to those later enacted in Massachusetts strongly suggests that the former served as a model for the latter."

In adding to and applying the findings of Champlin Burrage to American Puritanism, Perry Miller insisted strongly upon the distinction between separatist and nonconformist. But for those who have benefited from his work, as can be seen, this is, finally, a distinction to be made in the history of ideas rather than in their practice. Raymond P. Stearns is, perhaps, the exception which proves the rule. In his study of Hugh Peter, *The Strenuous Puritan* (Urbana, 1954), Stearns maintains the distinction even to insisting upon its institutional consequences (p. 76): "Hugh Peter's Rotterdam covenant was not unique. Similar in content and purpose were the 'Ten Vows' of John White's Dorchester congregation and the Covenant of the First Church of Salem, drawn up in 1629." If this is indeed the case, then, to some extent, nonconforming theory was also producing a practice distinct from that of separatism. But so far was John White from intending any similarity with Salem that, as Frances Rose-Troup shows in her biography, he found New England polity too separatist and withdrew his allegiance, while Stearns demonstrates later in his work that so far was the 1629 Salem covenant from Peter's intention that the first thing Peter himself did when he took over leadership of the Salem church in 1637 was to formulate a new covenant which (p. 111) "con-

his time, pondering the relation of his convictions to the practices asked of him, attempting to square his beliefs with the procedures, for he was a meek and cautious man despite his celebrity. Should he disagree to the point of having to make his difference public, he would not do so suddenly. He practiced in life what he preached about matters of doctrine, *"Zeale must be according to knowledge,* knowledge is no knowledge without zeal, and zeale is but a wilde-fire without knowledge."[14] America would make her discoveries to him before he would make his revelations to her.

On board the *Griffin,* which had taken eight weeks to reach Boston, the second Mrs. Cotton had given birth to a boy, the first child of the forty-eight-year-old preacher. He could not but look upon this event as a sealing of divine assurance that he had taken the right course in setting out for America and that his future was to be a fruitful one. In memory of that passage, he named the infant Seaborn.

The birth of Seaborn also gave his father his first opportunity since his departure from England to make a declaration about his current convictions as to what constituted the true church. A Christian child must be baptized and, in addition to his father, there were two other ministers on board ship, Thomas Hooker and Samuel Stone. But in consultation with his colleagues, John Cotton agreed that the passengers aboard the *Griffin* did not constitute a congregation and that, there-

---

tained articles designed to trap all persons who held Separatist or seditious tendencies."

As will be seen, the career of John Cotton adds further to the evidence cited in this note, and finally, it is pertinent to emphasize that Samuel Eliot Morison believes it valid to drill a generation of American school children as follows: "Governor Bradford to whom Endecott appealed for help, sent Dr. Samuel Fuller to Salem, and he cured many of the sick. While so doing he talked with the leading men about church organization, and they decided to form the First Church of Salem on the Plymouth model," *The Story of the "Old Colony" of New Plymouth* (New York, 1956), p. 119.

[14] John Cotton, *Christ the Fountaine of Life* (London, 1651), p. 145.

fore, none of the ministers was truly a minister at that moment because none wished to claim the office simply as the result of his previous ordination in the established church, each believing that he would have to have been elected by a congregation. Cotton, therefore, did not have the infant baptized, but awaited his arrival in the land of a truly settled ministry.[15]

When the *Griffin* arrived with her eagerly awaited passengers, the godly in Massachusetts rejoiced, for Cotton, and to a lesser extent Hooker, were the first truly eminent ministers who had come over to them; their presence went a great way towards changing the public aspect of New England from that of yet another refuge from the establishment to that of a divinely guided community. Just as Thomas Shepard in England noted, "I saw the Lord departing from England when Mr. Hooker & Mr. Cotton were gone,"[16] so the New Englander could note that the Lord was making His presence felt in the colony. A popular pun made the rounds to the effect that God had now favored Massachusetts with the three essentials: Cotton for clothing, Hooker for fishing, and Stone for building.

Some feeling existed that Cotton should enter into one of the new churches planned for the passengers of the *Griffin* and of the *Bird* which had come in the same day, but Boston easily won the contest for his services. It was only fitting, the majority felt, that the most eminent preacher in the colony should be located in the principal city where he could be heard by the most persons and could be readily accessible to the civil authorities for consultation. Boston, after all, had been named for his home parish, and Cotton confirmed the popular decision to settle him at Boston by announcing that the faithful at St. Botolph's wanted him "to minister in this country to such of their town as they had sent before

[15] Winthrop, *Journal*, I, 107.
[16] Thomas Shepard, "Autobiography," *Publications of the Colonial Society of Massachusetts* (Boston, 1932), XXVII, 375.

hither, and such others as were willing to go along with me, or to follow after me."[17] The greater number of colonists from Boston, Lincolnshire, was settled in Boston, Massachusetts, and Cotton had more than a spiritual attachment to the parishioners who remained in England and their requests. During his settlement in America, they sent him an annual stipend, or, as he put it, they "yeerly ministered, some reall testimony of [their] . . . love."[18] So at Boston he settled, and Hooker and Stone entered into the new establishment at Newtown, later Cambridge.

On the Saturday evening following his arrival, John Cotton was asked to speak to the church of Boston on the subject of a true church. After he had made his remarks, basing them on Canticles 6, both he and his wife were admitted to church membership and their child was baptized. The church he thus entered numbered about one hundred members, and there had been some twenty-two baptisms in it prior to his presentation of Seaborn. The minister of the congregation was John Wilson, who had received his M.A. from King's, Cambridge, but who had lost his fellowship because of nonconformity and had studied more than he had preached prior to his migration with Winthrop.

The course Pastor Wilson and his parishioners were pursuing was, perhaps, a logical extension of the thinking and practices Cotton had begun in Lincolnshire, but Cotton himself had not travelled the intervening ground. He had left many good ministers and many sound believers in the church at home, and whereas he did not object to confessing his faith in order to be admitted into the reformed church and was quick to acknowledge that he was no minister even with the ordination of the established church, he must have been troubled by how closely the practices of the Bay churches

[17] John Cotton, "Reasons for his Removal to New England," in Young's *Chronicles of Massachusetts*, p. 440.

[18] John Cotton, *Of the Holinesse of Church-members* (London, 1650), p. [iii].

bordered upon separation. These churches refused to communicate with new settlers from England until such settlers had been admitted to the covenant, and were even apprehensive about too full communion with one another, fearing that this would lead to an intercongregational structure which, in time, might resemble a hierarchy. Cotton was inclined to practice in Massachusetts what he had tried to practice in Lincolnshire, a purified church service within the broad framework of the Church of England.

When sermonizing in England on the same point in Canticles to which he spoke in order to gain admission to Boston church, Cotton had said, "Such Churches . . . and Congregations are Queenes whom the Ministers and Congregations do with mutuall free consent chuse either the other. . . . Of this sort are sundry Congregations in England, and very many in the reformed forain Churches: Other Congregations, which have Ministers thrust upon them without their liking and consent, and whom ministers have to them by some clandestine conveyances, are more like to Concubines."[19] This statement, repeated on the occasion of his examination before his entrance to the Boston church, would have been accepted, but Cotton was aware of a pressure to be less cordial to English congregations, even the allegedly reformed ones. Now far from England the majority of the colonists were tartly outspoken about the sins they had left behind. But it is extremely doubtful that Cotton was ready to deplore the condition of his English congregation and most likely that he was troubled that it seemed somehow implicitly to be expected of him.

On 10 October, the church of Boston kept a fast and on that solemn occasion chose John Cotton as teacher and Thomas Leverett, his friend from Lincolnshire, the talented persuader of bishops, as ruling elder. The office of teacher was distinct, in theory, from that of pastor, the former

[19] Cotton, *Exposition of Canticles*, p. 185.

supervising the doctrine of the congregation and specializing in sermons, whereas the latter supervised the practice of the congregation and presided over the services and administered the sacraments. The preparation of converts, the consoling of weak Christians, the advising in cases of conscience more properly fell, it was thought, under the scrutiny of the teacher, whereas matters of behavior were the province of the pastor. In practice, however the duties of the two officers were not so sharply separate and the pastor sermonized frequently just as the teacher administered the sacraments. Nevertheless, for a man with John Cotton's doubts as to the correctness of New England church procedures, the office of teacher was preferable, for in it he would not be so closely responsible for the details of church administration, about some of which he had grave misgivings. On the other hand, his scholarship, his meekness, and his great preaching ability admirably fitted him to lead the way in matters of Christian doctrine, and in this area he had no hesitations. For regardless of the ecclesiastical polity, be it episcopal, synodical, or local, the relation of man to God was the greatest reality. Debates about polity were, in the last analysis, debates about appearance, and so long as he could preach the doctrine in which he believed, he found it possible to accept the church organization.

Nevertheless, John Cotton was disturbed, from time to time, by the seeming disregard for ecclesiastical order which he found among his new neighbors. Shortly after his arrival, his fellow ministers had fallen into the practice of joining together with him to debate a point of scriptures at scheduled meetings. This comfortable practice strengthened the fellowship of the ministerial class and provided the intellectual stimulation which could not now be derived from proximity to universities, printing presses, and centers of population. To his surprise, however, Cotton learned that so zealous was the regard for liberty of the churches, that two men of Salem challenged the propriety of the meetings. Samuel

Skelton, the pastor, and Roger Williams, who had lately arrived there from Plymouth but who held no office, complained that such ministerial meetings could be the groundwork for a synod or an ecclesiastical court which, in time, might dictate to the now autonomous congregations. Cotton was gratified that the meetings continued in spite of this objection, but was concerned that liberty was guarded so exaggeratedly, for even those who joined him in hearty approval of the meetings affirmed that "they were all clear . . . that no church or person can have power over another church."[20]

In considering his position on polity in Massachusetts during his first years of settlement, John Cotton saw that the church of Salem, from which had come the objection against meetings, was not only the pioneer of the near-separatist practices now followed by his own church, but was also the fierce guardian of liberties and was fervently anxious to increase them. The expedient course, one which would reflect the cast of his opinions and yet maintain him honestly in his office, he probably saw, was not to attempt to return Boston to a more conservative position, but to check the zealous pace of reform at Salem so that Boston, if it did not become less independent, at least consolidated the position it now held rather than becoming even more closely separatist. He set about such a course, one which would result, in 1636, in his publicly accepting all he had found in Boston, and which he had formerly distrusted, on the understanding that reform in polity would go no further. This, in effect, meant that he had to deal with Roger Williams, the inspiring force at Salem.

Roger Williams had first arrived at Boston in 1631 at the age of twenty-seven. His reputation for nonconformity and piety had gained him an almost immediate invitation to officiate at Boston church in the absence of John Wilson,

[20] Winthrop, *Journal*, I, 113.

who was to return home to England to fetch his family. To the no small surprise of the inviters, however, Williams declined the offer, making clear that, now that he had come three thousand miles to avoid having to conform with the established church, he did not wish to compromise himself by having communion with a church which would not do as he had done; the members, he insisted, should publicly repent the communion they had held with the Church of England when they resided in the homeland. Such a declaration, of course, would have been, at the least, inexpedient, for it would have given the lie to the contention that the Boston church was not separated. Moreover, most persons felt Williams's demand to be misguidedly severe. To repent of communion with the establishment was to abandon those godly people, friends and relatives, who were still in that kingdom, to carry the rage for purification to destructive extremes; "as if things had been so far collapsed . . . that like a vessel once infected with the contagion of leprosy it must be broken in pieces, to be new cast and moulded, or else to be judged unclean, and unfit for the service of God."[21] In the opinion of the Boston church, scouring, not shattering, would do the job.

Nevertheless, Salem church proceeded to choose Williams as teacher to replace the recently deceased Francis Higginson, whereupon the Court addressed John Endicott to remind him of Williams's refusal at Boston, to add that the new teacher had "declared his opinion that the magistrate might not punish the breach of the Sabbath, nor any other offence, as it was a breach of the first table [of the ten commandments]," to marvel that Salem would therefore have acted without consulting with the magistrates, and to request that Salem "forbear to proceed" until a conference had been held.[22] Thus, but a short time after the Bay churches had been established, the inconvenience of the autonomy of each con-

[21] Hubbard, p. 118.   [22] Winthrop, *Journal*, I, 62.

gregation threatened to cause a schism. But, within the year, before the matter increased in friction, Williams, perhaps voluntarily, left Salem for Plymouth, where he expected a more friendly reception from the avowed separatists.

The community of Plymouth, however, was not prepared to accept what Williams believed to be the logical implications of separation. Having made the break from the established church, Williams maintained, they should go on to pronounce as unlawful attendance upon the sermons of any still practicing in that church and to bar any who were not true believers from sharing in religious practices. Since the oath of fidelity to the commonwealth invoked the name of the Lord, Williams went on to insist that to tender it to the unregenerate was unlawful because this was equivalent to having religious communion with them. In short, Roger Williams asserted that strict separation of the regenerate from the unregenerate in all matters in which the name of God was concerned was the only valid separation, and that if both regenerate and unregenerate must live together in civil concord, then the magistrate who ruled over both should not concern himself with matters of religious decorum. Religious practice was the proper concern of only a part of the community, and breaches should be matter for discipline in the church rather than by the state.

This doctrine promised to cause such dissension at Plymouth that Elder Brewster was relieved to hear that Williams, in 1634, desired dismission to return to Salem. "There being then many able men in the bay," Brewster reflected, "they would better deal with him then themselves could."[23]

Back at Salem, Williams was not immediately called to office by his somewhat chastened friends, but he continued to preach, or "prophesy," as such religious lecturing by unordained speakers out of the regular course of sermons

[23] Nathaniel Morton, *New-Englands Memoriall* (Cambridge, 1669), p. 78.

was called. Among other achievements, he had convinced the Salem women to follow the biblical model of wearing veils, and so impressed was John Endicott by this garb that he challenged John Cotton on the point when the Boston teacher denied that such a practice had a sound basis.

Upon the death of Samuel Skelton in 1634, Roger Williams was called to the office of minister of the church of Salem, and the anxious authorities, backed by Cotton and Hooker (not only prominent men but men so recently arrived that the extremities of Boston were a sufficient dose for them without their imbibing the elixir of Salem), decided to make their move. The first step was halted, however, for when John Cotton examined the treatise which Williams had written at Plymouth with special attention given to the three "offensive" points, he concluded that the wording did not, as was alleged, clearly imply that King James had lied in claiming to be the first Christian prince to discover New England, had blasphemed in referring to Europe as Christendom, or had misapplied various passages of the Bible to his reign. Moreover, in discussion Williams was willing to soften his stand, and, irritating as his opinions and their effects might be, he appeared to be a sincere, pious, and extremely personable young man.

For Cotton, dealing with Williams did not mean proving his errors to the authorities so that they would find him guilty of civil disobedience and take the means of silencing him. Rather, it meant convincing Williams of his own errors so that he would cease to pursue his course of action. In preaching his peculiar doctrine of absolute grace and conditional reprobation in England, Cotton had emphasized the fact that even natural men who had not yet been illuminated by grace could be persuaded to "walk according to the knowledge and helps, which they have received, and sin not against conscience, but only out of ignorance in the state

of unbeleef."[24] In America among the godly, he was all the
more convinced that men would act according to their consciences and that, if a saint were in error, all that needed
to be done was to enlighten his conscience on the matter. The
truth was one, and America did not present the impediments
to an informed conscience which had existed in England.
Williams's willingness to discuss the matter of his treatise
and to soften his assertions was evidence that the Salem
rashness could be checked by properly informing conscience.

In the following year, 1635, however, word reached Boston
that Williams was reiterating his Plymouth teachings about
the severing of religious relations with an unregenerate man,
even to the extent of refusing him an oath in a civil case.
Salem townsmen, led by John Endicott, stood stoutly behind
Williams and added further discomfort to the authorities
by removing the cross from the English ensign, claiming the
symbol to be idolatrous. At a time when Laud was setting
guards to catch any under prosecution who were slipping out
to Massachusetts, and episcopal factions at court were pressing
their rights to the land held by the Massachusetts settlers,
the Bay could ill afford such explicit support for the oft-
repeated claim that the colonists were anti-Church and anti-
King. But Salem seemed bent on providing that evidence.

Therefore, disciplinary civil action began in earnest in May
of 1635. Endicott was barred from serving as a magistrate
for a year, and in July the Salem petition for some land in
Marblehead Neck was refused "because they had chosen
Mr. Williams their teacher, while he stood under question
of authority, and so offered contempt to the magistrates."[25]
Williams, who had fallen ill that summer, countered by
writing to his church that he would not communicate with the
churches of the Bay and that unless Salem likewise refused
such intercourse he would not communicate with Salem either.

[24] Twisse, *A Treatise of Cottons*, p. 230.
[25] Winthrop, *Journal*, I, 155.

As offended as the Salemites were at what they regarded as unjustly vindictive action against their petition, they were, nevertheless, sufficiently level-headed to realize that the further step which Williams was advising was the beginning of anarchy. For in his threat to separate from them if they did not separate from others, he gave a glimpse of the continued splintering to which Salem could look should he be followed any further.

During the summer, therefore, Endicott made his peace with his fellow magistrates, but Roger Williams was not so easily convinced. Although Thomas Hooker and he dealt assiduously with Williams, Cotton learned that there was an alternative conclusion to such cases, little considered in old England. The man who professed his conscience was not convinced need not be flexible, for he was on the fringe of a howling wilderness. If he had the inclination and the courage, he could simply move on, placing himself further in the wilderness both physically and spiritually, rather than recanting or living a persecuted life. This course Williams considered preferable to accepting the arguments of Hooker and Cotton; he received his banishment with outrage at his being persecuted but with confidence in his ability to conquer the wilds.

"I desire not to sleep in security and dream of a nest which no hand can reach," said Roger Williams; "I cannot but expect changes."[26] John Cotton, on the other hand, while he recognized change, believed during his early New England years that the transformation would be in one direction, that of the consolidation of the holy commonwealth on earth. Necessary for that consolidation was the silencing of disturbing doctrines such as that of Roger Williams, but equally necessary before that commonwealth would be perfected was the silencing of those doctrines through the convincing of

[26] Roger Williams, "Letter to John Winthrop," *Publications of the Narragansett Club*, First Series (Providence, 1874), VI, 6.

conscience, and he was disturbed that in Williams's case the banishment had preceded such conviction.

Accordingly, he addressed a letter to Williams which began with his insistence that the civil authorities had banished Williams without his consultation or consent, although he could not deny that there was just provocation and due procedure in the expulsion. He insisted that Williams's rage for further separation had, in effect, resulted in Williams banishing himself, and he devoted the main part of the letter to showing Williams "the sandiness of those grounds" of separation. But Cotton's mind could not rest easy if he thought, or if he believed that Williams thought, that the cause of banishment was the tendency of Williams's doctrines to disturb the peace of the church and the state. Accordingly, Cotton took particular pains to spell out to Williams his stand on degrees of reformation because as a minister he was more concerned with the root of Williams's separation than he was with its effects. That root was Williams's inability to see the situation of the church in any shades other than black and white. Williams insisted that if a church were true, as the Bay churches claimed to be, and if it were different from the home church because it recognized imperfections in the home church, then it was impossible for that true church to have anything to do with the home church without tainting itself; therefore, it should not tolerate new members who refused to disown their former communion with the Church of England. With irony, Williams pointed up the zeal of the Bay churches in reforming manners, outward matters, while they tolerated corrupt principles, inward matters, such as affiliation with the home church.

Cotton attempted to show Williams that this dualism existed not because of any hypocrisy on the part of the members but because the greater sin was the subtler one. The iniquity of the home church is not so obvious to many of your fellow Christians as it is to you, Williams was told in effect, and you must learn to bear with these people and to appreciate that they are, nevertheless, truly repentant souls. Recognizing that Williams viewed the toleration of members of the home church as a stopping midway between Christ and antichrist, Cotton explained: "Wee conceive the Lord hath guided us to walke with an even foote between two extreames; so that we neither defile our selves with the remnant of pollutions in other Churches, nor doe wee for the remnant of pollutions renounce the Churches themselves, nor the holy ordinances of God amongst them, which our selves have found powerfull to our salvation."[27] Nonconformity rather than separation may have been merely a difference in rhetoric for some in the Bay, but John Cotton wanted to be understood as believing himself an active member of the Church of England who retained a keen sense of his obligation to it—had he not been saved in that church?—and warm feelings toward many who practiced in it in England. Roger Williams pocketed the letter before plunging into the woods; Cotton would hear his reply in a day more auspicious for the exile.

In 1635, at the time when he had been dealing in conference with Roger Williams, Cotton received a letter from England requesting his opinion on an enclosed treatise against persecution for cause of conscience.[28] The letter was but a fragment of the wide correspondence he held, for his reputation as a scholar and teacher was still strong in his homeland, but the topic was a particularly appropriate one for him to consider at the time. How utterly appropriate it was, he was not fully to appreciate until some ten years later, for Roger Williams was eventually to create his masterpiece not only

[27] John Cotton, *A Letter of Mr. John Cottons to Mr. Williams* (London, 1643), p. 11.
[28] This treatise is the first section of Roger Williams's "The Bloudy Tenent of Persecution," *Publications of the Narragansett Club*, First Series (Providence, 1867), Vol. III. Cotton's reply is the second section and Williams's examination and refutation of that reply is the third and main section.

on that topic but as a refutation of Cotton's handling of it. However, in 1635 Cotton's answer was but another letter of advice.

He began by affirming the difference between a man's claiming conscience as his reason for professing a certain point of doctrine and as his ground for practicing some act which he believed to be a religious duty; went on next to divide points of doctrine into fundamental, without which there was no salvation, and circumstantial, wherein differences could exist without prejudice to salvation; and to maintain that religious practices were also divisible in this manner. He continued his distinctions by pointing out that a man could hold his doctrine or pursue his practice meekly and peaceably or in disturbance of the civil peace, and concluded his preliminaries by saying: "let me adde this one distinction more: When we are persecuted for *Conscience* sake, It is either for *Conscience* rightly informed, or for erronious and blind *Conscience*."[29]

Proceeding upon this foundation, Cotton maintained that in fundamental points it was never lawful to persecute a person for a rightly informed or for an erroneous but blind conscience. A man in the latter state should be given wise admonitions, he said, "So that if such a Man after such Admonition shall still *per*sist in the Errour of his way, and be therefore punished; He is not *persecuted* for Cause of *Conscience*, but for sinning *against* his Owne *Conscience*."[30] In circumstantial matters, an erroneous person should be tolerated until God made the truth manifest to him. Of course, if he maintained his difference boisterously he could justly be punished for the civil disturbance he caused.

Cotton then proceeded to evaluate the arguments the treatise had offered in support of total toleration, omitting none. These fell under three headings: scriptural, historical, and patristic.

[29] *Ibid.*, p. 42.   [30] *Ibid.*

The first biblical support, one which became symbolic of the toleration controversy, was taken from Christ's commandment to let the tares and wheat grow together until the harvest. The author of the treatise took this to mean that those who walked in error in this world could be tolerated until they entered eternity, at which time Christ would pluck them out. Cotton countered by arguing that the field in which this crop was sown was not the world but the church, and since tares were very much like wheat, they signified not those who were clearly in error but hypocrites who were indeed unsound but who could not be detected and rooted out of the church by men. He matched the other scriptural arguments with his interpretations of the passages.

The historical supports Cotton met by citing other historical events, principally Elizabeth's sound harrying of the Roman Catholics. All his subsequent training had confirmed him in his conviction of the justice of the horrible sight he had seen as a boy in Derby during the terrible month of the Armada. For every patristic writing in favor of toleration Cotton either found another interpretation or another church father, crowning all these with: "*Calvins* judgement is well knowne, who procured the death of Michael Servetus for pertinacie in *Heresie*, and defended his fact by a Book written of that Argument."[31]

Informing the theory which he set forth in the letter were two practical considerations which Cotton had developed in nearly twenty-five years of service as a curate of souls, and which spokesmen for toleration either disregarded or concealed. The first was that no church, regardless of how reformed, could rid itself of hypocrites; the extension of the argument for toleration was that such purity was attainable, and, indeed, Roger Williams was bearing this out in separating himself from everyone in what appeared to be a ridiculous effort to be sure that he was not in church estate

[31] *Ibid.*, p. 52.

with any who were not spotless. The second practical consideration was the power of error to infect bystanders.

Both the letter to Williams and the letter to the English
advice seeker were sent without eliciting any immediate
response, for Roger Williams, his conscience unconvinced,
was busy surviving on the tangled path to Narragansett Bay.
But Cotton believed his assertions, and whereas Williams
may not have opened his ears to Cotton's admonitions, Cotton,
who upon his arrival in Massachusetts had felt that his conscience needed a great deal of enlightening before he could
approve of local church practices, and who had consequently
maintained his differences while seeking enlightenment, was
convinced by some of Williams's contentions. Writing to
inquiring friends in England in October 1635, he told them
that were he with them he would not "now partake in the
Sacraments with you, [even] though the Ceremonies were
removed."[32] He warned them against continuing to maintain
fellowship with the unregenerate in parish churches lest
this prove, ultimately, to be a fellowship with sin. Not only
did he justify his migration, but he went on to urge that
he be followed, insisting that to tarry in England was to
become corrupt. Roger Williams and his sympathizers when
they learned of such pronouncements on Cotton's part were
baffled at his sturdy opposition to their own practices and
could not but view him as inconsistent or hypocritical. On
the basis of the same evidence, meanwhile, many of the
faithful who tarried in England could only conclude that
men like Roger Williams had captured the mind of John
Cotton, who was now enthusiastically embarked on the road
of separation.

What Cotton had succeeded, in fact, in doing after three
years of settlement was to arrive privately at the position
which he had been holding publicly, by implication, ever
since his appointment as teacher of the church of Boston.

[32] Baillie, *A Dissuasive*, p. 66.

The cynic might view his progress as a massive rationalization designed to cover a lack of firm principles and the capitulation to the *status quo* consequent upon it. Because Cotton did conclude his change of heart by saying that the appearance, the form of the Boston church, was, indeed, the reality, the form of the true church, there would always be some valid basis for such scepticism. But for Cotton, acceptance of the New England way was a milestone arrived at only after vigilant striding between the separatists and the communicants of the parish church in England. Arrival at the milestone should be signalized, he felt, and he did this not only by delivering his concept of church polity in a sermon, but by doing so in Salem, the home of the late Samuel Skelton, whom he had rebuked by letter in 1629 for following many of the same practices he now accepted, and the site of the recent defeat of Roger Williams.[33]

In Salem, in 1636, John Cotton proclaimed that he now had found sufficient light to endorse what the churches had been doing ever since his arrival. The scriptural ground of his difficulty, he explained, had been that he had formerly believed that the covenant which the Lord made with man and his seed was made by the righteousness of faith at large, and that, therefore, all true believers should be admitted to the sacraments regardless of membership in the particular church in which they wished to communicate. He now saw, however, that the covenant was made by the faith of the seed of Abraham, that is, to such believers as were confederate with Abraham. He thus acquiesced in the necessity of a church covenant which made men confederated before they could practice in a church. Without such a covenant there was no true church.

John Cotton thus announced his attachment to the form of ecclesiastical organization which was so new as to be

[33] John Cotton, *A Sermon Preached by the Reverend Mr. John Cotton Deliver'd at Salem, 1636* (Boston, 1713).

nameless until some six years later he himself was to label it Congregationalism. He was fifty-one, well known for his learning, and deeply experienced in church matters. But the lessons he had learned in England were to be made to fit what he found growing in America rather than the reverse. The new land imposed its conditions upon him, and he, after extended debate, accepted them and then employed his talents to clothe these conditions in the mantle of respectability. His first act in that enterprise was to discover to the church of Salem the grounds he had found for believing as they did, even as he continued to warn them against those (like Williams) who separated from churches at the slightest breach. They "think they are sprinkled with the water of Separation: but believe it, they are Separated from Christ Jesus for ever."[34] If John Cotton was to go as far as Salem had gone, it was in order that Salem should go no further.

In civil matters, however, John Cotton displayed a powerful and, to the majority of the deputies, monotonous consistency. He had come from a land governed by crown, lords, and commons to a plantation which, he believed, should reflect the same system of organization.[35] "Democracy," he wrote in a 1636 letter, "I do not conceyve that ever God did ordeyne as a fitt government eyther for church or commonwealth. If the people be governors, who shall be governed?"[36] The best form was theocracy, which for Cotton meant separate but parallel civil and ecclesiastical organizations framed on the evidence of scriptures. Church and state, he believed,

---

[34] *Ibid.*, p. 40.

[35] The discussion of Cotton's theocratic ideal is based principally upon the *Discourse about Civil Government in a New Plantation Whose Design Is Religion* (Cambridge, 1663). Isabel M. Calder's argument that Cotton is the author (*New England Quarterly*, III, 82-94) seems convincing, but even should Davenport have been the actual penman, evidence of his relying upon Cotton's ideas is sufficient to justify regarding the discourse as representative of Cotton's opinion on the subject.

[36] Thomas Hutchinson, "Copy of a Letter from Mr. Cotton to Lord Say and Seal in the Year 1636," *History of Massachusetts Bay* (Cambridge, 1936), I, 415.

were of the same genus, "order," with the same author, "God," the same subject, "man," and the same end, "God's glory."

On the level of species, however, the two diverged. Here the end of the church was the salvation of souls while that of the state was the preservation of society in justice. This meant that the subject of the church was inward man and was limited to those only who were in a state of grace although the government, in order to preserve society, saw to it that outward men, ungodly as well as godly, attended the church meetings. Moving along parallel lines, church and state could avoid dissolving into one another by not delivering spiritual power into the hands of the magistrates, not, for instance, allowing the civil authorities to excommunicate from the church, and, conversely, by not holding a man responsible in church for his civil opinions, which procedure would bring about a type of papal excommunication. However, if the lines were not to dissolve into one another neither were they to diverge through the failure of one to lend full and sympathetic support to the other.

The rule that freemen be church members, even though it might result in power residing in the hands of a minority, was the only equable basis for citizenship. The godly could be trusted to be just to the ungodly as well as to the saints, but the ungodly, by definition, were not entitled to the same trust. The laws the godly would rule by were the laws of God, and in all hard cases, the clergy could be consulted without danger of a confusion of church and state.

The chief intrinsic obstacle to the well-being of such a state was the lack of any clear model of a constitution, for the Bible was susceptible of various interpretations. Moses' laws, Cotton affirmed, were ceremonial as well as moral, and the former were to be considered dead while the latter were still binding in a civil state. But who was to identify whether any particular precept was ceremonial or moral? Richard

Hooker, back in 1594, appreciated the fact that the Puritan insistence on God's laws was a marvelous vantage point for attack upon other forms but an indefensible position should it ever come into power. On behalf of the episcopalian party, he had warned the Puritans: "not to exact at our hands for every action the knowledge of some place of Scripture out of which we stand bound to deduce it . . . but rather as the truth is, so to acknowledge, that it sufficeth if such actions be framed according to the Law of Reason; the general axioms, rules, and principles of which Law, being so frequent in holy Scripture, there is no let but in that regard, even out of Scripture such duties may be deduced by some kind of consequence."[37] Hooker was speaking only of church government. The problem was greatly compounded in New England when John Cotton and his fellows attempted to apply their theocratic notions to the commonwealth as a whole. Almost immediately questions of scriptural interpretation arose, prompted by differences of opinion on matters of life and property, and Cotton's parallel lines began the vibrating and colliding which were to prove his theory unworkable. But as imperfect as the theory was and continued to be in practice, the fascination it held for Americans never faded entirely, and centuries after its defeat by the more practical doctrine that the state belongs to the godly and ungodly alike, American rulers still frame their rhetoric as an appeal to the godly and paint the promised future as one in which the laws of God and the laws of man will so coincide that the commonwealth will resemble an holy city.

When John Cotton took his freeman's oath at the General Court of May 1634, he was invited to preach to the Court. He did so, delivering the doctrine that "a magistrate ought not to be turned into the condition of a private man without just cause."[38] In so preaching, Cotton was supporting his

[37] Richard Hooker, *Of the Laws of Ecclesiastical Polity* (Oxford, 1793), I, 294.
[38] Winthrop, *Journal*, I, 124.

concept of the state, especially his notion of the role of the civil governor who was placed over the people by God speaking through them in their votes. Once the magistrate had been elected, he believed, further elections were not for the purpose of the people's choosing whomever they thought to be the best man at the time of voting, but were, rather, for the purpose of the people's reaffirming their initial choice. Defeat at the polls in seventeenth century Massachusetts Bay was far more than political; it was more closely equivalent to a congregation's expulsion of its minister. Just as the church chose and ordained its rulers but then abided by their administration and removed them only on grave consideration, so, in a theocracy, Cotton insisted, the same magistrates should be returned year after year. Elections did not and would not make Massachusetts a democracy "if it [the government] be administered, not by the people, but by the governors"[39] who were responsible to the people only for their honesty, not for their policy or their competence, and who were to be retained in office so long as they served faithfully under God.

His auditors in the Court listened respectfully, but the discussion which followed revealed their distrust of the doctrine. However sympathetic some of the magistrates may have been to this enlargement and consolidation of their power they had sufficient political instinct to question its official proclamation and they decided to consult other ministers before accepting it in a legal manner. Nothing more came of it legally.

In September of the same year, the discontent of the Newtown settlers, which had been bubbling ever since the settlement of that group with Hooker as their minister, boiled over into a meeting of the Court. Hooker complained that a fundamental error had been committed in placing towns so close to one another and the citizens complained that because of this they had insufficient accommodation for

---

[39] Hutchinson, I, 416.

their cattle and were unable to maintain their ministers. They professed themselves anxious to move to Connecticut, as yet unsettled by any English, and affirmed that aside from taking advantage of the fruitfulness and commodiousness of Connecticut, they would be placing a check on the ambitions of the Dutch to exploit that land. But they needed the permission of the General Court because in settling in Massachusetts Bay they had entered into a covenant which could not be unilaterally dissolved.

The members of the Court opposed to the removal of Hooker's congregation argued that the departure of such a number would weaken a precariously feeble commonwealth, divert new colonists away from the Bay, and place the Newtown people in danger of assault from the Dutch and the Indians. They offered to grant further land to Newtown from adjacent plots or to allow a removal northward within the bounds of the Bay patent. They concluded their arguments with an appropriate scriptural passage, Revelation 2:5, to show that the removal of a church from its neighbors was an adverse judgment of God.

This debate led to even greater legislative difference because so unclear was the model for such a decision that the majority of the assistants (magistrates elected at large by all freemen) opposed removal and the majority of deputies (representatives from each town) favored it. The Court was, theoretically, one body and the total majority, therefore, favored the removal, but now for the first time the question arose as to whether the majority of the assistants could veto a measure decided upon by the majority of the deputies. They insisted upon their negative voice and the Connecticut issue became a matter of constitutional interpretation.

Obviously, this was one of the civil situations in which the Court needed the expert help of a theologian and after Thomas Hooker declined the office because he was personally involved in the substance of the controversy, John Cotton was asked to preach. He took his text from Haggai, the Lord's urging of the people in his covenant to be strong and His promising to shake nations for them, and from it drew the doctrine that the strength of the magistracy resided in their authority, of the people in their liberty, and of the ministry in their purity. All matters should be decided by all groups concurring, and, therefore, if the magistrates disliked some matter they did have the veto power. Lest the people consider this dangerous, however, Cotton amply opened to them their rights to maintain their true liberties against any unjust violence.[40]

The sermon was an immediate success and the Newtown congregation accepted enlargement locally while the Court accepted the principle of the magistrates' veto. But only immediately. The deputies recognized that Mr. Cotton's "true" before their liberties and his "unjust" before the violences they could object to, severely limited their power, and they continued in meeting after meeting to press for more and more power while the Connecticut settlers waited only until warm feelings had cooled before presenting their suit once more and, the second time, succeeding.

Cotton's theocratic ideal was further undermined in December of 1634 when the inhabitants of Boston, in choosing seven men who would make division of the town lands, left out the magistrates who resided in Boston, "fearing that the richer men would give the poorer sort no great proportions of land, but would rather leave a great part at liberty for new comers and for common, which Mr. Winthrop had oft persuaded them unto."[41] The citizens of Boston were feeling the straitness of their physical bounds and taking that occasion to react against the tightness of the magisterial bounds, for there was talk that an aristocracy could soon be induced to settle and that the land was being held for such noblemen. There was some truth to the rumor but principally the magisterial

[40] Winthrop, *Journal*, I, 133 ff.   [41] *Ibid.*, I, 143.

faction was holding further land grants in check because of the expected increase of refugees from the policy of Laud, and because Winthrop had the foresight to perceive that Boston, eventually, could not succeed as an agricultural community but would have to rely heavily upon its trades. Encouraging farming by further grants of land, therefore, seemed to him to postpone the inevitable and to keep back the proper prosperity of the city.

In this connection, John Cotton was again called upon to deal with a civil matter in a sermon, and drawing upon the Israelite pattern he showed that it was the Lord's order that the elders, i.e., magistrates, be entrusted with such business. If the citizens were to ignore this, then at least they should have elected a mixed body which included some of the foremost residents. The chastened Bostonians agreed to a new election, but deputies and freemen clearly perceived that John Cotton's civil function was defining itself as that of a scriptural apologist for the magistrates and three years after his settlement they were not so eager to hear his voice raised in civil matters as they once had been. He stood for the theocratic model of restricted liberties. The function of the people was to obey the rulers with whom they had covenanted—this utterance they knew they could always expect from him.

Cotton's seconding of his model through sermons revealed also that if the parallel lines of church and state were to collide then the dominant course would be that taken by the state. He had gladly appeared at the request of the magistrates to support their claims, but they were too practical to wait for the time when he would convince the conscience of Roger Williams and banished him without consulting the ministry. Congregationalism with its insistence upon the autonomy of each congregation and its suspicion of any intercongregational body did not provide the needed machinery for correcting the aberrations of any given church, and the magistrates assumed that function by stepping in with civil charges when they deemed the aberration dangerous enough. Within the first five years of its establishment, Massachusetts Bay's theocracy was one in which the balance of power between the church and the state was already uneven on the side of civil authority. Enemies of the system would have painted a more incisive caricature if they pictured a puppet dressed in clerical garb dangling from strings in the magistrate's hands than if they set a crafty-eyed priest behind the throne of the governor whispering into his ear.

The greatest opportunity John Cotton received to exert his influence on the frame of the commonwealth came in May of 1636 when he was appointed a member of a committee to make a draft of laws agreeable with the word of God which could serve as the constitution for the young plantation.[42] Although the committee did not function as a body, Cotton, in October, presented his code. In keeping with his scholarly habits, his conservative frame of mind, and his desire to make the principled action equivalent to the expedient one, Cotton gave the greater part of his code over to outlining what already existed. His constitution was an act of consolidation rather than one of providing new and needed rules, and in spite of its title, *Moses His Judicials,* drew only its chapters on crime and inheritance directly from the scriptures. All the other provisions followed the concoction in existence at the time of his writing with scholar Cotton merely providing biblical support. Since expansion, not consolidation, was what was needed only a part of Cotton's code was incorporated into the "Body of Laws" which was eventually adopted. Cotton's code lived on,[43] however, as a model for religious

[42] The following discussion of *Moses His Judicials* is based on the perceptive study by Isabel M. Calder in *Publications of the Colonial Society of Massachusetts* (Boston, 1935), XXVIII, 86-94.

[43] "What is remarkable is that Cotton, who had no legal training and who was not an officer of the colony, should have had as complete a grasp as he did of the fundamentals of its government, of the laws already in existence, and of the needs in certain directions for guarantees of due process and civil rights." Haskins, p. 126.

communities which had no laws whatsoever, and influenced both the settlement at New Haven and that at Southampton, Long Island.

Three years after his settlement in Massachusetts Bay, John Cotton's reputation as an adviser on matters of polity, civil and ecclesiastical, had settled to a lower level than it occupied when his arrival was anticipated and when he was first ushered into office. Cotton's genius was for strengthening and consolidating what had been achieved rather than for showing the way to further accomplishments and he, therefore, did not volunteer public leadership except when such was obviously demanded of him. The decision which sent him to Boston and Hooker to Newtown was to prove a wise one for Massachusetts for it allowed each man to utilize his gifts to the utmost. Hooker, the restless refugee who had fled to Holland and again to Massachusetts, was to go on to found a new colony which was separate from and yet dependent upon its bigger brother, Massachusetts Bay; while Cotton, who had weathered fourteen years of Cambridge politics and twenty more of parish politics, was to become a master of the Massachusetts way, and then its greatest spokesman. In the first years of Cotton's settlement, pioneers, not cultivators, were needed in public affairs, and he had to accommodate himself to many things which occurred in spite of, if not in opposition to, ideas he held.

What was happening to John Cotton's political ideas and his reputation as a public adviser, however, was decidedly secondary, for the great excitement generated in Massachusetts when word of his probable arrival had come and the eager expectations of the wonders of his presence were based on his reputation as one of the greatest, if not the greatest Puritan preacher in England. And in this sphere he was so far from disappointing that he met and surpassed all anticipations based on his ability until his very triumph grew so large it threatened the newborn colony with destruction.

CHAPTER FOUR

PUPIL AND LESSON ON TRIAL
(1636-1638)

JOHN COTTON was ordained as teacher of the Boston church on 10 October 1633 and by December of that year his foremost parishioner, John Winthrop, could reflect: "It pleased the Lord to give special testimony of his presence in the church of Boston, after Mr. Cotton was called to office there. More were converted and added to that church, than to all the other churches in the bay. . . . Divers profane and notorious evil persons came and confessed their sins, and were comfortably received into the bosom of the church. Yea, the Lord gave witness to the exercise of prophecy."[1] The teacher's English practice of fifth-day lectures was happily received by his new congregation, for preaching was not only a spiritual necessity for the small colony, but, now that the great Cotton was settled, a spiritual luxury. Note-taking during sermons was regarded as a commendable practice which sharpened the note-taker's concentration and provided profit and enjoyment for groups within the congregation, who thereby filled the intervals between sermons with discussion of the doctrines recently opened by their preachers and with debates on obscure or ambiguous points. For such colonists, sermons were the great episodes in lives of material privations and recreational restrictions. So eagerly did they attend the Boston fifth-day lecture that soon Newtown, Dorchester, and Roxbury also enjoyed weekday preaching and a man with a stout horse and time at his disposal could attend a lecture almost every day. The popular following of lectures, as gratifying a reflection of the godliness of the colonists as it was, nevertheless threatened to prove inexpedient in the end, for the settlers were distracted from their necessary mundane

[1] Winthrop, *Journal*, I, 116.

occupations, and in October of 1634 an agreement had to be made whereby the ministers consented to reduce the lectures to two days: "viz., Mr. Cotton at Boston one Thursday . . . and Mr. Hooker at Newtown the next . . . and Mr. Warham at Dorchester one 4th day . . . and Mr. Welde at Roxbury the next."[2]

The emphasis on preaching in a community relatively devoid of pastimes resulted, inevitably, in the laymen comparing preachers and even choosing sides. Should a small gap open between the doctrines of two men, their followers tended to widen it in their discussions, and when a real difference developed, it was matter for public confrontation and private recrimination even though all concerned recognized that the difference was on a point which was not essential to salvation. Under these conditions, John Cotton preached his Christian doctrine.

The congregation which heard John Cotton was, like his English audience, made up both of the elect and the reprobate. But whereas both groups were church members in England and entitled to the sacraments, indeed, no ecclesiastical distinction was made between them, in New England only the elect were admitted to membership. With the entire commonwealth, in Cotton's view, being of the godly, for the godly, and by the godly, he no longer felt the need to preach directly to the reprobate, and as time went by his sermons no longer contained reference to the peculiar doctrine of conditional reprobation which squared so illogically with the doctrine of absolute election.

Cotton bent his efforts to preaching salvation on the assumption that not only was this the greatest single task of the preacher but that news of their salvation came to most men in this way only. Hearing, not reading, the word brings conversion, he insisted, and in support he cited the history of the church, during which, he claimed, there had never been a

2 *Ibid.*, I, 135-36.

famine of reading the word, but during which, nevertheless, there had been antichristian times because the word was not preached. He pointed out that the apostles always wrote to those who were already believers because they realized that faith comes not from reading. He insisted that "All the work that reading could reach unto, could not reach to beget and worke saving faith, which is the principall scope of preaching."[3] He therefore mounted the pulpit with the solemn conviction that he was the instrument of the Holy Spirit with a responsibility which had devolved upon him from Sibbes, which he had had demonstrated to him in the conversion of Preston, and which made its consequences felt to him daily. Conversion was an emotional experience, he knew, for he as a young man had been brought to terror by the preaching of others so that he sought for faith in himself. Faith he had found, not when his reason devised it, but when he felt its presence. Preaching was an articulation of that experience designed to bring others to a sight of their being in a blessed estate and to strengthen them once they were in it.

In general, Cotton adopted the terminology of Calvin and Perkins. He spoke of election, justification, sanctification, and glorification: those whom God chose He justified, absolving them of their sins by considering them paid for in Jesus Christ; those who were justified were also sanctified by receiving spiritual gifts which, while not indemnity from sin, aided them in leading a godly life. None could be justified or sanctified who was not elected from the beginning of time by God. All who were so elected were consequently justified and sanctified even though they lapsed back into sin.

But within the general Calvin-Perkins framework there was room for various differing interpretations, and Cotton's immense pulpit success, although rooted in his absolute devotion to his being God's instrument when he preached, flowered as the result of the peculiarity of his particular

[3] Cotton, *Christ the Fountaine*, p. 181.

emphases. A covenant is generally conceived to be a hypothetical proposition: the person concerned covenants to do something in exchange for something. Thus, in one application of the covenant of grace, *if* man believes in God and throws himself upon Him for salvation, *then* God will show him signs of his salvation. But Cotton, while in his sermons he used the covenant terminology, did not accept the proposition as such. Rather, he urged the utter inability of man to do anything for his own salvation, even bewail his own unbelief, and would not declare there was an *if* man could perform before the *then* which God would agree to. Such an interpretation, he feared, opened the way for a Roman Catholic covenant of works since once one admitted that man should perform an act prior to his being saved, man became an actor who could affect God's disposition toward him. If it were admitted that he could influence God's judgment by achieving a proper kind of belief, then why not by acting decorously, doing penance, or contributing to the church? Cotton taught that such conditions for salvation had been in effect prior to the crucifixion when man, under the covenant of works, had to obey the Law of Moses in order to be saved and was consequently damned because his corrupt nature was incapable of meeting the requirements of the Law. But now in the days of the Gospel, he maintained, the Law is completely dead as a means of salvation, and the covenant with the Lord prefixes no conditions upon man's part but freely gives him the necessary requirements for salvation. The covenant is not one to be entered upon before you know you are saved, but one which reveals its benefits to you when you are redeemed. The Spirit enters man not only to work faith in him, but also, first, to convince the soul of its own unbelief. From beginning to end, man can do nothing without the Spirit, not even lament his spiritless condition. Cotton preached: "For the order of Nature in giving the Covenant: not Obedience first, nor Faith first, nor any thing else first, but himselfe is *Donum primum & primarium,* and in him, all his goodnesse."[4]

The chief corollary of Cotton's fundamental insistence upon man's utter passivity in the first act of his redemption was that no man could trust gifts he had received. It is dangerous to point to greater spiritual gifts and to assume thereby that you must be saved, for, he cautioned: "Though his mind be inlightened, sometimes to feare, sometimes to joy, to humiliation, to inlargement, to zealous reformation, yet rest in none of these, for these you may have and yet want Christ, and life in him; common graces may and will deceive you."[5]

Another danger was taking so great a delight in the purity of the New England churches that one relied upon his association with a reformed church service to help him on his way to salvation. Of course, one should cherish the true ordinances of the church and refuse to part with them, but, Cotton went on: "while you enjoy them, trust not in them, nor thinke not to stand upon this, that you are blessed in regard of them; but looke at them all as losse, and drosse, and dung, *that you may win Christ.* Looke not so wishly at the Priviledges of the Ordinances, trust not in the outward letter of them."[6]

Finally, Cotton insisted, so completely was salvation an inner experience, dependent solely upon man's personal relationship with the Holy Spirit, that even the scriptures could be a false source of comfort to the unwary. As radical as he might sound, Cotton went to the logical extreme of his doctrine of salvation, and declared: "Let not men be afraid, and say, That we have no *revelation* but the *word*: for I do believe, and dare confidently affirme, that if there were no revelation but the word, there would be no spiritual grace revealed to the soul; for it is more then the Letter of

[4] John Cotton, *The New Covenant* (London, 1654), 14-15.
[5] Cotton, *Christ the Fountaine*, p. 27.   [6] *Ibid.*, p. 22.

the Word that is required to it: not that I look for any other matter besides the *word*. But there is need of greater light, then the *word* of it self is able to give; for it is not all the *promises* in Scripture, that have at any time wrought any gracious changes in any soul, or are able to beget the *faith* of Gods Elect: true it is indeed, whether the *Father*, *Son*, or *Spirit* reveal any thing, it is *in* and *according* to the *word*; but without the work of the *Spirit*, there is no faith begotten by any promise."[7]

If even the New Testament is dead to a man who has not the Spirit, of what use to a believer, then, is the Old Testament with the elaborate Mosaic code? Are not its conditions meaninglessly detailed for one under the covenant of grace? These questions Cotton answered by pointing out the great uses the Law might have as warning to the reprobate and incentive to those destined for salvation but not yet aware of their call. But when he came to the man already under the covenant of grace and attempted to show his need of the Law, his doctrine lacked the energy it had possessed when it spoke of grace: "There is none under a Covenant of Grace that dare allow himself in any sin; for if a man should negligently commit any sin, the Lord will school him thoroughly, and make him sadly to apprehend how he hath made bold with the treasures of the grace of God. . . . None that have a portion in the grace of God, dareth therefore allow himself in sin; but if through strength of temptation he be at any time carried aside, it is his greatest burthen."[8] The strict logic of the situation, as Cotton perceived it, was that no Christian who truly had the Spirit would act in contradiction to it. If a respondent insisted that the best of believers had been known to backslide and demanded to know the consequences of a relapse into sin, then all Cotton could say was that he was not damned by

[7] John Cotton, *A Treatise of the Covenant of Grace* (London, 1659), pp. 199-200.
[8] *Ibid.*, pp. 97-98.

his disobedience, but that his perception of it would be his "greatest burthen."[9] Actually, there were no external regulations in his religion, scriptural or ecclesiastical, which checked the behavior of the true believer, but he proceeded as the Spirit dictated. Since both scripture and church were of the Spirit, the believer would, of course, proceed in accordance with them and could be judged as a good or bad Christian according to whether he did so proceed or not, but, in the last analysis, he did not follow church and scripture but the Spirit which led him along the same path.

In a commonwealth where man's spiritual estate directly affected his civil estate, a doctrine which so distinguished between the Spirit and the word could be expected to find opponents. The sanctified were the best qualified for citizenship because their conversion argued a higher degree of responsibility in their behavior, but the separation of the Spirit from the word could lead to saints who recognized no external obligations, and who, in a sense, acted only as the Spirit dictated. Cotton did not regard this as a danger, for besides such an assertion being founded on a contradiction, that of the Spirit as manifested in a man working against itself when manifested in a church, it was weak because it did not take into account the theocratic civil government. In Massachusetts, he thought, not only would saint and church pursue parallel courses, but the commonwealth too would be guided by the Spirit. Any doctrine was open to ridiculous applications— indeed, it came to pass that Captain John Underhill was inhabited by the Spirit while taking a pipe of tobacco, and that, among other things, the Spirit moved him to resort to a neighbor's wife for private prayer behind locked doors[10]—

[9] For the "legalistic" position on the same point held by the majority of Cotton's colleagues, see Thomas Shepard, *Theses Sabbaticæ* (London, 1649), pp. 65 ff. Shepard argues that in His offices on behalf of man Christ "did not beleeve and repent, and perform duties of thankfulnesse for us," but that these are "personally required" of man.

[10] Winthrop, *Journal*, I, 275-77.

but this, on the face of it, was no reason why Cotton's doctrine should collide with that preached by other Bay ministers.

The peaceful coexistence of differing doctrines was prevented, however, by two aspects of life in the Bay. The first was the magistrates' insistence that if Massachusetts was a theocracy then godliness had important outward signs and piety was matched with a corresponding morality. Understandably, also, the magistrates, governing outward man, tended to reverse the relationship of the two qualities and to believe that morality argued piety and that without morality there was no piety; whereas Cotton's doctrine regarded morality as the possible result of a number of causes, one of which could be piety, so that behavior was an uncertain indication of spiritual condition. It might have been more logical and even more pious to agree with Cotton, but a state simply could not be ruled in accordance with such a doctrine.

The second aspect which led to a collision of doctrines was the laymen's constant habit of accentuating the differences between preachers. The more generally favored interpretation of the covenant was conditional. Peter Bulkeley, for example, preached: "After . . . you have broken your covenant with your sins, judged your selves for them, submitted your selves to the will of God, and come in the name of a Mediator, then by faith look at the gracious invitation of God, and consider his readinesse and willingnesse to enter into covenant with you."[11] He, like all other ministers except John Cotton and John Wheelwright, made a firm link between piety and morality, saying: "God hath so linked together the blessing of the Covenant (which is his to give) with the duty and way of it, (which is ours to walk in) that we cannot with comfort expect the one; but it will work in us a carefull

[11] Peter Bulkeley, *The Gospel-covenant* (London, 1651), p. 51.

[113]

endeavour of the other."[12] An enthusiastic listener to John Cotton could, if he dwelt on such matters, easily conclude that the great preacher was the only minister in the Bay who held forth a full covenant of grace, and could even hint that men like Peter Bulkeley, with their recognition of obligations men had to perform under the covenant, were actually preaching a covenant of works.

Ever since his first American sermon, John Cotton's difference from his colleagues, most obviously from his fellow minister in Boston, John Wilson, was noticeable to his congregation. There was no discrete point at which the congregation rejected Wilson's ministry, but gradually signs emerged that Mr. Wilson was in far less favor because of the content as well as the manner of his preaching. At the private meetings held to discuss sermons, notably the two large weekly gatherings at the home of Mrs. Anne Hutchinson, Cotton's words were weighed with care while Wilson's were criticized and dismissed. At Cotton's sermons the congregation took notes; at Wilson's there were frowns, dozing, and even abrupt departures.

The cumulative effect of such behavior was felt keenly by Minister Wilson and those few in the congregation who were sympathetic to him, especially John Winthrop, who had founded the Boston church with him. Should matters continue in such a way, they feared that a rupture, not only within the Boston church but also of the Boston church from other churches, was inevitable. But John Cotton, confident of his pulpit ability, gratified by the number and professions of his converts, and entrenched finally in a pulpit from which he could give full expression to his doctrines without fear of college masters or bishops, was oblivious to the friction. His enthusiastic following, he believed, was to be expected in a land where the Gospel could be preached free of restraints, and was cause of rejoicing, not of impending

[12] *Ibid.*, p. [iv].

[114]

danger. His partisans, taking confidence from his confidence, little fancied any difficulties would ensue. Was not John Cotton the most learned of the New England preachers? And if there were any difference between his covenant and that of others, was not that which most magnified the Spirit and most depressed man the correct one? What else was Protestantism?

If any corroboration of their convictions was needed, the followers of Cotton received it in October of 1635, when the Bay welcomed its most distinguished resident to date. Henry Vane, son and heir of Sir Henry, comptroller of the King's house, arrived to "enjoy the ordinances of Christ in their purity,"[18] and, accordingly, he sought out New England's most eminent Christian, John Cotton, not only by joining his congregation but by accepting lodgings with him. Within three months of Vane's arrival, the deference (bordering on adulation) shown him had prompted the twenty-three-year-old gentleman to take a hand as arbiter in a dispute between Winthrop and Thomas Dudley, men of far more years and political experience, and his efforts were proclaimed by all to be a success. In May of 1636, having spent six months in the colony, he was recognized to the limit of that political body's abilities and was elected governor.

Governor Vane and Minister Cotton shared the same roof and the same board, and had frequent opportunity to consult about one another's matters. Theocracy was just as it should be, Cotton reflected, and the Boston congregation, confident, now, that the days of fullest felicity were about to open, set about preparing their neighbors. They attended sermons in other churches and during the debate which followed they corrected the preached doctrine in accordance with their understanding of what Cotton believed. In private conference with laymen from the other communities, they embroidered the doctrine of the priority in time of the indwelling of

[18] Winthrop, *Journal*, I, 162.

[115]

the Spirit, citing their teacher and the governor as authorities. And they became more and more outspoken against the fatuousness of regarding sanctification, the possession of graces which are outwardly manifested, as any sign of justification since sanctification revealed itself in a show of talents which even a carnal person could reveal. In their enthusiasm, they formulated statements designed to oppose what Cotton did not hold, confident that, like them, Cotton when he did not agree would positively disagree. Thus, the Boston members were increasingly insistent upon bringing their less fortunate brethren the message that the Holy Ghost was united with the person of a believer so that one who was so blessed was more than a man.

The Boston opinions, however, were not received as good news by either the neighboring churches or the small but powerful minority within their own church. To these people, Vane's arrival now appeared to have been the signal for erroneous and seditious pronouncements, and although he was governor and the magistrates felt they could not proceed as efficiently as they wished, nevertheless, something had to be done about Boston's zealous insistence on complete reliance upon personal revelations. Certainly, Cotton, as singular as his doctrine might be, was being outstripped by his followers; the single best move was to inform him of the pitch at which things had arrived and ask him to urge his parishioners to inform their words and actions with greater responsibility. Accordingly, much to his surprise, John Cotton was told in a private conference in October 1636 that members of his church were broadcasting outrageous opinions about the indwelling of the Holy Ghost, and that the chief fomenter of such opinions was Anne Hutchinson.[14]

Cotton had known Anne Hutchinson in England, for she had lived outside of Boston at Alford. There, as in Massachu-

[14] The following estimate of Anne Hutchinson is based on that made by Cotton in *The Way Cleared*, pp. 38 ff.

setts, she was an intelligent and capable woman whose practical skill at times of childbirth and sickness and whose ready discourse gained her admittance into many homes. Cotton realized that she gossiped of matters of salvation, and from his dealings with converts was conscious that she had prepared many of them for his ministry by pointing out to them that their souls might receive grace for a season, avoid evil courses, exercise all duties, and yet still be under a covenant of works because the Spirit did not visit them. He had known many thus apprised of their false security by Mrs. Hutchinson to come under the true covenant. Admittedly, he had had occasion to speak to her about certain idiosyncrasies. She seemed to strengthen her faith through private meditations without regard to the public ministry; she did not seem able to discern her sanctification although she felt her justification; and she appeared more censorious of others than a servant of God ought to be. But these were far from the charges of heresy and disorder which now, in the October of 1636, his fellow ministers were urging against her. Were they not exaggerating the import of some of her less valid statements and making too much of her particular shortcomings? He knew her well and could hardly believe her to be so scandalous in opinion as she was represented to him, but he agreed to look into the matter.

Accordingly, he held a conference with Mrs. Hutchinson during which she represented her views as completely conformable with his own. Either his colleagues were in error or Mrs. Hutchinson assumed another visage when she spoke with him. The only solution was to ask his colleagues to provide witnesses who had heard her express gross opinions and confront her with them. This, however, his brethren were unable to do, and the matter therefore was momentarily laid aside.

At the end of the same month, having proceeded unchecked thus far, the majority of the Boston congregation decided to crown their blessings by appointing John Wheelwright to the ministry. Brother-in-law of Anne Hutchinson, he was a silenced minister who had come over the year before and had been admitted to Boston church. Realizing that there were no grounds for removing Wilson, the pastor, the congregation decided that it needed a second teacher and moved to appoint Wheelwright, who, like Cotton, preached an unconditional covenant. Cotton had no objection to such a proposal provided it could be carried amicably, but when he saw the zeal with which John Winthrop opposed the plan by arguing the sufficiency of the existing ministry and the disputatiousness of certain of Wheelwright's opinions, he publicly counseled that it would be best if Wheelwright did not take office but was dismissed to officiate over another church. Accordingly, Wheelwright departed for the new settlement at Braintree, but resentment against Wilson and Winthrop increased in the congregation.[15]

In November, the elders of the Bay churches concluded that refutation of the Boston opinions was a fruitless task without Cotton's cooperation because the opinionists were ambiguous in their public statements and quick to claim the protection of Cotton's preaching for any pronouncement called into question. If Cotton could, in an unambiguous fashion, spell out what he held, then his followers could be made to confine themselves to his doctrine or suffer the consequences of going beyond it. Accordingly, they submitted sixteen queries to Cotton for which they requested written answers, while on the civil front Winthrop engaged Vane in written debate "for the peace sake of the church, which all were tender of."[16]

The outcome of both debates was only further turmoil. A veteran of compromises, Cotton certainly did not believe them either dishonest or dishonorable, but he simply saw no need to back down on his doctrine. This was New England,

[15] Winthrop, *Journal*, I, 196-97.   [16] *Ibid.*, I, 201.

where, in the church, the godly minister said what he thought. Surely, his fellows did not agree entirely with him, but, then, entire agreement was not necessary on matters, belief in which, both sides admitted, had nothing to do with whether a man would be saved or damned. The consequences of his doctrine had no bearing, so far as he could see, on anything but the inner life of the individual, and in this sphere he was a master. Asked whether a Christian could be as sure of his salvation after he had fallen into some sin as before, Cotton refused to admit that the erring believer was any the less saved, and he stoutly denied that God offered anything to a man on a conditional promise.

Question thirteen was aimed at the crux of the difference: "Whether evidencing Iustification by Sanctification, be a building my Iustification on my Sanctification: or a going on in a Covenant of *Workes*." Such evidencing, recognized by all the ministers save Cotton and Wheelwright, equated the pious man with the proper man, the believer with the citizen. Under this interpretation, theocracy was a form of government in which church was not to be distinguished from state, in which Christian doctrine was public proclamation, rather than a government in which state and church ran parallel and mutually supporting courses so that the state's very enforcing of morality could insure the church's concentration on piety. Cotton, therefore, insisted that such evidencing did betoken a covenant of works (which, of course, was most proper for the state but not the church), unless the person who claimed to be justified because he had sanctifying graces also had concurrent signs of his justification to put forth. "Justifying faith," Cotton affirmed, "cannot safely build or rest upon any ground, save onely upon Christ and Righteousnesse." Cannot a man press the Lord for spiritual mercies with arguments drawn from the graces of Christ which he contains in himself? Cotton was asked. He retorted somewhat tartly that it was more proper to press

Christ with one's own misery, and if graces were used as an argument, then to press Christ with the emptiness of one's graces.[17]

What was to be done? Mr. Cotton was too learned a man to hold his doctrine without an elaborate casuistry, and none was his equal in debate. The correspondence continued back and forth until it became obvious to the elders that although they could not dissuade him from his inexpedient doctrine, at least they could hold him to it. If his followers made one move beyond it, then they could act. Since Vane was governor and would continue to be until May, a waiting policy was the best one.

The outcome of Vane's bickerings with Winthrop, however, was more dramatic. At the December 1636 meeting of the Court, the young governor requested dismission from his office and the country because of the urgency of affairs in England to which he was called. The council assented to his departure on this ground, but when one of the magistrates used some "pathetical passages" in describing the loss of such a governor at such a time, Vane "brake forth into tears" and admitted that howsoever pressing his English affairs were he would have remained had not he been troubled by the dissension in doctrine and the imputation that he was the cause of it. This, of course, was not considered fit ground for dismission and the decision was revoked only to be passed again when Vane pleaded that the other matters he had first broached were sufficiently pressing and to be withdrawn again when Vane changed his presentation.[18]

The same meeting of the Court was stormy in other respects. The elders took occasion to meet and continue

---

[17] John Cotton, *Sixteene Questions of Seriovs and Necessary Consequences Propounded unto Mr. John Cotton together with His Answers* (London, 1644). The copy in the possession of the Massachusetts Historical Society contains a manuscript continuation of the debate between Cotton and the elders.

[18] Winthrop, *Journal*, I, 202.

orally the written debate they had been having with Cotton, but Vane took offense at this since he had not, as governor, been informed of the ministerial meeting. Hugh Peter, who now had the Salem church pursuing a tranquil course, did not hesitate to inform Vane that before he arrived the churches had been at peace, and at this session, as if it were a new phenomenon, sharp note was, at last, taken of Vane's youth.

Finally, in a very pointed gesture of sympathy, the Court called John Wilson to deliver a sermon before it, and he, fast becoming a man of no reputation in his own church and of increasing reputation as an embattled saint in all other Bay churches, publicly deplored the new opinions which, he said, were leading to schism. The Boston representatives to the Court, as well as Wheelwright and Cotton, denied that the specific opinions which Wilson cited (one was that sanctification was no evidence of justification) were so grave in their implications. When all the other officers, civil and ecclesiastical, seemed to concur heartily with Wilson, there-fore, Cotton returned home to enter into alarmed negotiations with Winthrop. Schism was a harsh and an untrue word to apply to his doctrine, he felt, and he sought to convince Winthrop that matters had not proceeded to the extremity Wilson depicted and the majority of the magistrates affirmed, and would not so proceed if they were not deliberately pushed to that point. The enthusiasts in the Boston congrega-tion cut his ground from under him, however, for even as he was attempting to move Winthrop to a more temperate course the congregation, to his alarm, moved to censure Wilson for his speech to the Court. Cotton successfully opposed the proceeding, dismayed that affairs had come so close to the stage that Wilson had been criticized for describing.

The year 1636 closed on a Massachusetts badly divided. The governor and most of the congregation of Boston were believed by the vast majority of freemen and elders outside of Boston to hold dangerous opinions; two ministers, John Cotton and John Wheelwright, did not give satisfaction to their fellow ministers on points which were suspected to be at the foundation of the dangerous opinions; and, worst of all, there seemed to be no procedure which could be employed for a reconciliation. Cotton and Wheelwright held nothing illegal or blasphemous, and, indeed, it was dangerous to dispute too far with Cotton because he commanded the respect of the Bay's influential backers in England, and, most probably, could summon the theological support of the great English Puritans, for they, after all, would find it easy to glorify the presence of the Spirit since they were not forced to contemplate its civil consequences. The lay followers of Cotton, indeed, may have been guilty of heresy, but there were no witnesses and although many strange opinions were known to have come out of Boston, as that the letter of the scriptures holds forth nothing but a covenant of works, the covenant of grace being in the spirit of the scriptures, or that a man may have communion with Christ and yet be damned because he had not the Spirit, these opinions could not be laid directly at anyone's door, and Mr. Cotton was sincere and skillful in qualifying those passages of his which seemed to be at the root of such opinions.

All moderation was fast disappearing from the scene. From an underground rift in the Boston church on the extent to which the Spirit inhabited the believer, and, therefore, the extent to which one's sanctified behavior gave grounds for concluding him to be a true believer, contention had grown to the proportions of a bloodless civil war. Addressing a group about to depart for England in February, Cotton asked them to report that the controversy was about magnifying the grace of God, one party advancing the grace of God within man and the other advancing the grace toward man, so that they could tell any in England who wished to strive for grace that New England was the best place for them.[19] The pleasant coating Cotton thus put on the situation for consumption in the homeland was not far from his true opinion of the matter. He recognized that there were differences, but he did not consider them cause for heat. He failed to realize the width of the rift because, in part, he was the substance of rather than a party to the difference. For the situation to improve, the Boston congregation had to rest content enjoying Cotton's ministry without comparing it with the ministry of others to their detriment. They had also to admit that the true believer's merit consisted, in part, of what he himself had achieved so that their opponents could then grant that the doctrine, unlike the polity, need not be the same in all churches. They had no intention of so doing.

On 18 January 1637, a general fast was kept in all of the churches in Massachusetts Bay to seek a betterment of conditions both at home and abroad. In Germany, the reformed churches were in a low condition; in England, the bishops were enforcing "popish" ceremonies with unabated rigor while the plague took hold in many communities; in Connecticut and other frontier settlements, the Indians were rising against the colonists; and in Massachusetts, the largest congregation differed with all others. Cotton delivered the fast-day sermon in Boston and based his doctrine on Isaiah 58:4, "Behold, ye fast for strife and debate," insisting that on such a day his listeners should turn their thoughts to pacification and reconciliation. The attempted censure of Wilson had taught him that the time had come for him to be forceful on the matter of peace.

Following his sermon, on which he "had bestowed much time, and many forcible arguments,"[20] the congregation

---

[19] *Ibid.*, I, 209.

[20] John Winthrop, "A Short Story of the Rise, Reign, and Ruine of the Antinomians, Familists & Libertines, That Infected the Churches of New England," *Publications of the Prince Society*, Vol. XXI (Boston, 1894), 203.

invited John Wheelwright to prophesy.[21] He began by declaring that the common cause of all the calamities for which the fast was being held was the failure in the afflicted areas to maintain Christ properly in worship and doctrine. As Wheelwright continued, it became increasingly clear that the true maintenance of Christ was not opposed so much by prelates, Indians, and continental monarchs, as it was by the holders of a specific view of salvation. He scorned those who held sanctification as grounds for their salvation, and indicated that the way out of the dilemma which Christianity faced was renewed vigor in seeing that "all is taken away from the creature, & all giuen to Christ." The doctrine that man was utterly incapable of putting forth one act of saving grace before or after conversion unless Christ were in him to do it for him was, Wheelwright said, like the wells in the Old Testament which the Israelites used to wash in, and, symbolically, needed in order to keep clean from sin. The course for his listeners to pursue, he went on, was to keep their well open: "If the Philistines fill it wth earth, wth the earth of their owne invencions, those that are seruants of the Lord, must open the wells agayne." None in the congregation doubted for a moment who the Philistines were and what duty was being urged upon them. The way out of the current dissension was to redouble their zeal for the Spirit in man so that their neighbors could not fail to be convinced.

Such a sermon was the opening for which the authorities had been waiting. Sedition they defined not as an overt act or even as a counseling to such, but held that "when the minds of the people being assembled are kindled or made fierce upon some suddaine occasion, so as they fall to take part one against another, this is sedition."[22] Wheelwright had

---

[21] John Wheelwright, "A Sermon Preached at Boston in New England vpon a Fast Day the XVIth of January 1636," *Publications of the Prince Society*, Vol. IX (Boston, 1876), 153-79.

[22] Winthrop, *Short Story*, p. 204.

provided them with ample material against the day in March when they were to convene for the quarterly session of the Court.

In Boston, however, Wheelwright's sermon was heeded as the solution to the difficulties and, accordingly, the Boston members set out to keep the wells open. They frequented the lectures of other ministers, raised questions in public about their doctrines, attempted to persuade them that they held little other than a covenant of works, and, in general, labored to remove the dirt as quickly as the Philistines could heap it. Winthrop sadly observed in February: "It began to be as common here to distinguish between men, by being under a covenant of grace or a covenant of works, as in other countries between Protestants and papists."[23]

Heretofore, Cotton, Wheelwright, and through them the Boston congregation, had been dealt with privately by the elders in a church capacity because the controversy appeared to be one of doctrine. But the Court which met in March was now pursuing the matter as one of sedition, and the elders who had met with no success in theological debate now yielded to and furthered the Court's conception. The Court fired its first salvo by declaring that no person could be questioned outside for what he said in or to the Court, thus supporting John Wilson, who had come under attack upon his return to his church after preaching at the Court's December session. In this manner, it also freed Winthrop and all other discontented Bostonians from any constraint which could be placed upon their testimony. With such assurances, evidence was procured against one Steven Greensmyth, who had vented his opinions before the wrong witnesses. He became the first of the Boston members to feel the sting of the law: "Steven Greensmyth, for affirming that all of the ministers (except Mr. Cotton, Mr. Wheelwright, & he thought Mr. Hooker) did teach a covenant

[23] Winthrop, *Journal*, I, 209.

of works, was for a time committed to the marshal, & after enjoined to make acknowledgment to the satisfaction of every congregation, & was fined 40 pounds, & standeth bound in 100 pounds till this be done."[24]

A minnow having been so successfully dispatched, the Court turned to bigger prey and proceeded to examine Wheelwright about his sermon. The Boston church petitioned that it might be present (the Court was held in Boston) as freemen, since this was a case of judicature, and also, in the petition, questioned the propriety of the Court's proceeding in a case of conscience before the church had dealt with its member. But the Court flatly rejected the petition on the grounds that the procedure was private and consultative rather than public and judicial. Wheelwright justified his sermon, stating unequivocally that he spoke against all who walked in the way he had defined, and when the elders of other churches were called they freely admitted that their way was the way Wheelwright had condemned. Therefore, over the protests of Vane and the Boston deputies, Wheelwright was found guilty of sedition since he had increased rather than quieted dissension on a day appointed for harmony. But with irate Bostonians outside the door, the Court members, conscious that a recantation on Wheelwright's part would be more effective than sentencing on theirs, postponed further action until the May Court. The coming Court was also to be the annual Court of election, and, all in all, its members felt it better to hold it in Newtown rather than Boston. However, Vane refused to put such a proposal to a vote, whereupon John Endicott of Salem did so, and after this proposal carried, the Court adjourned.

With civil discipline now an active factor in the controversy, John Cotton's concern increased. His sympathies were with Vane and the majority of his congregation who, he could not but believe, held nothing other than what he taught

[24] *Records of Massachusetts*, 1, 189.

although they might maintain it raucously. He had preached peace and reconciliation in January and considered Wheelwright's sermon ill-advised in manner although, considered in the abstract, valid enough in content. When pressed by the Court to say whether the elders of the other churches were not therein calumniated, he demurred, "They knew what themselves taught in that point better, then I."[25] In the winter of 1636-1637, then, he did not wait for his colleagues to approach him, but confident that the controversy was being generated more by heat of temperament than by difference on the fundamental truths of religion, he entered into correspondence with Thomas Shepard, pastor of Newtown, to see whether tempers could not be moderated. To date, no one had produced witnesses to the alleged heresies of Anne Hutchinson or others, which led him to believe that the real differences were exaggerated. The whole affair, he was confident, was one which needed only brotherly love to restore tranquility. This was not, after all, England under the bishops.

In the lull before the May Court, the Boston freemen prepared a petition asking for revocation of the decision against Wheelwright, while their opponents prepared to stamp out the disturbing opinions once and for all. When the Court assembled, Vane refused to proceed to a new election until the petition on Wheelwright's behalf had been acted upon, but the majority insisted that the Court was primarily one of election and that this must come before any other business. Accordingly, over Vane's protest, they proceeded to election, naming Winthrop governor, and Dudley, a firm foe of the Boston opinions and a man who had been known to protest that Winthrop was too mild, deputy-governor. Vane, together with William Coddington and Richard Dummer, the two magistrates from Boston, was left out of all office.

[25] Cotton, *The Way Cleared*, pp. 59-60.

The Bostonians had expected such a rebuff to their magistrates and consequently had deferred selecting their deputies
until the election at Court was completed. On the day after
the election, they sent Vane, Coddington, and Atherton
Hough to the Court as deputies, and although an attempt
was made to unseat them because of an alleged irregularity
in their election, they remained as deputies.

Dissension need not have gone any further, however, for
Thomas Shepard was to preach the election sermon and
John Cotton had arrived at certain compromises with him.
In reporting on this in his sermon, Shepard assured his
listeners that the differences had been reduced to a very
narrow scope: he and Cotton had agreed that justification
and sanctification occurred together in time, thus prohibiting
the stressing of one to the exclusion of the other; and while
Shepard granted that a man must know himself to be justified
before he can know himself to be sanctified, Cotton in turn
agreed that no man who was justified would be empty of
notable works. With the opinionated Bostonians out of power
and Cotton joining in a declaration of harmony, Wheelwright's sentence was again delayed for it was hoped that
he would now contribute to the growing temperateness of
the times. As Governor Winthrop reflected, now that the
Court clearly had power to crush the opposition, a gesture
of reconciliation and moderation was in order.[26] John Cotton
had done his part on the other side.

But whatever beneficial effect Shepard's report and the
delay of Wheelwright's penalty might have had was obliter-
ated by the epochal order passed at the same Court: "It
is ordered that no town or person shall receive any stranger,
resorting hither with intent to reside in this jurisdiction, nor
shall allow any lot or habitation to any, or entertain any
such above three weeks, except such person shall have
allowance under the hands of some one of the council, or

[26] Winthrop, *Journal*, I, 217.

of two other of the magistrates, upon pain that every town that shall give or sell any lot or habitation to any such, not so allowed, shall forfeit 100 pounds for every offense, & every person receiving any such, for longer time than is here expressed, (or than shall be allowed in some special cases, as before, or in case of entertainment of friends resorting from other parts of the country for a convenient period of time) shall forfeit for every offense 40 pounds; & for every month after such a person shall there continue 20 pounds; provided, that if any inhabitant shall not consent to the entertainment of any such person, & shall give notice thereof to any of the magistrates within one month after, such inhabitant shall not be liable to any part of this penalty."[27] Cotton and Vane, who just a year ago thought that they had embarked on cooperating in a model theocracy, now saw the death blow not only to the model they had attempted to administer, but to any meaningful theocracy. The intent of the order was undeniable: the magistrates now were to specify the opinions which were allowable for settlers in Massachusetts Bay. Even though a would-be settler were an acknowledged Christian and acceptable as a member of the church he could be turned away by the civil authorities. Winthrop flatly admitted in correspondence with Vane that "A man that is a true christian, may be denied residence among us, in some cases, without [it being said that we are] rejecting Christ."[28] Cotton and Vane well realized what sort of religious person would no longer be allowed to settle in the Bay, and the latter retorted ineffectually, "It is not the refusing of some religious persons against which we except, but against the libertye which is given by this law of rejecting those, that are truly and par-

[27] *Records of Massachusetts*, I, 196. The order was renewed indefinitely in the following year.

[28] John Winthrop, "A Defence of an Order of Court Made in the Year 1637," *Publications of the Prince Society*, Vol. 1 (Boston, 1865), 82.

ticularly religious."[29] Cotton realized that the balance between church and state was now badly one-sided, for the elders' examination of fit candidates for church membership was gravely restricted when the magistrates screened those candidates for their doctrines beforehand.

The other Bay ministers, however, saw the balance of power go into the hands of the magistrates without a murmur. They had contributed to this change through their failure to deal effectively with the Boston members and their teacher in a church way and by nevertheless insisting that doctrinal offenses had been committed which somebody should punish. Now they had to accept the consequences both in the order about new settlers and by allowing Wheelwright's sermon to be exposed to civil rather than to theological debate.

As the Bostonians, Court and ministry arrayed against them, pondered the way out of the encirclement, John Cotton considered removal to New Haven with his guest, John Davenport, who had arrived within the year.[30] But he could not bring himself to the admission that even Massachusetts was not to be the final earthly home for a man who had weathered the winds of English controversy by finally allowing them to blow him to New England. He therefore surveyed the Boston scene looking for a likely way to pacify the congregation so that with a visage of harmony on the face of Boston an attempt could be made to regain part, at least, of what seemed to have been lost. So long as the Bostonians remained openly disputatious, they would only justify the severity of the measures against them and give color to the claim that magistrates needed to rule on fit residents because many Christians carried themselves uncivilly.

On their part, the magistrates realized that the greatest contribution toward strengthening their stand now would

[29] Henry Vane, "A Brief Answer to a Certain Declaration, Made to the Intent and Equitye of the Order of the Court," *ibid.*, p. 92.
[30] Cotton, *The Way Cleared*, pp. 52-53.

be some concerted support from the churches, and although
such a course was to be pursued cautiously among churches
eagerly jealous of their independence, they decided to call
a synod which could pronounce authoritatively on matters
of doctrine. This would supply a ground for further action
against those who held undesirable opinions, and provide the
civil authorities with a guide in their screening of new settlers.
The call went out, and as Vane set sail in August to return
to England and other contentions, the elders prepared themselves for the synod to begin 30 September 1637. Cotton
welcomed the coming meeting, for he had a fundamental
distrust of the independence of congregations and although
the move did not come except at the seeming expense of
his doctrine, he felt that a more formal means of communica-
tion between churches should exist. Rather than impinging
on his doctrinal liberty, such synods, he believed, would
support it by clearing the ambiguities and confusions which
the preachers held about one another's pronouncements,
relying, as they had to, upon the word-of-mouth reports of
listeners. A synod would also preserve the liberty of the
churches by filling the gap into which the civil government
was inclined to move all too rapidly, and therefore might
go some way toward restoring what he regarded as the true
balance of a theocracy.

The preparations for the synod consisted chiefly of gathering up for public refutation all of the offensive opinions
which had been vented, and in extracting from Cotton's
sermons and conferences those things which were distrusted
so that Cotton could settle them beforehand in a peaceable
way and brotherly harmony would prevail when matters
of outright error were discussed. Before the synod, therefore,
Cotton was sent a list of questions, the chief aim of which
was to effect a clarification of the extent to which he thought
a man contributed to his own salvation. The drift of the
elders was to have him admit that, at the least, a man

must have faith before his union with Christ was complete. This, of course, Cotton could not grant, but, anxious to cooperate, he felt he could be helpful if he qualified his answer, and replied that a union with Christ, salvation, took place "not without, nor before the habit (or gift) of Faith, but before the act of Faith; that is, not before Christ hath wrought Faith in us (for in uniting himself to us, he worketh Faith in us:) yet in order of nature, before our faith doth put forth it self to lay hold on him."[31] But the elders insisted that faith is an instrumental cause in man's procuring Christ's righteousness because they feared that Cotton was leaving no distinction between the saved person and the saviour. Their respondent would not grant this, however, and retorted that a man's faith is cause of his salvation to about the same extent that a vessel's emptiness is the cause of its being filled with oil.

Cotton was eager to compromise wherever possible and readily granted that "some of the Schoolmen . . . and some others (even of judicious Protestants)" shared his colleagues' opinions, but since they did not differ in basic matters he saw no reason to become alarmed at their differences. Unlike them, he simply could not believe that a dangerous or seditious application of his principles could be or had been made by his parishioners. As a result, he saw no possible complication resulting from his continuing affirmation that "No spirituall act can bee done by us without Christ habitually permanent in us."[32]

All in all, the pre-synod conferences were terminated to the satisfaction of the elders because they felt they had so committed Cotton that he could not lend support to the erroneous opinions they planned to refute, and to the satisfaction of Cotton because he believed that although the elders could gather erroneous opinions enough, they could not produce any in his congregation who held them.

[31] *Ibid.*, p. 41.   [32] *Ibid.*, p. 42.

On 30 September, the representatives of all the churches in the Bay and Connecticut (which was under its jurisdiction) gathered in the church at Newtown and proceeded to refute eighty-four errors. These ranged from such statements as, "To be justified by faith, is to be justified by workes," to "Christs worke of grace can no more distinguish betweene a Hypocrite and a Saint, then the raine that fals from Heaven betweene the just and the unjust."[33] Cotton recognized that his doctrine provided a clear point of departure for almost all of the eighty-four errors, from those adjudged to be mistakes to those considered blasphemous. For example, in the two errors just cited, the first could almost be a quotation from his preaching if faith were understood as the product of man previous to Christ's aiding him; the second, while far from any actual statement of his, was probably a misrepresentation of the belief that sanctification did not evidence justification, and that, therefore, no amount of seeming grace in a person could define him as a saint rather than a hypocrite. At least, the terminology was to be clarified and all would be harmonious.

As the synod got under way, Cotton joined in the condemnation of the errors as they were stated, qualifying his assent whenever he felt the terminology was ambiguous. In this arena, he was confident of his ability to resist any encroachments upon his doctrine and was careful to see that precise wording of the errors removed them from any connection they might have with his doctrine. He would have continued to pursue such a course when, contrary to his fondest expectations, the lay representatives of his church at the synod began to pull shy of condemning what he considered to be flagrant errors. Before the synod, he had thought his cause was Boston's cause and that the synod, for the most part, would storm positions for which there were no defenders. Now as a member of the attacking party, he was alarmed to perceive

[33] Winthrop, *Short Story*, pp. 102, 119.

that those whom he had thought would second him were, on the contrary, reluctant to see the castle of errors entirely reduced. At this point and only at this point did the amazed John Cotton realize what the elders of the other churches had been so disturbed about. The Boston teacher was the same man as the St. Botolph's vicar whose adherents had rudely awakened him one day with the sound of stained glass shattering, and his reaction now was the same—strive for harmony, avoid extremes. His best course, he felt, was to emphasize his basic agreement with his fellow elders in an attempt to check the newly discovered recalcitrants in his own congregation; the luxury of lovingly emphasizing his particular differences would have to be surrendered. To his dismay, when his attitude became apparent the dissenting Bostonians absented themselves from the synod. Now the assembly made quick work of it. Cotton's conclusion was that he considered "some of the Opinions, to bee blasphemous: some of them hereticall: many of them, Erroneous: and almost all of them, incommodiously expressed."[34]

The magistrates regarded the outcome of the synod with delight and now felt they could proceed with full force against holders of the proscribed opinions as traducers of the magistrates and ministers of the commonwealth. Cotton, stunned by his belated recognition of a gap between himself and members of his congregation, would be temperate in his opposition, if he opposed at all; Vane had departed for England; and no Boston dissenter held influential office.

Accordingly, Anne Hutchinson, considered the ringleader of those in error, was called to public trial before the Court sitting at Newtown in November.[35] But Cotton was not stunned into total silence. He felt that although Mrs.

[34] Cotton, *The Way Cleared*, p. 48.
[35] "The Examination of Mrs. Ann Hutchinson at the Court in Newtown, November, 1637," Thomas Hutchinson, *The History of the Colony and Province of Massachusetts-Bay* (Cambridge, 1936), II, 366-91.

Hutchinson did disagree with him more than he had formerly thought, she was far from the flagrant blasphemer report made her out to be and he attended the trial with an alert ear for she was his parishioner and, he knew, when the pupil is on trial for doctrine the teacher is obviously implicated. His strategy would be to allow her to argue her case, as indeed she must, but to reason with her about her error should any appear and to temper her less judicious statements. Hugh Peter of Salem had testified that many of the ministers had hoped to see Mrs. Hutchinson dealt with by the Court last May, but at that time Cotton had interposed, saying that: "he thought it not according to God to commend this to the magistrates but to take some other course, and so going on in the discourse we thought it good to send for this gentlewoman, and she willingly came."[36] The words passed in this springtime interview between Anne Hutchinson, Cotton, Wilson, Peter, Zechariah Simmes (of Charlestown), George Phillips (of Roxbury), Thomas Shepard (of Cambridge), John Eliot (of Roxbury), and Thomas Weld (of Roxbury) became in November the chief evidence in her trial.

The formal declaration of the purpose of the examination of Anne Hutchinson was made by Governor Winthrop at the outset: "Mrs. Hutchinson, you are called here as one of those that have troubled the peace of the commonwealth and the churches here; you are known to be a woman that hath had a great share in the promoting and divulging of those opinions that are causes of this trouble, and to be nearly joined not only in affinity and affection with some of those the court had taken notice of and passed censure upon [notably Wheelwright and some of the petitioners on his behalf who were fined and sentenced], but you have spoken divers things as we have been informed very prejudicial to the honour of the churches and ministers thereof, and you have maintained a meeting and an assembly in your house

[36] *Ibid.*, p. 372.

that hath been condemned by the general assembly as a thing not tolerable nor comely in the sight of God nor fitting for your sex, and notwithstanding that was cried down you have continued the same, therefore we have thought good to send for you to understand how things are, that if you be in an erroneous way we may reduce you so that so you may become a profitable member here among us, otherwise if you be obstinate in your course that then the court may take such course that you may trouble us no further."[37] Mrs. Hutchinson quickly responded, "I am called here to answer before you but I hear no things laid to my charge," and the wrangling got under way with the magistrates attempting to avoid specific charges and to lay at her door all the troubles that had occurred in Boston while she demanded details certified by witnesses. During this dispute, Winthrop made it clear that the fathers of the commonwealth were embraced in the fifth commandment and that this, too, had been breached by Mrs. Hutchinson's conduct.

The large catchall case against her went badly, for Mrs. Hutchinson was adept at matching scripture phrase for scripture phrase in her justification of weekly meetings, so that finally the magistrates had to turn to specific instances of misconduct on her part. They claimed that she had said that all of the ministers save John Cotton preached a covenant of works, the same charge that had dispatched Steven Greensmyth in March. But Mrs. Hutchinson denied this and demanded witnesses so that the prosecution, in effect, was taken from the hands of the magistrates and placed in those of the ministers who had consulted with her earlier in the year.

Consequently, Hugh Peter spoke out, but Mrs. Hutchinson protested the legality of his evidence, saying that "it is one thing for me to come before a public magistracy . . . and another when a man comes to me in a way of friendship

[37] *Ibid.*, p. 366.

privately." Peter countered that at the interview, "She did not request us that we should preserve her from danger or that we should be silent," and on the strength of this went on to reveal that she had told him that Cotton preached a covenant of grace while all other ministers preached a covenant of works. He added an absolution for Cotton, saying, "that day being past our brother Cotton was sorry that she should lay us under a covenant of works, and could have wished she had not done so."[38]

Mrs. Hutchinson, however, maintained that Peter's report was inaccurate, and remembering that John Wilson had taken notes of the meeting she asked that he produce them. But Wilson declined, saying the notes were not complete, and Weld, Simmes, Phillips, Shepard, and Eliot all spoke to confirm Peter's statement. At the same time, Phillips professed his ignorance of the context of the meeting but Simmes attempted to mend this chink by vehemently asserting that he had known her to be erroneous ever since their common voyage to America. Winthrop, hoping that in the face of such testimony Mrs. Hutchinson would repent, decided, when she denied the accuracy of the report, that the best alternative was adjournment. The other most likely procedure would have been to call Cotton, the one person at the spring interview who had not yet testified, and he was wary of what that minister would say and anxious to keep his imposing presence out of the debate.

On the next day, however, Anne Hutchinson had reconsidered only to the extent of demanding that what had been alleged against her be said under oath. This caused considerable consternation, for, as Magistrate Brown pointed out, "An oath is of a high nature, and it is not to be taken but in a controversy, and for my part I am afraid of an oath and fear that we shall take God's name in vain, for we may take the witness of these men without an oath."[39] The ministers

[38] *Ibid.*, p. 372.   [39] *Ibid.*, p. 377.

demanded to know what they had said against which Mrs. Hutchinson and other witnesses could testify once an oath were taken, but she declined to reveal this, assuring them that she could produce oaths against theirs and insisting that they swear. But the ministers maintained that since they were not specifically contradicted there was no controversy and they could not take an oath. Faced with this stalemate, Winthrop was forced against his will to ask John Cotton, whom he wished to keep from the public controversy, to give his recollection of the disputed interview.

Cotton prefaced his remark by pointing out, "I did not think I should be called to bear witness in this cause and therefore did not labour to call to remembrance what was done." His apology of imperfect memory was not meant as an excuse for his abandoning the defendant, however, but rather as a gesture toward his colleagues, for he then went on to say that although Mrs. Hutchinson, to his regret, distinguished between his ministry and that of the others, the substance of what she said was merely that he preached a covenant of grace more clearly than they. He went on: "If you put me in mind of any thing I shall speak it, but this was the sum of the difference, nor did it seem to me to be so ill taken as it is and our brethren did say also that they would not so easily believe reports as they had done and withall mentioned that they would speak no more of it, some of them did; and afterwards some of them did say they were less satisfied than before. And I must say that I did not find her saying they were under a covenant of works, nor that she said they did preach a covenant of works."[40] Cotton thus attempted to demonstrate that if he had been slow to detect the true feelings of his congregation, nevertheless his brethren were being more zealous than accurate in mending his error. Hugh Peter sparred with him in order to gain an admission that Mrs. Hutchinson's statements as reported by him

[40] *Ibid.*, p. 382.

amounted to what the ministers had alleged, but Cotton refused to be drawn into this interpretation.

In view of the gravity of Cotton's statements and the obvious reluctance of any of the ministers to challenge their accuracy, the examination appeared to have arrived at an inconclusive termination. If the ministers of the Bay had had their day at the Synod, Cotton was now having his in tempering their fervor at the trial. But Anne Hutchinson, her cause looking bright now, unhappily took the opportunity to give the Court an excerpt from her spiritual autobiography in order to show them "the ground of what I know to be true." In so doing, she spoke of the Lord guiding her to distinguish "between the voice of my beloved and the voice of Moses, the voice of John Baptist and the voice of Antichrist."

This rhapsody unreeled another line for the Court, and the hook was baited at the close of her speech by Magistrate Nowell: "How do you know that that was the spirit?" Mrs. Hutchinson rose to the lure: "How did Abraham know that it was God that bid him offer his son, being a breach of the sixth commandment?" Thomas Dudley played out the line: "By an immediate voice"; and Mrs. Hutchinson swallowed the hook: "So to me by an immediate revelation." Dudley frantically reeled in, "How! an immediate revelation," and Anne Hutchinson's fate was sealed.[41]

Having failed to establish convincingly any practice or opinion of hers which threatened civil harmony, the authorities were furnished suddenly with not to be hoped-for proof volunteered by Mrs. Hutchinson in public. As Winthrop later wrote: "For here she hath manifested, that her opinions and practise have been the cause of al our disturbances, & that she walked by such a rule as cannot stand with the peace of any State; for such bottomlesse revelations, as either came without any word, or without the sense of the

[41] *Ibid.*, pp. 383-84.

word, (which was framed to humane capacity) if they be allowed in one thing, must be admitted a rule in all things; for they being above reason and Scripture, they are not subject to controll."[42]

Bickering about Mrs. Hutchinson's meetings and statements ended as the Court members vied with each other in adjudging the heinousness of her claim of immediate revelation. Mr. Bartholomew, deputy from Salem, now recalled statements of a similar nature which he had heard her make and Zechariah Simmes confirmed this and added details. At one point it was remarked that Mrs. Hutchinson had had the effrontery to claim that Thomas Hooker, in a sermon, had said that he had had a revelation that England would be destroyed. John Eliot stoutly affirmed, with the approval of all, that such a report ran counter to Hooker's mind and judgment and this was looked upon as another calumny on her part. (Appraised of this some time later in Hartford, Hooker admitted that he had so preached.)

Now John Cotton could perceive the radicalness of his pupil, the assembled authorities felt, and now he could no longer protest against their rigorous examination of her. He was asked to give his opinion of her claim that she had had a revelation that she would be delivered from affliction by a miracle. To the disappointment of the Court, however, Cotton prefaced qualifications: he refused to deny that she could expect a miracle by way of the ordinary course of providence; he would hold her unsound in the point only if she expected a miracle above the course of nature. But the members of the Court felt the term "miracle" was plain enough without Mr. Cotton splitting it so as to provide a possible refuge for Mrs. Hutchinson. They had, by a wonderful mercy of God, been provided with a firsthand example of "the most desperate enthusiasm in the world."

Moreover, Thomas Dudley protested that Cotton's be-

[42] Winthrop, *Short Story*, p. 177.

[140]

havior had given him no satisfaction whatsoever and he
turned to questioning him more closely while Cotton stood
on the distinction which Dudley said "wearied" him. Peter
and Eliot joined Dudley, but Winthrop, feeling that sufficient
advance had been made, and fearing the effect on the Boston
congregation should Cotton be driven closer to Mrs. Hutchinson, cut this short: "M. Cotton is not called to answer to
anything but we are to deal with the party standing here
before us."

With the impetus provided by the new turn, Weld and
Eliot gladly testified under oath, and Coddington, the Boston
deputy, was the only one who tried to stem the tide that
was sweeping Anne Hutchinson to banishment. Cotton, after
Coddington's remark, again stood on his distinction and
suggested that Mrs. Hutchinson might not have been completely reckless. This prompted Peter to remark, "I profess
I thought Mr. Cotton would never have took her part."

However, Winthrop again steered away from Cotton and
called for a vote to deprive Mrs. Hutchinson of her civil
liberties, including residence, and for her imprisonment until
such time as banishment took effect. Only Colburn and
Coddington, deputies from Boston, opposed the measure, with
one deputy abstaining. Winthrop pronounced sentence, and
on Mrs. Hutchinson's asking wherefore she was banished,
he closed the session by telling her, "Say no more, the court
knows wherefore and is satisfied."

The Court had not accomplished all it had desired in its
examination of Anne Hutchinson, for the evidence brought
out at the trial, while serving to confirm all other towns in
their estimation of the matter, did not appear to have chastened
Boston. The Bostonians, indeed, did not believe that Mrs.
Hutchinson had acted expediently in striking out on her
own rather than in staying close to the testimony of her
teacher, John Cotton. Nor did many of them believe that
there was absolutely no danger in guiding one's conduct by

immediate revelation. However, banishment seemed a harsh penalty for the course Mrs. Hutchinson had pursued.

The civil authorities, therefore, determined upon a further measure which, it was hoped, would humble Boston and bring about a speedier acceptance of their order. Since at many stages of the controversy matters had come almost to blows, the Court now called attention to the violence which could result from an uncontrolled dependence upon revelation by disarming fifty-nine Bostonians. In its order, the Court alleged its fear that the supporters of Mrs. Hutchinson and Mr. Wheelwright might "as others in Germany, in former times . . . upon some revelation, make some sudden eruption upon those that differ from them in judgment."[43] The Court, with Mrs. Hutchinson's recent aid, was pushing her sympathizers into a context from which they had no logical escape. Further support of Mrs. Hutchinson would be evidence of rebellious intent and would justify the ridiculous severity of the disarmament order, while silence in the face of the order would signify assent. The latter alternative, in turn, implied necessarily that they must examine her in the church also in order to determine whether there was ground for her admonition or excommunication. Since even Cotton's remarks had been insufficient to stem the Court's fervor, the majority felt that the time had now come for a general reconciliation and accepted the inevitability of trying Mrs. Hutchinson in church. Cotton, whose policy at the synod had been abandoned by his parishioners and whose shield for Mrs. Hutchinson had been discarded by her in Court, contemplated the church meeting as a last chance to support his opinion that the reality was far less turbulent than the appearance. As Mrs. Hutchinson's teacher, he would play a large part in her examination, at which time he could bring out her fundamental piety and dissuade her from her more irresponsible utterances. The examination could very well

[43] *Records of Massachusetts*, I, 211.

result in a confession of error on her part which would be satisfactory to all, for she was quartered over the winter in the home of Joseph Weld (brother of the minister, Thomas) in Roxbury, and she was visited weekly by consulting elders, notably Shepard, Davenport, and himself.

In March of 1638, Anne Hutchinson was tried before the church of Boston. Sixteen opinions, duly testified to by witnesses, were presented as hers, and she was requested to declare whether she still held them or had since renounced them. Mrs. Hutchinson entered the same protest that she had made at the Court examination: her opinions had been solicited in private and, without any dissent being expressed there, she was now called to answer for them publicly. But Cotton interrupted the dispute over this and, as her teacher, began to reason with her about the first error, "That the Soules of all Men by nature are mortall & die like Beastes." He showed her many places of scripture contrary to her opinion, urging her, "Sister, doe not shut your Eyes agaynst the Truth. all thease places prove that the soule is Immortall."[44]

On the whole, the dealings with Mrs. Hutchinson went on much more tranquilly than at the Court. She debated principally with Cotton and Davenport, and occasionally a more curt word would be put in by Winthrop, Wilson, or one of the visiting ministers who were witnesses against her. When she had been brought to a halfway change of position which promised better things to come, Wilson moved that she be placed under admonition pending the next meeting, at which time the effects of the admonition could be gauged.

Some members of the congregation, however, were reluctant to proceed to a measure so grave since Mrs. Hutchinson's opinions might have been more nearly of the nature of mistakes than the "damnable heresies" they were termed by Wilson. These objectors were criticized by Simmes and the

[44] "A Report of the Trial of Mrs. Ann Hutchinson before the Church in Boston, March, 1638," *Publications of the Prince Society*, Vol. XXI (Boston, 1894), 292.

question was raised as to whether the church "may proceede: to any Censures, when all the Members doe not consent thearto: or whether the Church hath not power to lay a Censure upon them. that doe hinder the Churches proceedings." Cotton answered the query by saying that the church was bound to take every pain to convince each member so that there would be no dissenters and proceedings could go forth unanimously, but "if yet some Brethren will persist in thear Dissent: upon no Ground: but for by Respects of thear owne. or owt of naturall affection. than the Church is not to stay her proceedinge, for that."[45]

The church then passed admonition, and since Mrs. Hutchinson's error was in doctrine rather than in practice, the censure was pronounced by the teacher, Cotton. He accepted this occasion as an opportunity finally to lay all contention to rest and to encourage Mrs. Hutchinson to recant. He began, therefore, by admitting his own faults: "I confes I have not bine ready to beleeve Reports, & have bine slowe of proceedinge agaynst any of owr Members, for want of sufficient Testimony to prove that wch hath bine layd to thear Charge. But now they have proceded in a way of God, & doe bringe such Testimonie: as doth Evince the Truth of what is affirmed, it would be owr sine if we should not joyne in the same, wch we are willinge to doe."[46] He then turned to Mrs. Hutchinson's family, asking them to put aside their natural reluctance at the censure of their mother so that they would not be instruments of "hardninge her Hart & Nowrishing her in her unsound Opinions." Next, he addressed the women of the congregation, granting that they had received much good from their conferences with Mrs. Hutchinson, but admonishing them, "Let not the good yow have receaved from her, make yow to receave all for good that comes from her." Finally, Cotton turned to Mrs. Hutchinson, and despite the banishment sentence and the presence of visiting

[45] *Ibid.*, p. 309. [46] *Ibid.*, pp. 310-11.

magistrates and ministers, praised her for her good parts and urged her, therefore, to consider the dishonor she had brought to Christ and His church and the door to libertinism which some of her tenets opened. He was interrupted once by Mrs. Hutchinson, who said, "All that I would say is this that *I did not hould any of thease Thinges before my Imprisonment*." He replied, "I confesse I did not know that yow held any of thease Things, nor heare till hear of late: but it may be it was my sleepines & want of watchfull care over yow."[47]

This mildly tendered and mildly acknowledged interruption was not to pass so insignificantly, however. When the church assembled on Thursday to continue the trial, Mrs. Hutchinson admitted the impropriety of most of her opinions but now pursued the tenor of her interruption on the previous Sunday by insisting that she had held none of the opinions until she was imprisoned. The outraged ministers who had witnessed against her proclaimed this to be an open falsehood since they had heard her express the views in question as early before her imprisonment as their spring conference with her. But the harassed defendant, brought to an admission of error, stuck at this point and refused to acknowledge their claim as to the age of that error. On this ground, excommunication was moved. When it was protested that she was not yet convinced of her lie and, therefore, not acting against her conscience, Cotton, who had been silent at this appalling turn of events, finally resolved to give her up irrevocably and said: "This now is not for poynt of Doctrine, wherein we must suffer her with patience, but we now deal with her in poynt of fact or practise, as the makinge & houldinge of a Lye: now in poynt of groce fact, thear may be a present proceedinge."[48]

Only Mrs. Hutchinson's immediate family held out now, and Wilson proceeded to pronounce excommunication, with Cotton pointing out that he himself was to deal in matters of doctrine but that "it belongs to the Pastors Office to instruct

[47] *Ibid.*, p. 315.   [48] *Ibid.*, p. 334.

& also to correct in Righteousnes, when a Lye is open & persisted in, in the face of the Congregation after proved by
Witnes."

With such an action administered by the Boston congregation, the dispute was, in effect, over. What dissension remained
was individual and private rather than collective and public.
The elders and magistrates, having gained full victory, were
anxious to salve the wound, while the Boston members, a
bit truculently, also resumed their former relationship to
the commonwealth.

John Cotton had grievances aplenty to nurse, and although
the idea of migrating to New Haven, where he could preach
as he pleased to whom he pleased, interested him, he was,
without too great difficulty, persuaded to remain by the more
levelheaded citizens, like Winthrop, who recognized that
his departure would be a signal to England that all was not
well in New England and would give the lie to American
protestations that the recent controversy was a clear matter
of the good defeating the bad. Certain persons in authority
were inclined to look at Cotton with distrust, as "the *Trojan*
Horse, out of which all the erroneous Opinions and differences
of the Countrey did issue forth."[49] Thomas Shepard told
his diary that "Mr. Cotton: repents not: but is hid only,"
and cited Cotton's commendation of Mrs. Hutchinson at the
church trial, which, he wrote, "gave her a light to escape
thorow the crowd w^t honor," as well as Cotton's peculiar view
on revelation.[50] But the ordinary God-fearing citizen, a man
like Edward Johnson of Woburn, found no trouble in believing that the great Mr. Cotton had been misrepresented by
his adherents so that the popular representation of the recent
stir was that Mrs. Hutchinson's group, perceiving that John
Cotton, "this holy man of God . . . was and yet is in great
esteeme with the people of God," misrepresented him in

[49] Cotton, *The Way Cleared*, p. 53.
[50] Shepard, *Autobiography*, p. 386n. Modernized spelling.

"daily venting their deceivable Doctrines. Like subtill Logicians," they would say, "I'le tell you Friend, Neighbour, Brother, if you will forbeare to speake of it till you hear farther, this is the judgement of M. Cotten, when he, it may be, had never heard of it, or at least wise, when they brought this their bastardly brat to him, they put another vizard on the face of it."[51]

As unsophisticated reports go, this was not too inaccurate an one. John Cotton never took a firm position on any issue until he had canvassed the range of possibilities and elaborately qualified and defined his own intent. His followers might shatter the windows at St. Botolph's or deface the King's arms, but he was firm and sincere in deploring their actions, while, at the same time, maintaining doctrines which, many would say, were the seminary of these actions. In Mrs. Hutchinson's case, he had been unwilling to prosecute as a heretic a woman whom he believed guilty only of some unwarranted conclusions as to the nature of man's relationship to God. But to use what influence he had in an unqualified defense of Mrs. Hutchinson would have been to blur the differences between his ideas and hers and to part with the doctrinal independence he had won in the pre-synod conferences by again associating his doctrines with the errors he had joined in condemning. Consequently, he pursued the untracked path, defending Mrs. Hutchinson insofar as he shared tenets with her, and abandoning her to her fate when she injudiciously introduced matters over which he had no control.

The American atmosphere, however, was different from that of the England in which he had developed his habits. He had learned this with regard to polity and he had again to learn it in matters of doctrine. If the Puritan in America was freer to express his beliefs in word and deed, he also had

[51] Edward Johnson, *Wonder-working Providence of Sion's Saviour in New England*, ed. by J. Franklin Jameson (New York, 1910), p. 125.

a far narrower range of choice once the issue was joined. What had been a multicolored spectrum at Cambridge and a slightly less chromatic variegation at St. Botolph's was now muted considerably through what he took to be a confusion of church and state. The close blending of the two threatened to contain most of the abhorrent features of the Holy Roman Empire, chief of which was the facile interchange of excommunication and banishment. He had, upon his settlement, refused to be paid by taxes and he preached against the proposal that the magistrates should raise funds for the support of the ministry, both as a result of his fear of confusing church and state. But now the distinction was blurring and he had, during the controversy, chosen a line in the range of possibilities which was not clearly visible to others. As a result, not only had he seemed myopic to some, but he doubted his vision himself. Now that he had agreed, for the sake of appearances in England, not to go to New Haven, what was to be left for the exercise of his superior powers?

↬ CHAPTER FIVE ↫

THE TEACHER'S ART AND ATTITUDE
(1639)

IN HIS *Moses*, Martin Buber makes the following observation about the nature of change in a theocracy: "A chief or shaman, whose authority is supported by a superhuman power, can be combated in two ways. One is to attempt to overthrow him, particularly by shaking faith in the assurance that he will receive that support, and to take his place. . . . [This] in general leaves the structure of society unchanged. The second method is to cut off the main roots of the leader's power by establishing, within the tribe but external to the official tribal life, a secret society in which the actual, the true, the 'holy' communal life is lived, free from bounds of the 'law;' a life . . . in which the wildest instincts reach their goal on the basis of mutual aid, but in holy action."[1]

What Buber thus observes in the institutions of the biblical Israelites was, on a more sophisticated level, acting itself out in Massachusetts during the Antinomian controversy. Anne Hutchinson's group stood for "divine freedom" as opposed to "divine law," and while their promptings are not to be dismissed, as the Court saw fit to do rhetorically, as a rage for unlicensed behavior, neither are they to be regarded as a premature enlightened movement toward democracy.[2] For the Court in acting selfishly, if one wishes so to put it, to preserve its own powers was also, consciously or not, acting to preserve the holy commonwealth of Massachusetts so that

---

[1] Martin Buber, *Moses* (Oxford, 1946), pp. 186-87.
[2] For a period, the definitive treatment of the Antinomian controversy was that of C. F. Adams in *Three Episodes of Massachusetts History* (Boston, 1892), 2 vols. The relation of events in the preceding chapters differs from his account to some extent and the interpretation in that and the present chapter differs widely.

For a brief consideration of the legal aspects of the trial of Anne Hutchinson, see Haskins, pp. 49-50.

[149]

it might perpetuate itself through time. Like other religious philosophies, American Puritanism recognized the possibility of the existence of divinely designated leaders who were so seized by a Holy Spirit that they carried out Its wishes without particular regard for existing laws. But unless their possessed actions resulted in justice and law, their influence was not lasting, and if the power which these infrequently appearing seers are acknowledged to have is extended, as Anne Hutchinson wished to do, to all who sincerely believe, then, in effect, the power and the glory is no longer God's. For, as Buber points out: "without law, that is, without any clear-cut and transmissible line of demarcation between that which is pleasing to God and that which is displeasing to Him, there can be no historical continuity of divine rule upon earth."[3] Mrs. Hutchinson, in the final analysis, refused to recognize that line of demarcation, and the community's instinct of self-preservation, which brought about her banishment, did not impel only the magistrates as men in power but moved the populace as believers striving to perpetuate their holy commonwealth. Toleration of the society Mrs. Hutchinson promoted would have meant extinction of the Massachusetts they believed in, as, indeed, the Rhode Island to which Mrs. Hutchinson went abandoned all claims to being a holy commonwealth.

John Cotton, although the leading public preacher of the presence of the Holy Spirit in the believer, was outstripped by his followers and embroiled in a controversy from which he could not but emerge with some dishonor. Nevertheless, this did not diminish his concern about the basic distinction between himself and the Antinomians, on the one hand, and himself and his more legalistic colleagues, on the other. Although he was received cynically by extremists on either side, he continued to inveigh against Antinomians who "abrogate the Commandements, and in summe hold forth,

[3] Buber, p. 187.

Grace without Christ, Christ without Faith, Faith without the word of promise applyed particularly to me by the spirit, And the word of the Gospel without the word of the law."[4] At the same time, he maintained his insistence upon the divinity within man, the impossibility of any believer leading any part of his life, pursuing any of his activities, even the most base, except as a divinely stirred being: "A wind-mill moves not onely by the wind, but in the wind; so a water-mill hath its motion, not onely from the water, but in the water; so a Christian lives, as having his life from Christ, and in Christ."[5]

Placed in the realities of the battle between "divine freedom" and "divine law" in Massachusetts, Cotton was saying that the danger of the law becoming emptied of the spirit was acute in New England and this threat, though it may not have justified, certainly caused the Antinomian reaction. The conclusion, he urged, was a never-ceasing return of the bearers of the law to the wells of the spirit so that their edicts would always be fresh and pure, not staled by the false and the arbitrary. His teaching after the controversy frequently included the lesson of the need of the believer to allow the spirit to irradiate his conduct. He maintained a continual insistence that if men did their duties in order to pacify their consciences they were not "risen with Christ: But if it be our death that we come not off in duties with spirituall life, and if we see others doe not grow, it is our griefe, then are we risen and live with Christ."[6]

Cotton's constant emphasis on saturation in and by the Spirit knew no bounds but was applied as forcefully to commercial ethics as to church matters. When, for instance, Robert Keayne, Boston's most prominent merchant and the man whom the magistrates trusted to collect weapons when the

[4] Cotton, *Exposition of Ecclesiastes*, p. 274.
[5] John Cotton, *The Way of Life* (London, 1641), p. 277.
[6] John Cotton, *The Churches Resurrection* (London, 1642), pp. 29-30.

Bostonians were disarmed, was called before the Court to answer for the extortionate prices he charged, the church met to consider whether or not to excommunicate him for covetousness. On that occasion, Cotton laid down certain rules of business in his lecture based on medieval conceptions of the "just price": a man must not sell above the current price; he must not include in his price any recompense for losses he may have suffered either through want of skill or through providence (such as shipwreck); but, he may, when God has made a commodity scarce, then raise its price. He argued that covetousness was not habitual in Keayne but, rather, proceeded from his misguided business principles and that, therefore, the offender should be admonished but not excommunicated by the church.[7]

Behind Cotton's explicit lesson to his congregation on the rules of trade and his pronouncement that Keayne was guilty of false principles but not of covetousness was his conviction that a Christian was a Christian in all that he did; that "though you may have a godly man busie in his calling from Sunne rising to Sunne setting, and may by Gods providence fill both his hand and head with businesse, yet a living Christian when he lives a most busie life in this world, yet he lives not a worldly life."[8] To be sure, he wanted Keayne admonished so that he would correct his principles, but the action was most necessary because it would once more bring Keayne's procedures under the influence of the Spirit which should irradiate and purify them. Cotton taught, "If you live with Christ you may so buy as you bought not, and so use the world, as though you used it not. That what you doe, you do it not as worldlings, as if that were your Soveraign good that you set your hearts upon, but you buy and sel by the rules of Christ, to the praise and glory of Christ and the good of the church where you live, and such buying and selling

[7] Winthrop, *Journal*, I, 315-18.
[8] Cotton, *Way of Life*, p. 270.

will never darken the sight of Christ: You will see him cleere enough for all your businesse and ther's no calling God sets a man in, that hinders him from Christ, but the more just and diligent we are in our calling, the more we shall see Christ."[9]

Kindred doctrines could and did become rationalizations of zealous and successful business practices within the world, even though they allegedly aimed at a world beyond, but just as Cotton differed from the legalists and therefore was attractive to the Antinomians, so he differed from the Protestants whose ethic contributed so much to the generating of modern capitalism. He never reversed justification and sanctification and refused to agree that signs of the latter argued the existence of the former state. He insisted upon piety irradiating conduct without making the facile transfer to conduct arguing piety. Thus, he differed from most of his class, for, as Max Weber pointed out, one of the ideas essential to the thesis of the Protestant ethic is that "the methodical development of one's own state of grace to a higher and higher degree of certainty and perfection in terms of the law [is] . . . a sign of grace."[10] Cotton, of course, caused a great deal of difficulty in Massachusetts by refusing to grant just this point, and his experience illustrated both his own exclusion from Weber's thesis and his society's inclusion in it.

Moreover, holy commonwealths prosper when asceticism is required of everyone who would be certain of salvation. John Cotton's forceful preaching tended to undermine this with his frequent urging that "it be true, that once justified, for ever justified, once blessed, for ever blessed . . . and though after that time we should immediatly fall frantick, not able to put forth an act of reason, much lesse an act of

[9] Cotton, *The Churches Resurrection*, p. 26.
[10] Max Weber, *The Protestant Ethic and the Spirit of Capitalism* (London, 1948), p. 133.

faith, yet wee are blessed."[11] One of Cotton's frequent auditors, Roger Clap, recalled in his diary that he was in doubt of his salvation until he heard the preacher explain "that a small running stream was much better than a great land flood of water, though the flood maketh the greatest noise."[12]

John Cotton, then, acted as a constant brake to the commonwealth's rush toward legalism and capitalism, insisting time and again on the need to refine all duties by the inner test of the Spirit. He proved no more than a brake; his society went where it was going anyway. But his attitude transmitted itself to many another American spokesman. Time and again his emphasis was on Christ in man. His images of this, varied though they were, tended to center on water—rivers, seas, watermills. The following portion of one of his sermons may well stand as a metaphoric summation:

"First a Christian wades in the rivers of God his grace up to the ankles, with some good frame of spirit; yet but weakly, for a man hath strength in his ankle bones, *Acts* 3. and yet may have but feeble knees, *Heb.* 12. 12. So farre as you walk in the waters, so far are you healed; why then in the next place, he must wade till he come to the knees, goe a thousand Cubits, a mile further, and get more strength to pray, and to walk on in your callings with more power and strength.

"Secondly, but yet a man that wades but to the knees, his loynes are not drenched, for nothing is healed but what is in the water. Now the affections of a man are placed in his loynes, God tries the reines; a man may have many unruly affections, though he be padling in the wayes of grace; he may walk on in some eavennesse, and yet have many distempered passions, and may have just cause to complaine of the rottennesse of his heart in the sight of God: why then,

---

[11] Cotton, *Way of Life*, p. 335.
[12] Roger Clap, *Roger Clap's Memoirs with an Account of the Voyage of the "Mary and John" 1630* (Seattle, no date), p. 22.

thou hast waded but to the knees, and it is a mercy that thou art come so farre; but yet the loynes want healing, why, wade a mile further then; the grace of God yet comes too shallow in us, our passions are yet unmortified, so as we know not how to grieve in measure, our wrath is vehement and immoderate, you must therefore wade until the *loynes bee girt with a golden girdle*; wade an-end, & think all is not well untill you be so deep, & by this you may take a scantling, what measure of grace is poured out upon you. And if thou hast gone so farre, that God hath in some measure healed thy affections, that thou canst be angry and sin not, &c. it is well, and this we must attain to. But suppose the loyns should be in good measure healed, yet there is more goes to it then all this; and yet when a man is come thus farre, he may laugh at all temptations and blesse God in all changes: But yet goe another thousand Cubits, and then you shall swimme; there is such a measure of grace in which a man may swimme as fish in the water, with all readinesse and dexterity, gliding an-end, as if he had water enough to swimme in; such a Christian doth not creep or walk, but he runs the wayes of Gods Commandements; what ever he is to doe or suffer he is ready for all, so every way drenched in grace, as let God turn him any way, he is never drawn dry."[13]

In varying ways, the attitudes of Cotton, the legalists, and the Antinomians all received sustenance from the eschatological expectation. God, they believed, was coming and would one day re-enter history in person. His presence had been felt in history throughout the biblical times, and the prophecies which the Spirit made in scriptures had been fulfilled, in part, and were during the very days in which they lived being further fulfilled. Such an expectation was a main source of strength to the ideal of a theocracy, for if God's days on earth were not coming, then the legalists need

[13] Cotton, *Way of Life*, pp. 104-05.

not insist so much upon religious duties throughout life, but might release the non-church-members to do as they pleased, thereby separating the church, the place of believers who were going to heaven, from the state. But if the prophecies were working themselves out in time at that time, then a theocracy was an important part of the fulfillment. The Antinomians relied heavily upon the coming of the millennium within their century, for at that day law would, once and for all, disappear in favor of "divine freedom." If this were not to be, then their society based on an intimate relation to God's Spirit was directionless, for, by definition, it could not mold itself into a self-perpetuating organization.

The expectation of the Antinomians was keener but no more necessary to their philosophy than that of the legalists. Yet another group dismissed such theory entirely, and argued (with more effect out of Massachusetts than in it) that church and state be separated since in history God's rule is to be restricted to religion. But even in Massachusetts, as the eschatological expectation waned, so Caesar had rendered unto him the things that were his with less and less regard for the unity of church and state.

Ardent theocrat that he was, John Cotton shared the eschatological expectation in 1639 and taught in accordance with it. The Puritan movement of which he had been a member ever since his Cambridge days had been, at times, a badly defined one, but the common idea, shared by all who called themselves Puritans, was that a holy commonwealth could be established on earth. To that end, Cotton had experimented with polity in Boston, Lincolnshire and had hesitated in a time of persecution to go so far away as America since he was confident that within his lifetime Christ in His progress was making Himself felt more and more strongly in England. When he did agree to go to America, it was not in abandonment of this expectation, but in confidence that New England would not only be among the first places to feel Christ's increasing presence, but might very well lead the way for the homeland.

Besides its obvious and important effect on what Cotton taught, the eschatological expectation had an effect on the way he taught it. Together with his disbelief in the capability of the Bible to save souls in the mere reading, Cotton had a far greater lack of confidence in the written sermon as anything other than edification or consolation for the believer. The first step in conversion, he believed, was the pricking of the hardened heart of the future convert, afflicting it with "sorrow and griefe for sin; *griefe for sin*, and *care for reformation* of it."[14] This was accomplished when the sinner *heard* the word of God applied so that he received a simultaneous conviction of his own sins and the greatness and goodness of the God against whom he had committed them. The heart which the Spirit pricked by means of the preacher's spoken word was not the fleshly organ but "the will of a man, which lyes in the heart, for as the *understanding* lyes in the *head* or braine, so the *will* is seated in the *heart*: so as a good frame in the heart, and wisedome in the braine, makes a compleat man."[115]

To the end of pricking the heart and bringing about conversion, the preacher, Cotton held, might use "rhetorical elegancies," but, he cautioned, the rhetoric must be "suitable to the matter, grave and holy; else its bastard Rhetorick," and it must be present only to contribute to the end of the discourse, affecting "the heart with the sense of the matter in hand."[16] The latter caution served in practice to make the sermon closely resemble a lesson, as the teacher set about to persuade his audience of God's mercy and His justice. Recognizing that "the appetite desires new dishes more,"[17] he dressed the ancient message of the Bible in a

[14] *Ibid.*, p. 127.   [15] *Ibid.*
[16] Cotton, *Exposition of Ecclesiastes*, p. 9.
[17] John Cotton, *A Practical Commentary or an Exposition . . . upon the First Epistle Generall of John* (London, 1656), p. 76.

new spirit, but, in effect, this dressing was a use of metaphor to illustrate meaning, not to supply it. The sermon sought to prick hearts, to start an experience in the listener, not to supply that experience. Over a century later, another American Puritan, Jonathan Edwards, was to agree that the sermon must move the heart, but was also to perceive that it best did so when the imagery of the preacher provided the listener with a religious experience, when metaphor fused with meaning, in short, when the sermon became an art. Cotton's idea of the use of imagery, however, was that it was an accompaniment to meaning, and as the lecture progressed he abruptly abandoned or mixed his metaphors far more frequently than he sustained them. The main object was to bring home the particular point under discussion and he laid hold of whatever illustration seemed most effective regardless of its aesthetic relationship to what had preceded and what would succeed it. Rarely did Cotton sustain a metaphor so long as he did that of the waters of grace, cited above, and even there he mixed creeping, running, and walking in with swimming.

In preparing a sermon, then, Cotton had no desire whatsoever to construct a product detachable from its immediate delivery and capable of satisfying another audience under other circumstances. His sermon was to be delivered to a particular audience in such a way that a listener whose heart was pricked could call to memory each detail as he lay on his cot during the long New England night, the sins running from his wounded will. Consequently, Cotton began by extracting an affirmative proposition, a doctrine, from the biblical text, and explaining its meaning mainly through the help of other passages; "By comparing Scriptures together, you shall have the full meaning of every part of Gods Counsell."[18] He then divided, subdivided, and redivided

[18] John Cotton, *The Powring Out of the Seven Vialls* (London, 1642), "Seventh Viall," Sig. Bbb.

[158]

his doctrine with many a firstly, secondly, and thirdly—a sixteenthly was uncommon but not a rarity—so that God's message was thoroughly grasped. Then he gave explicitly numbered "reasons" in support of the doctrine, and followed the edification with an application in the form of a series of numbered "uses" to which the doctrine was to be put.

John Cotton, then, regarded the sermon as an act rather than a product and he constructed it with the intent of its having a future in its human consequences rather than in its form. This belief in the transitory nature of the work itself was strongly reinforced by the eschatological expectation which emphasized the passing of all that man had constructed. As that expectation deprived the work of Cotton and most of his contemporaries of an aesthetic existence, so it also provided it with a vigor and an urgency which may be called the mark of its style. Impelled as it was by an acute consciousness of its place in time, of its nature as an act in Christ's steady march toward the millennium, the Puritan sermon such as Cotton's took on a sturdy if ungraceful tone. From the time when Sir Thomas More's artful works, replete with fables, were answered by Tyndale's single-minded battering, to Martin Marprelate's sinewy snarling at the more stately monuments of the bishops, to the day of John Cotton's New England sermons, the Puritan work had derived strength from its conscious appropriateness to the moment in history. Thomas More for the Roman Catholics, and later various polemicists on behalf of the Anglicans, had written with conscious artistry but, compared to their respondents, with a dying fall. Richard Hooker's magnificent document begins on such a bittersweet note: "Though for no other cause, yet for this; that Posterity may know we have not loosly through silence, permitted things to pass away as in a dream, there shall be for men's information extant thus much concerning the present state of the Church of God, established amongst us, and their careful endeavours which would have upheld

[159]

the same."[19] No Puritan, including John Milton, was capable of this prose style, because what dominated the great artistic prose works of the period was a consciousness of their own structure being all that would come between them and mortality. They sustained themselves by their very construction, as works of art must do.

But the Puritan prose work was powered by history. It was a bark confidently tossed on the swift-flowing stream of time, moved and sustained not by its own structure but by the waters which were carrying it to the ocean of the millennium. As such, it was, as often as not, ill constructed, even in the fundamentals: metaphors were mixed, point of view was not recognized, the unit of thought frequently failed to find its grammatical counterpart. But the very ramshackle nature of its construction argued a confidence in its appropriateness to the stream which would move it, and if there were holes in the bark, the rivers of time flowed in and out of them, as often whirling the work on as sinking it. How often the Puritan could leap over the gap in construction or conclude a nervous creation with words like, "Thou dost not think so now, but thou wilt find it so one day." If, however, there would ever come a day when that river turned from its bed and became a pond, a backwash of history, then the bark would be waterlogged. Precisely this came to pass with the most popular literary creation of early New England, the sermons of John Cotton. But American literature never rid itself of the eschatological tone, and just as the belief in a millennium, as Ernest L. Tuveson has shown, became secularized into a belief in progress,[20] so many of the monuments of American literature secularized the goal but retained the tone of John Cotton, rather than converting to that of Richard Hooker. Such great American works are more frequently propelled by a sense of the

[19] Hooker, *Ecclesiastical Polity*, I, 127.
[20] Ernest L. Tuveson, *Millennium and Utopia* (Berkeley, 1949).

American experience as one of changes hastening along to one millennium or another than by an inner principle of aesthetic form. [21]

While John Cotton was thus oblivious to the literary product as a work of art, he was, nevertheless, devoted to a fuller life than that of the storybook Puritan. In England he had preached: "We may conform to the civill customes of the World, the Holy Ghost doth not forbid those . . . so that in pretence of mortification we must not fill our spirits with morosity and rusticall rudenesse, good manners and civill respects stand well with Christianity."[22] This remark reflects his birth and breeding in Elizabethan England and while the American experience frequently represented a narrowing range, Cotton never lost his confidence in the

[21] The roll of authors who are in the tradition stemming from Puritanism includes such diverse writers as Thomas Paine, Herman Melville, and William Faulkner. All seize an urgent power from the rhetorical assumption of the tremendous appropriateness of the work to the cosmic problems facing man, and all have a hasty disregard for the single well-focused point of view, limited but sustained metaphors, and an accurate mirroring of the unit of thought in the unit of grammar. Emerson is perhaps the most striking example of a modern writer with a "millennial" style. His famous inconsistency is rooted in a distrust of the artifact and a keen desire to substitute an informing spirit for literary form. As Vivian C. Hopkins says, "However definite the value which Emerson places on specific works of art, his regard for the spirit that creates all artifacts keeps him from sorrow at the loss of the greatest masterpieces." Speaking of Emerson's use of images, she says, "Each symbol is figured merely as a stimulus to send the reader on to new intuitions. Emerson thinks of the symbol as having effect not so much through perfect fusion of idea with image, as through the expression given to the object by the idea, in the moment of flowing through it." *Spires of Form* (Cambridge, 1951), pp. 103-04, 130.

Students of American literature searching for a continuity which can be traced back to the Puritans might well explore the eschatological expectation. Manicheism has been overemphasized as a probable source of literary continuity: first, because the doctrine itself does not convey any stylistic consequences; but more importantly, because the Puritans, strictly speaking, were not Manichees and if one applies the term loosely so as to include them, then, obviously, all literature concerned with good *versus* bad becomes fair game and the analysis loses precision.

[22] Cotton, *Commentary on John*, p. 124.

[161]

ability of the Christian to be comfortable and mannerly.[23] In England, he had also preached that pastimes were not in themselves unlawful, but were so only "when men make an occupation of recreation, as stage-players, and musicians." His argument was that "men should have a calling besides."[24] Playing at cards, too, he was willing to accept as lawful so long as it was not abused for gain. Of course, these remarks were addressed to listeners who had these recreations ready to hand and Cotton was acknowledging their lawfulness in exchange for his listener exercising moderation. In America, where the diversions did not precede the settlers there was no need to institute them simply because they were lawful; men could better employ themselves in other pastimes. But music, secular as well as religious, continued in favor, and Cotton was a prime agent in the group which translated the psalms for *The Bay Psalm Book*, supplying that book with an introduction, while his son, Seaborn, when a Harvard student, transcribed into his notebook the ballads of "The Love-Sick Maid," "The Last Lamentations of the Languishing Squire," and "The Two Faithful Lovers."[25]

The Elizabethan conceit of the playwright as a god, and vice versa, did not escape Cotton, but he used it as a reproof to the Jeremiahs in his congregation who felt the best was behind them: "God . . . presenteth every age with a new stage of acts and actors . . . if a Poet would not present his spectators but with choyce variety of matters, how much

---

[23] Countless irrelevant exceptions might be taken to the historical accuracy of Hawthorne's *The Scarlet Letter*, but he captured much of the reality of American Puritan experience, including this one. His use of color imagery to set forth the England which the settlers remembered in rainbow hues while Boston is represented in muted and less varied tones presents a visual contrast which finds its invisible counterpart in the development of men like John Cotton. In the scenes set in Governor Bellingham's mansion and the election day marketplace, the contrast is especially effective.

[24] Cotton, *Commentary on John*, p. 127.

[25] Zoltan Haraszti, *The Enigma of the Bay Psalm Book* (Chicago, 1956), pp. 19-27, 63-64.

lesse God?"[26] One of the purposes of the Book of Ecclesiastes, Cotton maintained, is "to teach us not to defraud our selves of such lawful delights, as the Lord alloweth us, in the good things we enjoy: we shall do him and our selves also injury in so doing."[27] He lived accordingly. Although his younger colleague, John Norton, noted with admiration that John Cotton was in his study twelve hours a day, writing sermons and polemical works, studying, and praying, Cotton was engaged in study as a "lawful delight" as well as a professional necessity. When he preached that "Evening meditations should rather be Devotionall then Scholasticall,"[28] he was cautioning himself as much as any in his congregation. His books were an item of comfort almost to vanity with him and a certain pride in his prodigious learning crept negatively into his sermons from time to time. For instance, he warned his listeners not to think that: "Ministers and Schollers eat the bread of idleness. . . . No calling more wasteth and grieveth him that is occupied therein, then theirs doth. The Ploughmans employment is a pastime to theirs; his labour strengtheneth his body, but theirs wasteth body and spirit; whence it is the one so long a time outliveth the other."[29]

The natural environment of America waged a quiet war with Cotton's twelve daily hours in the study and while Pliny's *Historia Naturalis* was still regarded as the single best place to learn what one wanted to know about nature, Cotton was far from oblivious to the New England flora and fauna. When explaining Canticles he went to the Roman authority to learn the properties of the various birds, beasts, and plants mentioned so that he could appreciate the full signification of the symbols, but in explaining the frogs in the sixteenth chapter of Revelation he was forced to take account of the new environment and its refusal to contribute to his explanation: "And like unto Frogs are they for their continuall

[26] Cotton, *Exposition of Ecclesiastes*, p. 131.
[27] *Ibid.*, p. 38.   [28] *Ibid.*, p. 193.   [29] *Ibid.*, p. 33.

croking; nothing but one kinde of tune: their own matters they never leave croking of not like these Frogs here in *America* that have a severall tune in each part of the yeare, but they are always in one, or two, or three at the most."[30]

Just as the various explicit headings in the sermon were insurances of clarity and aids to memory, so the meter and rhyme of poetry were helpful guides for channeling meditations or commemorating events. Cotton, like most of his colleagues, wrote poetry for his private consolation, using the mechanics of that medium to help him direct his thoughts but abiding by few of the more aesthetic demands of verse. For the most part, his poems, like the majority of New England verse of the period, commemorated grave events. The great proportion of elegiac verse in his Massachusetts stemmed not so much from the frequently alleged natural morosity of the people as from the way the requirements of poetry imposed a restraint on the flow of grief and therefore provided the writers with a controlled outlet for the natural sorrow which was felt at what needed also to be regarded as a joyous event, the entry of the saint into the church triumphant. An articulation of grief, restrained by rigid mechanical rules, was a check on excess and a help toward appreciating the glory of the moment more than its sadness. The best consolatory stanzas John Cotton wrote occur in a poem which he composed in order to restrain his grief at the loss of his Lincolnshire pulpit and the anticipated rudeness of his future home:

> I Now may expect some changes of miseries,
>> Since God hath made me sure
> That himself by them all will purge mine iniquities,
>> As fire makes silver pure.
>
> Then what though I find the deep deceitfulness
>> Of a distrustful heart!

[30] Cotton, *Seven Vialls*, "Sixth Viall," Sig. E2.

Yet I know with the Lord is abundant faithfulness
    He will not lose his part.

When I think of the sweet and gracious company
    That at BOSTON once I had,
And of the long peace of a fruitful Ministry
    For twenty years enjoy'd:

That joy that I found in all that happiness
    Doth still so much refresh me,
That the grief to be cast out into a wilderness
    Doth not so much distress me.[31]

The poetic numbers do their task for John Cotton and grief
is caught and smoothed. Significantly, when the poem turns,
in the final four stanzas, from private consolation to explanation of why Cotton had to leave Lincolnshire, then it
degenerates into jagged doggerel. The first of these final
four stanzas runs

For when God saw his people, his own at our Town,
    That together they could not hit it,
But that they had learned the language of Askelon,
    And one with another could chip it:

The task of the second half of the poem is edification and
while Cotton needed to be consoled for the events for which
the first half of the poem attempts to console him, he did
not need to be edified as to the reasons for those events.
Accordingly, when the verse turns didactic its amateurism
becomes painful. John Cotton's best verse was not emotion
recollected in tranquility but emotion tamed by law. When
he turned from consolation to edification, his small skill
fled him.

Feasts, poems, recreations, all were lawful, and with
regard to these John Cotton held, as he held with regard
to matters of greater weight, that the practice was secondary

---

[31] Norton, *Abel Being Dead*, pp. 29-30.

to the spirit which prompted it. So long as the poem or the song, the glass of strong water or the game was approached by a good person for a good end it was a good thing. The numerous festivals of the Roman Catholic calendar and the Anglican insistence upon the maintenance of sports and revels had left him and his fellows with a deep distaste for historically fixed celebration. The abuse, they were confident, far outstripped the use, and the date being fixed to an event so that the same ritual occurred annually only allowed for an accumulation of man-made and creature-satisfying indulgences far removed from the spirit of the initial celebration. Therefore, Cotton, and New England with him, were opposed even to the celebration of Christmas. But they had their holidays of thanksgiving, unfixed to any date, occurring as occasion arose. Thus the celebration was the result of an awareness of divine blessing, sanctified and informed by the spirit, never repeated in remembrance of the same occasion, never receiving a set calendar date, and, therefore, never accumulating practices which would mediate between the cause and the manner of celebration. Modern America's inclusion of Thanksgiving, with a capital letter, in its calendar of national holidays is, of course, a commemoration of the Puritan practice, odd for most citizens because of its lack of relation to any specific historical event. Folklore has been busy for over a century attempting to provide some reason for the feast which would fix it to an historical event.

When John Cotton maintained in Anne Hutchinson's interest that she might in all soundness expect a miracle to occur on her behalf in the ordinary course of providence, he was drowned out in the storm of disapproval which broke about her head. But, indeed, he was enunciating a doctrine which was not far if at all removed from the opinions most of his colleagues held in their calmer moments. The inevitable accompaniment to the macrocosmic eschatological expectation was the microcosmic reading of daily happenings as evidences of God's particular favor or disfavor. Strayed cattle, drowned sailors, and sunning snakes held their significances for the New Englanders, but, on the whole, while remarkable things did happen there was no set formula to be applied to their interpretation. Many among the first generation of settlers indulged in interpreting petty phenomena—the vulgar far more than the learned; John Cotton was consistently reluctant to support such a way of deciphering God's will. While the Book of Revelation might unfold itself in great political and religious events, he thought, when God meant to speak to men privately He did so through awakening their souls rather than through little external signs and events.

The deciphering of the cryptic messages written in the trivial occurrences about him was the Massachusetts freeman's answer to the same spiritual yearnings which moved the Anne Hutchinson group to magnify the nature and effect of their union with Christ. The wilderness into which he had been cast was abnormally cruel and chaotically meaningless if it were not a special arena of God's progress toward the millennium, and the wonderful communal achievements in church and state were insufficient to satisfy his hunger for special recognition from God. Consequently, he remained alert and sensitive to his surroundings, anxious to note God's signature in what the day brought. Whereas the Antinomians went to one extreme in internalizing God's progress so that necessary precepts of conduct were destroyed, he tended to the extreme of seeing God's messages out in the open in objects, so that no one could accuse him of "desperate enthusiasm" although certain might smile at his gullibility. Consequently, when, for instance, news reached Massachusetts that Anne Hutchinson was delivered of a monstrous birth, he indulged himself in relating each of the reported particulars of the monster to specific heresies allegedly held by Mrs. Hutchinson.

Cotton, however, was wary of such interpreting, preferring to steer between this and Antinomianism, but, if driven to one or the other extreme, then siding with the latter. Shortly after the exile of Anne Hutchinson's group, it was revealed that Mrs. Dyer, a follower of Mrs. Hutchinson, had had a monstrous birth in Boston prior to her exile but that on John Cotton's advice she had kept it secret. The avid cryptographers, Winthrop among them, were dismayed at Cotton's silence because they thought he had thereby deprived them of important evidence of God's disposition toward such as Mrs. Dyer at a time when such information would have been welcomed. When questioned, Cotton replied that if it was God's providence, then it was also a providence that although many women attended Mrs. Dyer in her labor, only two were present at the delivery, which argued that the Lord wanted the event kept secret. Besides, he frankly added, if it had been his own case he would have wished it concealed for if the Lord meant to edify by it, then, surely, considering the manner He chose, the edification was intended for the parents.[32]

Certainly, God set external seals on His special care for John Cotton, the recipient thought, and he acknowledged them. He had been born at the beginning of eventful anti-Catholic times; his father's business, once marginal, had prospered when he went to the university, freeing him from severe financial concerns; when his first wife died after a happy but childless marriage, he was able to find another worthy helper; if he had any doubts about the correctness of his going into exile, his decision was blessed by the birth of his first child on shipboard. Since then his wife had given birth to a daughter, Sarah (named for her mother) in 1635, and, shortly after Anne Hutchinson's church trial in the winter of 1637, another daughter, Elizabeth (named for the queen who struck a blow against Catholicism and, perhaps,

[32] Winthrop, *Journal*, I, 267-68.

also for her father's first wife). His family was to grow larger with the addition of John in 1640, Mariah (named for her father's mother) in 1642, and Rowland (for his father's father) in 1643.[33] But these and many other blessings were not to be termed extraordinary and their meaning was private and for his own edification. The extraordinary messages from God which he was fond of remembering were internal, such as the fact that he had received the strongest assurance of his justification up to that time on the day of his first marriage.[34] He believed that when God spoke to individual men He almost inevitably did so in this manner.

With such habits of mind forming his perception of reality, John Cotton left the Antinomian controversy behind him, and, in 1639, stood on the threshold of his period of greatest public service. To that point, his public career appeared singularly disastrous, involving as it did a reversal on polity and a severe rebuff, if not defeat, in doctrine. But the realities as he perceived them sustained him and as he entered his fifty-fourth year the news from abroad brought expectations of a millennium to a wonderful height. The fifth vial mentioned in the Book of Revelation was being poured and New England was being called to make its grand entrance into Christian history.

[33] *A Report of the Record Commissioners, City of Boston* (Boston, 1883), Vol. IX.
[34] Mather, *Magnalia*, I, 258.

THE TIME OF THE FIFTH VIAL
(1640-1644)

UNSUCCESSFUL in his efforts to chastise Scotland by arms, Charles I, in April 1640, summoned Parliament from an eleven-year recess. He urged upon this body his need for subsidies, but when he found money would be forthcoming only if he made concessions to the Puritan cause which had become interwoven with the people's liberties, he dissolved it, raised funds from private lenders, and set out on his second expedition against the Scots. This campaign proved more disastrous than the first. Charles's army was beaten at Newburn and the victors crossed the Tyne, apologizing and assuring the King of their loyalty as they advanced into England. A truce was made with them only by guaranteeing them, among other things, eight hundred and fifty pounds a day. To extricate himself from the expenses and obligations thus incurred, Charles, in November of 1640, needed again to call a Parliament.

To the English Puritans, the success of the Scotch polity in combination with Scotch arms augured a better day for the reformation of religion in England. The turn of affairs represented a severe check to Archbishop Laud, who, since 1633, had been strengthening the enforcement of uniformity and emphasizing the sacerdotal character and powers of the church. Moreover, every Englishman knew that the convening of a Parliament in 1640 meant that grievances would be dealt with before grants and the Puritans felt that the time was now at hand when the English church would be reformed according to their principles.

The situation in England was reflected in Massachusetts immediately in the rate of immigration. To 1640, an estimated 21,200 people had come to Massachusetts Bay, divided roughly into 4,000 families and arriving in about 300 separate voyages. In 1640, not only did the wave of immigration cease but the undertow pulled many back to the homeland. Thomas Hutchinson, writing in 1764, said that since the date of Charles's defeat at the hands of the Scots, "More persons have removed out of New-England to other parts of the world than have come from other parts to it."[1]

After seven eventful years of settlement, then, years which seemed to bring an increasing number of changes and expansions to which he could relate himself only with difficulty, at a rate of speed which was far outstripped by his times, John Cotton was finally facing a situation designed for his talents. The first pioneering days were over and the time for consolidation had arrived. Always in lag of new developments—the Salem polity and the rise of the more legal Christian doctrine—he was, on the other hand, the greatest biblical scholar and ecclesiastical theorist in New England. Both of these talents were in prime demand now, for the stirring news from abroad demanded a Christian historical interpretation and the established practices at home needed to be knit more closely to a theory based on scripture so that they would have the validity necessary to call the Massachusetts polity to the attention of those who would have to ponder such problems in England.

The sixteenth chapter of the Book of Revelation was that on which the eschatological expectation of New England was most firmly based, and preaching on that work Cotton was able to locate current events in God's chronological scheme. In the text, the Spirit described the pouring out of the seven vials, and before Charles's reign, the first four vials had been poured, as Cotton proved to his listeners. "*When the first Angel poureth out his Viall upon the Earth,*" he said, "*it* is upon the lowest and basest Element in the *Antichristian* world, and that can bee no other, but the lowest

---

[1] Hutchinson, *History of Massachusetts*, I, 82.

sort of vulgar Catholiks, and they were the first that had the wrath of God pour'd upon them."[2] This occurred, he went on, during the reign of Henry VIII and continued through the reformations of Luther and Calvin. The second vial which, in the text, was poured upon the sea, which then became as the blood of a dead man, was the wrath of God loosed against the Roman Catholic religion, as opposed to the behavior of Roman Catholics, which was submerged by the first vial. Junius, Chamier, Whitaker, and Perkins, who wrote against the Council of Trent, were the human instruments for the pouring of this vial, and when Queen Elizabeth, in 1581, assented to the law against foreign-ordained priests she was the instrument of the pouring of the third vial. Queen Elizabeth also supplied the human agency for the pouring of the fourth vial by opposing the house of Austria, for the "sun" upon which the fourth vial was poured in Revelation symbolized either this monarchy or the Pope whom the monarchy reflected. The first four vials having been aimed in time at different aspects of Roman Catholicism from the days of Henry VIII to the present, a New Englander could reflect with excitement that he had been a witness in his lifetime to the latter three gigantic fulfillments of the divine scheme for human history. Moreover, his expectation of great things yet to come was equalled and pricked on by his desire not only to witness the pouring of the next vials but to partake in that act, to be an instrument chosen from eternity for the important penultimate role in human history, just as not only Henry VIII and Luther had been, but also people whom he had seen with his own eyes, like Elizabeth, or heard and talked with, like Perkins.

The fifth vial, said Cotton, was aimed not only at the Pope, but "at the government of all National, Provinciall, and Diocesan Churches." Beza, Cartwright, Baynes, and Parker were active in this event, and now the church of

[2] Cotton, *Seven Vialls*, "First Viall," Sig. B2v.

Scotland had entered with full force. Cotton continued: "Concerning the undertakings of the *Scots* in our native Country, since the world began was it never known (for there are no Histories of note but are commonly known) such a patterne as this, that ever a whole Nation did rise to take up such a quarrell, with so much justice, wisdome and piety, a thing to be wondred at, that a whole nation should carry such a matter in such a way."[3] Indeed, the divine pattern was so far realized that many in Massachusetts believed that they were placed where they were, close to the Indians, so that they might bring the savages in after news reached them of the conversion of the Jews.

The most immediate instinct, however, was to get into the thick of things, and those who could hastened to England to increase the ranks of the parliamentary party: John Winthrop's son, Stephen, became one of the Parliament's major-generals; Samuel Desborough of Guilford was made Keeper of the Great Seal of Scotland; Hugh Peter became Cromwell's chaplain; Edward Hopkins took a seat in Parliament and was made Warden of the Fleet and Commissioner for the Navy and Admiralty; George Downing, one of the nine original graduates of Harvard, became Scoutmaster General in the English army in Scotland, and then Cromwell's ambassador to the Low Countries; and a host of others with New England experience returned to England to play less prominent roles in the rebellion.[4] They were Englishmen and their return was prompted by the same spirit which informed the following words of New England minister William Hooke: "There is no Land that claimes our name, but *England*, wee are distinguished from all the Nations in the world by the name of *English*. There is no Potentate

[3] *Ibid.*, "Fifth Viall," Sig. B2.
[4] William L. Sachse, "The Migration of New Englanders to England, 1640-1660," *The American Historical Review* (January, 1948), LIII, 251-78. For a more general treatment, see also Sachse, *The Colonial American in Britain* (Madison, 1956).

breathing, that wee call our dread Soveraigne, but King
CHARLES, nor Lawes of any Land have civilized us, but
Englands; there is no Nation that calls us Countrey-men,
but the *English*. Brethren! Did wee not there draw in our
first breath? Did not the Sunne first shine there upon our
heads? Did not that Land first beare us, even that pleasant
Island, but for sin, I would say, that Garden of the Lord,
that Paradise?"[5]

As much as John Cotton agreed with his colleague William
Hooke—indeed, he had spent but seven of his fifty-five years
out of England—nevertheless, he was cautious about the
widespread zeal to return to England, and he warned, "If
men be weary of the Country and will back again to *England*
because in heart they are weary . . . I feare there is no Spirit
of Reformation."[6]

Faced with the events in England, Cotton was not so
confident of the imminence of the second coming that he
failed to speculate on the problem of governing the homeland
should Charles capitulate. Characteristically, while the deed
sped ahead of him, he pondered the philosophical basis for
the action and, thus, in the early part of 1640 preached on
the relation of Christians to kings. The law, he held, was
supreme and, therefore, if the laws of a state are against
religion, as were those of ancient Rome, then the Christian
has no recourse but to submit. But, on the other hand, "if
the law be for the maintenance of Peace and Trueth, and true
Religion," and the prince, nevertheless, goes against or beyond law and contrary to the oath he himself has taken,
then his war against the saints and their religion is illegal
and "in such a case as this, It is . . . lawfull to take up arms
of defence."[7] In matters of doctrine, Cotton strongly opposed

[5] William Hooke, *New Englands Tears, for Old Englands Fears* (London, 1641), p. 16.
[6] Cotton, *Churches Resurrection*, p. 21.
[7] John Cotton, *An Exposition upon the Thirteenth Chapter of The
Revelation* (London, 1655), p. 109.

the position which is conventionally termed legal and preached the precedence and sufficiency of the Spirit. But in civil matters he adhered to the law as the only guide and insisted that all submit: "If Laws be made, let a man yield active obedience to them, if they be good, and passive if they be evill; but against Law, contrary to the stream of Law, to make a man think himselfe bound, in such a case it is to flatter Princes and Powers, not to yeeld professed subjection to them."[8]

Cotton's hate for Roman Catholicism, bred in him by Protestant parents, nurtured by his consciousness developing in the England of the 1580's, and matured by his studies in theology, was impelled by the eschatological belief that Rome would be destroyed after the pattern in Revelation. That hate, however, was not so blind that it deprived his reaction to Roman Catholicism of positive tenets for his theocratic theory. And now, in 1640, preaching on Revelation, he was able to extend his remarks about the dangers of Roman Catholicism and the right of the people to take up arms so that he could make application to the civil situation in Massachusetts, one which was not entirely to his liking because of the frequent obfuscation of the distinction between church and state. Pointing to the horrible example set by Rome, he warned that it was dangerous "to annex civill penalties, *ipso facto*, upon such as are cast out of the Church."[9] And applying his lesson to New England, he urged that excommunication not be taken as a just cause for depriving a man of the privileges of the state or for depriving him of "civill Commerce." Men, he maintained, "may discover such hypocrisie as may make them unfit for the Church, but yet they may not altogether be unfit for the Common-wealth."[10]

Human nature, to be sure, could be divided into two gross classes, the elect and the damned, but finally this was a

[8] *Ibid.*, pp. 111-12.
[9] Cotton, *Exposition of Ecclesiastes*, p. 166.
[10] Cotton, *Exposition upon Revelation*, p. 238.

distinction for the church invisible, thought Cotton, and life on this earth would be incredibly naïve and inept if conducted with regard only to these two classes. He was soon to engage Roger Williams on just this point because, he believed, Williams's assumption that the blessed and damned division was one which could govern all affairs on earth was impractical. Rather, Cotton recognized that although all that ultimately counted was man's spiritual relation to God, on earth this could have many shades ranging from outright reprobate, to civil reprobate, to hypocrite, to weak Christian, to strong Christian (to mention only the high tones), and that outward matters, civil matters, must be conducted in accordance with this realization. To attempt to look at human beings as either blessed or damned would lead either to abandoning any hope for a holy commonwealth on earth through refining the pure into so small a number that their church would be a minute fraction of the whole community (as Williams was to do), or to attempt an unworkable tyranny. On the other hand, the Roman Catholic refusal to make any distinctions, and, therefore, its complete confusion of church and state, led to other enormities, he thought. He attempted to maintain a commonwealth based on a recognition of the variety of human nature as manifested in this world. In preaching Christian doctrine, his words reflected only the gross, the all-important distinction between those who were and were not saved, but in dealing with other matters, with the variety of human nature and the consequent difficulty of establishing a sound theocracy, he was cautious. Although he was disturbed by the Court's usurpation of the church's liberty in giving the civil authorities the right to pass on fit residents, he did not believe that the church should compensate by dictating to the Court; faced with a period of consolidation in New England which could well set the pattern for establishment in England, he continued to insist, "Let not any Court, *Ipso facto*, take things from the Church; If such a Law were made (the

Fathers live not for ever;) and if such a Law were once established, that a Church-member standing so long excommunicated, the Common-wealth then should proceed against him; were this established, it would make a Beast of the Church; we are subject to erre, and our posterity that comes after us may erre (it may be feared) worse."[11]

The immediate advice John Cotton had for those who would listen at the beginning of the 1640's was a warning against a false security in New England based on the belief that the colony had so far surpassed the homeland that the reformation of the church was a resurrection such as the sixteenth chapter of Revelation described. "I cannot say, here is a Resurrection of Churches, such as the text speaks of," he said, although he hoped the Lord would bring them to it.[12]

After he had prefaced such cautions, however, after he had emphasized the constant need for a personal reformation and a personal resurrection, a constant devotion on the part of the listener to his own salvation and a constant search for signs of it, a constant commitment to the Spirit in man and a constant attempt to lead a life according to the Spirit, after he had speculated on the problems of polity facing his commonwealth and about to face England, then, finally and importantly, he did turn to the practical problem of just what those in New England could do to help on the gigantic work going forth in England. That contribution, he affirmed, was clearly one of guidance and he was becoming increasingly sure that the great American migration had taken place so that the Lord could have a laboratory model of ecclesiastical polity ready for mass production when the time of the fifth vial arrived. "We came not hither to speak hardly of other Churches," Cotton affirmed, and he went on to reflect that he had less cause than many others to think badly of the national church because of the liberality of Bishop Williams toward

---

[11] *Ibid.*, p. 19.
[12] Cotton, *Churches Resurrection*, p. 21.

him. But reflecting further on his own experience, he admitted that the episcopacy was so rooted in things of this earth that so far as the bishops and their subordinates were concerned, "the summe of the matter is, *quid mihi dabis?*"[13] Now he could speak these things though earlier he had been silent about them, because now the "Word of God calleth for it." Those who enjoyed the Bay polity, he said, "should be wickedly silent if we should not let the people know, what the mercy and blessing is, which we doe enjoy." New England's prayers for itself had, in great part, been answered, but the halting place had not been reached: "Let us therefore pray both night and day, in season, and out of season for our brethren in our native countrey, for whom God hath wrought all these great things, and for whom greater things yet remain to be done, for whom our work is to wrastle with God, that they may not perish for lack of knowledge, nor mistake a false Church for a true, (and false it is, if it be either Cathedrall, Provinciall, Nationall, or Diocesan)."[14] And while the prayers of the people of the new Israel went forth to wrestle with God, their leaders could make a practical contribution toward the homeland's discovery of the true church. "Great pitty were it," said Cotton, "that they should want any light which might possibly be afforded them."[15] He and his colleagues were determined to emit what light they had.

The colonists' interest in England did not go unreciprocated. The constant threat to their charter now seemed a thing of the past and Commons, in 1642, removed all tariffs on goods passing between New England and the homeland. In the same year, letters came to Cotton at Boston, Hooker at Connecticut, and Davenport at New Haven, urging them "to come ovar with all possible speed, all or any of them, if all cannot," to aid in "the seatlinge and composeing the

[13] Cotton, *Seven Vialls*, "Fifth Viall," Sig. A4.
[14] *Ibid.*, "Seventh Viall," Sig. Bbb4v.
[15] *Ibid.*

affaires of the church."[16] The letters were signed by members of both houses of Parliament, including Lord Say and Seal, Lord Brooke, Arthur Haselrig, Oliver St. John, and Oliver Cromwell.

Politically acute Thomas Hooker took little time in deciding to refuse the invitation, reckoning that at most the New Englanders would find three allies in the large number of clergymen called to settle the state of affairs. He did not think it, in Winthrop's words, "any sufficient call for them to go 3,000 miles to agree with three men."[17] Davenport was more sympathetic to the invitation but was irreplaceable in his young colony. Cotton, however, was anxious to attend. More than the others, he had left a great reputation and many friends in England; indeed, those few who were tentatively counted as allies by Hooker were headed by Thomas Goodwin, Cotton's disciple in nonconformity, and Cotton felt confident in his power to be a moving force in any assembly met to consider polity. Before his plans to heed the call could materialize, however, news arrived of the fresh breach between King and Parliament and he reluctantly resigned himself to affecting the Westminster Assembly as best he could through propagandizing the model which had been developed in the Lord's laboratory.

Although no New Englander attended the Westminster Assembly, the way of the churches in New England became a matter of widespread interest to those assembled. They recognized the experimental role which the Americans had played. Whereas reformed English congregations had led sporadic existences on the continent for a century, in New England a group of believers had erected a reformed polity which embraced thousands of people and which was, allegedly, within the confines of the Church of England. Those who favored independence of congregations and regarded *An*

[16] Hutchinson, *History of Massachusetts*, I, 100-101n.
[17] Winthrop, *Journal*, II, 71.

Apologeticall Narration[18] as their manifesto could draw strength from the fact that their polity had been tried in America and had worked, while the Presbyterians realized that one of their chief functions in debate would have to be to show the unsoundness of the New England polity. News from New England, then, was of prime importance. Details and theory of the church way, the demand for which dated from Cotton's written admonitions to Skelton and the supply of which was rising as the Westminster Assembly gathered, were important points of evidence.

The manner in which the Salem and Boston churches were gathered had, in a few years, become the core of a pattern which was followed by every new church in the Bay. Although all residents were required to attend services, and thus the assembled group took on the appearance of a parish congregation in England, not all were admitted to the sacrament of the supper and could have their children baptized. Nonconformity in America had established a character not only distinct from that of the parish church in England but also vastly removed from the most radical reforms the more successful members of the Westminster Assembly had previously been able to institute, reforms for which Cotton had provided a working model at St. Botolph's some ten years earlier. Just how far removed the American churches were in practice is illustrated by Winthrop's description of the founding of the Newtown church. Letters describing similar occasions circulated widely among the English Puritans. Winthrop's description went:

[18] On page five of *An Apologeticall Narration* (London, 1643), the authors say: "We had the example of the wayes and practices (and those improved . . .) of those multitudes of godly men of our own Nation, and among them some as holy and judicious Divines as this Kingdome hath bred; whose sincerity in their way hath been testified before all the world, and will be unto all generations to come, by the greatest undertaking (but that of our father *Abraham* out of his own countrey, and his seed after him) a transplanting themselves many thousand miles distance, and that by sea, into a wilderness, meerly to worship God more purely, whither to allure them there could be no other invitement."

"Mr. Shepherd, a godly minister, come lately out of England, and divers other good Christians, intending to raise a church body, came and acquainted the magistrates therewith, who gave their approbation. They also sent to all the neighboring churches for their elders to give their assistance, at a certain day, at Newtown, when they should constitute their body. Accordingly, at this day, there met a great assembly, where the proceeding was as followeth:

"Mr. Shepherd and two others (who were after to be chosen to office) sate together in the elder's seat. Then the elder of them began with prayer. After this, Mr. Shepherd prayed with deep confession of sin, etc., and exercised out of Eph. v -that he might make it to himself a holy, etc; and also opened the cause of their meeting, etc. Then the elder desired to know of the churches assembled, what number were needful to make a church, and how they ought to proceed in this action. Whereupon some of the ancient ministers, conferring shortly together, gave answer: That the scripture did not set down any certain rule for the number. Three (they thought) were too few, because by Matt. xviii an appeal was allowed from three; but that seven might be a fit number. And, for their proceeding, they advised, that such as were to join should make confession of their faith, and declare what work of grace the Lord had wrought in them; which accordingly they did, Mr. Shepherd first, then four others, then the elder, and one who was to be deacon, (who had also prayed,) and another member. Then the covenant was read, and they all gave a solemn assent to it. Then the elder desired of the churches, that, if they did approve them to be a church, they would give them the right hand of fellowship. Whereupon Mr. Cotton, (upon short speech with some others near him,) in the name of their churches, gave his hand to the elder, with a short speech of their assent, and desired the peace of the Lord Jesus to be with them. Then Mr. Shepherd made an exhortation to the rest of his body, about the nature of their covenant, and to stand firm to it, and commended them to the Lord in a most heavenly prayer. Then the elder told the assembly, that they were intended to choose Mr. Shepherd for their pastor, (by the name of the brother who had exercised,) and desired the churches, that, if they had any thing to except against him, they would impart it to them before the day of ordination. Then he gave the churches thanks for their assistance, and so left them to the Lord."[19]

Although the procedure had become somewhat routine after a decade, the assent of the magistrates and elders consulted was not automatic. Two months after the gathering described, when another assembly was held in Dorchester for the same purpose, approbation was withheld and plans postponed. The reasons assigned for the dissent of the authorities were the unsound grounds upon which most of those gathered based their conviction of salvation. But the ceremony at the rim of the forest which Winthrop described in such detail was intended by its participants to be the factual pattern for re-established churches in England.

To the six salient features of the Salem church,[20] practice had now added the necessity for the consent of the magistrates and the elders of the other churches. Thus, while the independence of the Bay churches from the English way had become systematized, so also had the similarity of the Bay churches with one another. Independence of congregations was a fact only in terms of the daily intramural procedures of a given church. The authorities both supervised the foundation and interposed if dissent arose within a church, as they did in Boston in 1637. Whereas the dependence of a church on the cooperation of the magistrate and the good will of its neighboring churches was recognized, its independence from subordination to the laws of any other church was jealously guarded.

[19] Winthrop, *Journal*, I, 173-74.
[20] *Vide*, chapter III, p. 76.

Like the children in a family, the churches maintained an equality with one another while soliciting mutual good will and depending upon the aid of the parents, i.e., the magistrates, who, as Anne Hutchinson was reminded, were entitled to the full respect enjoined in the fifth commandment.[21]

Little in the Bay polity disagreed with the description of the visible church compiled some fifty years earlier by Henry Barrow, who was persecuted and, finally, executed for his beliefs. While the Bay settlers were sincere in their protests that they had learned from other models than that of the separating Barrow, the freedom their distance from England provided had resulted in an organization very much like that followed by those against whom Cotton had protested in his 1630 letter to Hugh Goodyear at Leyden. The church, Barrow had affirmed, consists of a company of faithful and holy people gathered in the name of Christ Jesus and worshipping him aright.[22] The officers he assigned to this church were the same as those employed by a Massachusetts congregation, except for the Relievers, or widows in charge of ministering to the ill, who were not installed with the official title, but whose office, in some way, was unofficially filled. And Barrow's pattern was the accepted one for the attaining and holding of office: "They orderly proceed to ordination by fasting and prayer, in which actions the Apostles vsed laying on of hands. Thus hath everie one of the people interest in the election and ordination of their officers, as also in the administration of their offices, vpon transgression, offence,

[21] On this point, Cotton's catechism drilled generations of Massachusetts children:

"*Quest. Who are here* [fifth commandment] *meant by Father and Mother?*

Ans. All our Superiours, whether in Family, School, Church, and Common-Wealth."
John Cotton, *Spiritual Milk for Boston Babes in Either England* (Boston, 1656), p. 4.
[22] Henry Barrow, *A True Description out of the Word of God of the Visible Church* (London, 1589), p. 1.

abuse, &c. having an especiall care vnto the inviolate order of the Church, as is aforesaid."[23]

One of Barrow's statements left room for various interpretations and opened an area of attack for the Presbyterians in their objections to the Massachusetts way. Barrow had said that Christ gives "them" the keys to the kingdom of heaven, and it was a matter of some debate to interpret the reference of his pronoun. Most of the separatist congregations which gathered on the continent in the early seventeenth century had been so democratic in their procedures as to refer all matters of entrance and excommunication to a vote of the entire congregation, even to allowing the majority of the congregation to vote out and thereby unfrock its pastor. They would have said that the recipients of the keys were the believers as a whole. However, in the Bay churches although such matters were formally settled by a vote of the congregation, this vote was taken only after the elders had decided upon the measure and had moved it. Samuel Stone of Hartford described this kind of church organization as "a speaking *Aristocracy* in the Face of a silent *Democracy*."[24]

Since Henry Barrow was a separatist, John Cotton and his colleagues studiously avoided any explicit recognition of his contribution to their system, for their inclusion in the Church of England was for them more than a matter of rhetoric. Their system was, at the least, however, Barrowistic, and regardless of whom they recognized as parents, what was obvious to them and their English correspondents alike was that their initial task in Massachusetts was not one of formulation so much as it was one of practical operation. The late sixteenth and early seventeenth centuries yielded them theory enough; the problem was practice and the queries from England during the first decade of American settlement were directed at that aspect of the New England way.

John Cotton was one of the earlier suppliers of information

[23] *Ibid.*, p. 3.   [24] Mather, *Magnalia*, I, 437.

about New England procedures. In 1634, well before he was convinced of the correctness of the procedures he had found on his arrival, he had begun a brief description of the constitution and order of public worship of the Boston church, and this he had published once the reformation seemed under way in England.[25] The order of worship he described in the completed treatise was prayer; a psalm; reading and preaching of the word; prophesying by the gifted members of the congregation; discussion of questions addressed to the minister; administration of the sacraments; a psalm; collection for the ministry, the poor, and other needs of the church; and dismissal with a blessing.

Descriptions similar to this and that of Winthrop (cited above) prompted a fairly regular flow of questions not only from those seeking to confute the American churches, but also from well-wishers who desired more light, or who were troubled, as Cotton had been initially, by what they considered the separatist aspect of the Bay practice. Of principal concern was the question of the extent to which the Church of England had to be renounced by one who wished to gain membership in a reformed church which claimed, nevertheless, to be part of the Church of England. Cotton was quick to assure the questioners that only one "Sheba," the banished Roger Williams, had held it necessary to renounce the home church totally, and that the believers in the Bay required repentance "onely in generall so farre as we have polluted our selves with any corruption."[26]

Other questions repeatedly directed to the Massachusetts ministers were designed to elicit a clear notion of the degree to which the congregation had power over the admission of new members, irrespective of the judgment of the elders, and the amount of public examination to which an applicant had

[25] John Cotton, *The True Constitution of a Particular Visible Church Proved by Scripture* (London, 1642).
[26] John Cotton, *A Coppy of a Letter of Mr. Cotton of Boston* (London, 1641), p. 2.

to submit. Unfriendly visitors had described the application for church membership as an ordeal during which the applicant had to stand before everyone, make public confession of his faith, and undergo prolonged questioning designed to illuminate every detail of his spiritual autobiography. There were some, it was said, who "choose rather to goe without the Communion then undergoe such publique confessions and tryals, but that is held their fault." The writer of this report dryly noted in the margin: "Whether Popish Auricular confession, and these publique confessions be not extremes, and whether some private Pastorall or Presbyteriall collation, left at liberty, upon cause, and in case of trouble of conscience, as in the Church of England is approved, be not better then those extremes, I leave to the wise and learned to judge."[27]

Cotton, however, saw the confession as the farthest thing possible from an ordeal. With his abounding confidence in the Spirit's motions in a true believer, he maintained that all questions were sure to find a quick response. "The difference will ever hold," he said of sermons, "between the word read, and preached,"[28] and he was confident that this difference held between a confession of faith by formula and one by the motion of the Spirit. In his exuberant desire to further reliance on the Spirit, however, he buried his allies in England beneath a formidable description of the New England confession, one which confirmed their opponents' criticism. All the applicant for church membership had to do in his confession, Cotton insisted, was to say what anyone who had been justified could say:

"How it pleased God to worke in them, to bring them home to Christ, whether the Law have convinced them of sinne, how the Lord hath wonne them to deny themselves and their owne righteousnesse, and to rely on the righteous-

---

[27] Thomas Lechford, *Plaine Dealing* (London, 1642), p. 7.
[28] John Cotton, *A Modest and Cleare Answer to Mr. Balls Discourse of Set Formes of Prayer* (London, 1642), p. 43.

nesse of Christ, then they make a briefe confession, or else an answer to a few questions about the maine fundamentall points of Religion, that it may appeare indeed whether they be competently endued with the knowledge of the truth, and sound in the faith, and about the Godhead, the Trinity, the worke, our first estate of innocency, the fall, our redemption, Christ his Natures, his Offices, Faith, the Sacraments, the Church, the Resurrection, the last judgement, such as every Christian man is bound to learne and give account of; we refuse none for weaknesse, either knowledge or grace, if the whole be in them, and that any of the Church can give testimony of their Christian and sincere affections, and then the Church consenting to the admission, one of the Elders propounded to the party, the covenant that hee must enter into with God and the Church, whereunto the party expresly covenants, then is reciprocally received the Churches covenant back againe by the voyce of the elder. This is all the secret we have among us, neither have we any more secret carriage, than this which no godly man that ever came over to us have ever disliked, you come not more willingly to have communion with us, then we receive you, upon no harder termes then have been declared."[29]

Before the Westminster Assembly gathered, John Cotton added another published description of the way he practiced in New England. Here again, he described the make-up of the church, the manner of calling officers, the duties of the officers, the order of worship, and the relationship of churches. "Looke what power one Brother hath over another in the same Church," he explained, "the same power hath one Church over another in Brotherly communion."[30]

There were four issues on which a decided difference existed between the Presbyterians in the Westminster Assembly on the one hand, and the American Puritans and Independents

[29] Cotton, *A Coppy*, p. 5.
[30] Cotton, *True Constitution*, p. 12.

in England on the other. First, the Presbyterians wanted the new church establishment in England to be as comprehensive as the one it replaced. To that end, they did not insist that all members be regenerate, but only that the elders, who would have strict governing powers within a particular church, be reformed believers. In this insistence, they were closer to the Genevan model than were their New England brethren who had combined a devotion to Calvin's Christian doctrine with an acceptance of the polity of such English reformers as Henry Barrow. The second issue concerned the power of a church member, the Presbyterians maintaining that a congregation which took a democratic part in church action violated the church order set forth in the Bible. Thirdly, the Presbyterians disliked the limited use of synods in the New England system and insisted that such gatherings should be held regularly and should be recognized as the lawful authority over all churches. Finally, the Presbyterians were uneasy about the amount of toleration which independence of congregations might admit since they feared that with no central authority over the congregations, any frenzy seizing a particular church would have to be allowed as godly for want of power to exterminate it.

Recognizing that they had committed themselves theoretically to positions of which the Presbyterians disapproved, Cotton and his colleagues did not, initially, attempt a theoretic defense of their position. The important point, first, was to emphasize the workability of the New England way, to show that the consequences of their practice were not so baleful as the Presbyterians claimed they were. Thus, in defending his insistence upon a regenerate church body, Cotton was eager to show that the entrance procedure at Boston church was not a difficult one rather than to develop his theological arguments for excluding the reprobate. The emphasis upon the issues of difference between Presbyterian and Independent and upon the practical aspects of the New England system was strong in 1643 when the two most significant expressions of the system to date were published. They were both in the form of answers to questions or propositions which had been sent to Massachusetts prior to the Anne Hutchinson affair in Boston. The first was a relatively short answer by John Davenport to nine positions sent by a Somersetshire minister named Barnard,[31] while the second was a more elaborate answer by Richard Mather to thirty-two questions addressed to the New England elders.[32] Mather's answer had been reviewed by Cotton and others before it was dispatched for publication.

Both of these publications justified Massachusetts practices by citing their happy effects rather than through adducing scriptural supports. The New Englanders were, at this point, illustrating their way, not defending it. For example, in response to a question designed to show how few of the residents of Massachusetts Bay were actually church members ("Whether the greatest part of the *English* there (by estimation) be not as yet unadmitted to any Congregation among you, and the Reasons thereof"), Mather did not insist upon admitting only the regenerate, but interpreted statistics: "For the heads of Families, those that are admitted are farre more in number then the other."[33] On the question of whether baptized children were automatically admitted when they came of age, Mather again answered in practical terms by saying that the churches had not been in existence long enough to develop a principle on this point.

Mather carefully picked his way through questions designed to show that the Bay churches had, in effect, separated. How hard put he was to do so was reflected when he claimed, "If we were in *England*, we should willingly joine in some

[31] John Davenport, *An Answer of the Elders of the Severall Churches in New-England unto Nine Positions Sent over to Them* (London, 1643).

[32] Richard Mather, *Church-government and Church-covenant Discussed* (London, 1643).

[33] *Ibid.*, p. 7.

parts of Gods true Worship, and namely in hearing the Word, where it is truely Preached in sundry Assemblies there."[34] His readers well knew that hearing the word was not an actual form of communion with a church; after all, the unregenerate were not only allowed but required to listen to preaching in Massachusetts. Indeed, even the great separatist, John Robinson, had admitted that it was lawful to hear the word preached in a parish church so far was such a practice from signifying consent with the Church of England. Mather denied that English church members were refused communion in the Bay because the New Englanders regarded themselves as separated. Rather, he explained, if newcomers wish to stay they are admitted to membership after examination, not because the truth of their previous church is denied, but because any church may err in admitting a member and it is best to have this double assurance. Mather's remarks on whether the parish assemblies in England were considered by the American elders to be lawful were similarly hedged with numerous qualifications.

In effect, the Presbyterian pressures were molding the acknowledged separatists at Plymouth and the nonconformists at Massachusetts Bay into one body. Plymouth had become increasingly conservative so that it could no more abide the strict separation of Roger Williams than could the Bay, and the Bay settlers, in spite of their sincere intentions to the contrary, had found Plymouth practices to be agreeable. Therefore, when Mather cited the hearing of the word in English churches as an example of the Bay's opposition to separatism, he was distinguishing his polity only from that of such extremists as Roger Williams and not at all from the avowedly separated Plymouth. Indeed, he openly announced a united front with Plymouth in answer to the thirtieth question:

"Whether all and every of your Churches (including

[34] *Ibid.,* p. 27.

Plimouth, &c.) do precisely observe the same course both in Constitution and Government of themselves?

"If those words (precisely the same course) mentioned in this Question, be not meant of particular and individuall circumstances, but only of the substantialls or generall circumstances, then for ought we know there is no materiall point, either in constitution, or government, wherein the Churches in *N.E.* (*viz.* In the bay, in the jurisdiction of *Plymouth,* or *Connectacute,* and *Qulipiake* [New Haven]) do not observe the same course."[35]

Finally, Mather handled with some gingerliness the question of whether a church practicing another form of discipline would be granted similar liberties and recognized as a sister church should it desire to settle in New England. The qualifications of new settlers are decided by the magistrates, he said, and since Christ has erected only one true discipline, a church departing from it could not be recognized as a sister.

Although John Cotton was a consultant on these practical answers, it remained for him to produce the most influential of all New England statements. In 1644, *The Keyes of the Kingdom of Heaven* was published with the endorsement of Thomas Goodwin and Phillip Nye, thereby signalizing that it was not still another New England description but a document which was to take its place as the chief argument of the party which had brought out the *Apologeticall Narration* in the preceding year. A few years before its appearance, Cotton had added to his sketchy descriptions of the Bay procedures a lengthy treatise in which, in addition to description, he included justification from scriptures. This circulated in manuscript so widely that Presbyterian attacks on it were in print before it arrived at the press. Cotton insisted, when it finally was in print (as *The Way of the Churches of Christ in New-england, 1645*) that the publication was against his wishes and that *The Keyes,* which had been written subsequent

[35] *Ibid.,* p. 82.

to it but published previous to it, represented his final thoughts on the subject. There was nothing in *The Keyes* which manifested a difference in attitude from the statements of Davenport and Mather, but here, for the first time, the New England way was derived from authority rather than set forth descriptively. John Cotton's sketches of his practice were much like those of others, but his theory, constructed after the fact, was first in time and eminence.

In their preface, Goodwin and Nye signified that they considered Cotton's theory to be: "That very *Middle-way* (which in our apologie we did in the generall intimate and intend) between that which is called Brownisme, and the *Presbyteriall-government,* as it is practised; whereof the one doth in effect put the chief (if not the whole) of the rule, and government into the hands of the people, and drowns the *Elders* votes (who are but a few) in the major part of theirs: And the other, taking the chief and principall parts of that rule (which we conceive is the due of each *Congregation,* the *Elders* and *Brethren*) into this Jurisdiction of a common *Presbyterie* of severall *Congregations,* doth thereby in like manner swallow up, not only the interests of the people, but even the votes of the *Elders* of that *Congregation* concerned, in the major part thereof."[36]

Cotton began by saying that the keys of the kingdom were the ordinances of Christ (preaching, the sacraments, and censure), and that they conveyed no power civilly or legislatively to anyone but were held in stewardship. The power of the keys, he granted, was given to Peter, but not to him as the sole vicar of Christ who would at his death transmit the power to another individual. Rather, in receiving the keys, Peter stood as a representative of all who were ever to share their power, whether they were apostles, elders, or church members.

[36] John Cotton, *The Keyes of the Kingdom of Heaven* (Boston, 1843), pp. 7-8.

Peter received two keys. The first was a key of faith (or knowledge) and was common to all believers. The second was the key of order which was the power "whereby every member of the Church walketh orderly himself, according to his place in the Church, and helpeth his Brethren, to walk orderly also."[37] The power of this key, Cotton argued, was divided between the elders and the congregation: the former having the authority but the latter the interest. He explained that this division of the key was not arbitrary, but that each area was clearly marked: "The Gospel alloweth no Church authority (or rule properly so called) to the Brethren, but reserveth that wholly to the Elders; and yet preventeth the tyrannie and oligarchy, and exhorbitancy of the Elders, by the large and firm establishment of the liberties of the Brethren, which ariseth to a *power* in them."[38] He then enumerated the practical manifestations of the power of each group. The brethren could choose their officers; send forth their elders for the public service of Christ;[39] propound just exceptions to the admission of a new member; join the elders in judging matters of public scandal; resort to a synod to settle dissension; withdraw from the communion; and

[37] *Ibid.*, p. 29.
[38] *Ibid.*, p. 36.
[39] This power of sending forth elders was intended as a shield from a barb frequently hurled in Presbyterian and episcopalian attacks on the Congregational system. How, the New Englanders were asked, can the savages be converted if there is no supervising authority which binds congregations to one another and ordains ministers? For if a minister is no minister without a congregation, then no missionary can be a minister since the savages are hardly capable of electing him to such a post over them. If, however, some hierarchy is recognized, then that hierarchy appoints the ministers and can dispatch missionaries. Here Cotton mentions briefly that congregations too can send forth missionaries; but, of course, the objection still stands that within the bounds of strict Congregationalism once the missionaries are sent forth they lose their ministerial power. The fact that the Congregational system developed essentially untroubled by such problems reflects how trifling the settlers believed was the original claim that they came to convert. The eschatological expectation, of course, worked strongly against any such ambition since pagans were not to become Christians in significant numbers until the Jews had been converted.

commune with other churches. The last, Cotton cautioned, was not done by way of subordination. He made clear also that the brethren could not excommunicate their elders and that the relationship between members and their elders was like that between a jury and a judge: "though the Brethren of the Church do with one accord give up their vote for the censure of an offender, yet he is not thereby censured, till upon the sentence of the Presbytery."

The elders manifested the power they derived from the key of order in that they could preach the word and administer the sacraments; call the church together; examine new applicants for membership; ordain the officers whom the brethren had chosen; maintain order in the church meeting; prepare the matters to be dealt with in the church meeting; advise the church of the proper procedure in matters of difficulty; dismiss the church after meeting; watch that none of the people lived inordinately without proper occupation, idly in their occupation, or scandalously in any of their activities; deliberate in synods; and withhold the ordinances should the church grow blasphemous. Cotton symbolized the relationship between the congregation and its elders in a popular image of the day: "A Queene [she would serve better than a King at this date] may call her servants, her mariners, to pilot and conduct her over the sea to such an Haven: yet they being called by her to such an office, shee must not rule them in steering their course, but must submit herselfe to be ruled by them, till they have brought her to her desired Haven. So is the case between the Church and her Elders."[40]

Having derived all of the practices of the Congregational system directly from Christ's entrusting the keys to Peter, Cotton now turned to synods and examined their place in this structure. There were three just causes, he argued, for summoning a synod: when a church desires greater knowledge

[40] Cotton, *The Keyes*, p. 54.

[194]

or greater peace; when a church suffers a serious breach which cannot be healed by the members themselves; and when a corruption infects the majority of the churches. Although he was cautious about the necessity for summoning synods, because of the key of authority which the elders held, Cotton was definite about the power of a synod. Once it was summoned for just causes, it could not only counsel but could command what was to be believed and done, so long as these commands dealt with fundamental matters of doctrine and practice. The brethren had liberty only to ratify what the elders did in synod although they could question their procedures in a brotherly manner and to a limited degree.

Finally, Cotton turned, in *The Keyes*, to outlining the relationship the ecclesiastical structure he had derived bore to the state: "The first subject of the ministeriall power of the keys, though it be independent in respect of derivation of power from the power of the sword to the performance of any spirituall administration, yet it is subject to the power of the sword in matters which concern civill peace."[41] Two of these matters were the disposing of men's goods, lands, lives, liberties, worldly honors and inheritances; and public administrations (such as holding fast-days, preaching election sermons, offering thanksgiving for a general blessing), which were for the good of the state as a whole. Two other matters in which the church was subject to civil authority were of greater interest at that time. "The establishment *of pure Religion, in doctrine, worship, and government,* according to the word of God, as also the reformation of all corruptions in any of these," concerned the civil peace. Cotton said magistrates helped by stirring up the churches and ministers to conduct their religious affairs properly and by punishing willful opposers and disturbers of pure religion. However, he added cautionary words: "Neverthelesse, though we

[41] *Ibid.,* p. 95.

[195]

willingly acknowledge a power in the Civill Magistrates, to establish and reform Religion, according to the Word of God: yet we would not be so understood, as if we judged it to belong to the civill power, to compel all men to come and sit down at the Lords table, or to enter into the communion of the Church, before they be in some measure prepared of God for such fellowship."[42] The magistrate, then, was to see that all attended the church respectfully, but the church reserved the right to select its members free from magisterial interference; in this respect, theory was attempting to mend practice.

The final relationship the church bore the state was one of possible persecution by unjust rulers. This, of course, was a larger threat to Cotton's English audience than it was to his fellow Americans, but his past devotion to the law rather than his comparatively freer location was the source of his affirmation that when the church was afflicted by unfriendly civil authorities it had to submit "in patient suffering their unjust persecutions without hostile or rebellious resistance."

With the publication of *The Keyes* in 1644, the Independents had a platform but the Presbyterians now had a well formed target. They had suspected Cotton ever since his emigration because American church polity had maintained and strengthened its radical character ever since that eminent man had arrived on the scene. Since they did not know the extent of Cotton's differences from his fellows, for not only was there a natural caution in America to preserve a public silence on this point but also Cotton himself was reluctant to make his disagreements public except after a long period of contemplation and a considerable amount of qualification, they naturally concluded that he had been one of America's pathfinders, that his influence had, to a large extent, preceded the details of Massachusetts polity. As Robert Baillie, one of the more vigorous

[42] *Ibid.*, p. 97.

[196]

Presbyterian polemicists, said, Cotton was "if not the Author, yet the greatest promoter and Patron of Independency."[43] Baillie's fellows agreed with him and attacks upon the New England way included, if they were not in great part consumed by, attacks on Cotton's writing and conduct.[44] A blow could as well be struck for Presbyterianism by exposing Cotton's earlier attachment to Mrs. Hutchinson as by citing strong biblical support for a synodical state church. Ironically, those who found fault with Massachusetts for tending toward separatism, now opened their ears and happily accepted all the evidence they could receive from separatists, like Roger Williams, who were so extreme as to find disfavor with the Bay colonists and could surely expect at least equal severity should Presbyterianism come to power.

John Cotton, the majority of the English Puritans knew, was the American with the widest reputation for scholarship and pulpit ability; of all the American ministers he had been consulted most frequently by the prominent Englishmen interested in Massachusetts; of all of the American ministers, he had been the one to supply England not only with descriptions of his practice, but with the theoretical basis for it. John Cotton, the majority of the English Puritans concluded, was the prime mover in New England's ecclesiastical polity.

Speaking of the Independent system, Baillie noted that "of all the by-paths wherein the wanderers of our time are pleased to walk, this is the most considerable; not for the number, but for the quality of the erring persons therein."[45] He then went on to trace the genealogy of the New England way and in so doing repeated the popular belief of his fellows at the Westminster Assembly: "Master *Robinson* did derive his way to his separate Congregation at *Leyden*; a part of

---

[43] Baillie, *A Dissuasive*, p. 58.
[44] The most influential of these attacks were Thomas Edwards, *Antapologia* (London, 1644), and Samuel Rutherford, *The Due Right of Presbyteries* (London, 1644).
[45] Baillie, *A Dissuasive*, p. 53.

them did carry it over to *Plymouth* in *New-England*; here Master *Cotton* did take it up, and transmit it from thence to Master *Thomas Goodwin*, who did help to propagate it to sundry others."[46] Baillie had his lines somewhat tangled —Robinson might as accurately have been said to have gained notions at Leyden as to have delivered them there; Cotton's contact with or influence from Plymouth was far from direct; and the Cotton-Goodwin relationship was of a different origin—nevertheless, his main perception was a reality for most in England, Puritans as well as Anglicans. The Bay settlement was, basically, a separatist establishment.

Baillie knew of Cotton's stand against the separatists while he was in England and he cited Cotton's letter of criticism to Skelton in 1629. This was the same Cotton, Baillie noted, who now in 1644 demanded a confession of faith from believers wishing to receive the sacrament although these believers were members of good standing in the Church of England. Was it not clear, then, that the great promoter of Independency had been converted by the separatists and that Independency, therefore, was nothing other than subtly maintained Brownism? The nature of the edifice was not so important for Baillie's end as was the color in which he could paint it.

While Baillie was certainly on sound ground in exposing Cotton's position in 1644 as a near contradiction of the position he held during his English ministry, Cotton, of course, could not therefore accept Baillie's interpretation of his conversion. Although changing one's mind over a period of a decade was not necessarily a shameful thing, he was not going to allow his change to be characterized as a conversion to separatism. Throughout his conversion to the New England way, and now in his consolidation of it, Cotton had insisted upon his church being well within the boundaries of the Church of England. His deepest allegiances were to such

[46] *Ibid.*, p. 54.

reformers as William Bradshaw, Robert Parker, and William Ames, who were not separatists, and he maintained his insistence that they were sufficient guides for what he practiced. In *The Keyes*, he had been conservative in the liberties he had granted to the congregation. Although in practice, as Richard Mather said, there might now be small difference between Plymouth and Boston, nevertheless, Cotton felt, the paper war could be won or lost over the issue of whether Massachusetts had remained within the home church. Therefore, in his reply to Baillie, he attempted the difficult task of adhering closely to his published description and theory of the Boston church and yet maintaining a clear distinction between its derivation and that of Plymouth. For a polemical war requiring such theorizing as he had done and such qualifying as he was to do, Cotton was eminently qualified.

In handling the distinction between separatism and his way, Cotton was the gracious Christian reproaching a less charitable brother: "Though we put not such Honor upon those he calleth Brownists, as to own them our Fathers; yet neither doe we put so much dishonor upon them, 'as to heap coals of contumely upon their heads.' We look not at them with contempt, but compassion: Neither doe we bear witnesse against their Schism in any words of contempt and reproach, (which are the characters of contumelie) but in words of spirituall and just reproof; even in such terms, not which scornfull wit, but which holy Scripture suggesteth."[47] He then reiterated the New England watchword that he did not separate from other churches but only from those who were unfit for the Lord's table, and that, therefore, Independency was a misnomer since his way was not independent of the Church of England. Accordingly, he attached to the New England polity the label which it was thenceforth to wear: "If there must needs be some note of difference to decypher our estate, and to distinguish our way from a Nationall Church-way,

47 Cotton, *The Way Cleared*, p. 10.

I know none fitter, then to denominate theirs Classicall, and ours Congregationall."[48] The true line of descent of Congregational practice, Cotton went on, ran not from separatism but from the old nonconformity of Elizabeth's day (such as he had practiced in Cambridge); secondly, from renewed consideration of the second commandment (such as he had debated with Bishop Williams in one frame of mind and with Goodwin and Davenport in another); and lastly, from the writings of not Barrow or Robinson but Parker, Baynes, and Ames, all of whom had remained within the Church of England.

The separatists, then, were denied as parents, but not as brothers. Nothing of the character of Congregationalism as Cotton defined it was missing from the Plymouth system established in 1620. In acknowledging Baynes, Ames, and Parker rather than Barrow or Robinson, he was maintaining a distinction most necessary for the paper war but substantively slight. Just as Robinson and Ames, once they found themselves together in exile in Holland, had compromised their differences so that, finally, the major distinction between them was Robinson's admission of separation from the Church of England, so Plymouth and Massachusetts Bay were similar. The difference between a Robinson or an Ames as a parent amounted, in practice, to no larger a difference than that between a Boston man and a Plymouth man: they practiced the same church way and were even, upon letters of recommendation, admitted into the communion of one another's churches, but the former had declared his separation from the Church of England while the latter had not. Cotton knew this, but he realized also that if the similarities between men like Ames and Robinson could give the Presbyterians occasion to slander his fellows with the name of Brownists —a name which even Robinson denied—then it also gave him valid opportunity to claim that Ames, not Robinson,

[48] *Ibid.*, p. 11.

was the guide for Massachusetts Bay. His insistence on this distinction, echoed by others, came, in time, to be taken as a substantive rather than a rhetorical one and was developed after the fact into an elaborate set of separate genealogies, each with its own source, its own heroes, and its own practice, with little regard for occurrences such as Cotton's admonishing Skelton in 1629 and his capitulation to Salem's practice in 1636.[49] The rhetoric which was so effective through history, however, failed to shake the Presbyterians' profound distrust of Congregationalism or to diminish their ardor for painting that form in the colors of Brownism.

The men of position who had urged John Cotton to remain in Boston after the controversies which shook his church had ample reason to congratulate themselves. A man of singularly small official influence in America to that date, Cotton from 1639 onward continued to add to his English reputation. If he and his English allies failed, eventually, to establish Congregationalism as the national church form, his pronouncements at least clothed the hastily established New England churches in the robes of theological respectability. Moreover, as Cotton became the Massachusetts spokesman on polity, the public nature of his position and the *ad hominem* content of the attacks on him forced him into somewhat of a defense of the procedures against Mrs. Hutchinson. Baillie did not scruple to strengthen his attack on Cotton's Independency with remarks designed to show Cotton's unsoundness in Christian doctrine as evidenced by his relationship with the banished heretics. Indeed, there was a strong suspicion, when the much-circulated manuscript about the Hutchinson controversy finally reached the London press in 1644, that Thomas Weld, its editor, had been a dupe of the Presbyterians who had gladly cleared the way

[49] For a more detailed discussion of the relation of the Bay polity to that of Plymouth, see "The Salem Puritans in the 'Free Aire of a New World,'" *Huntington Library Quarterly* (August 1957), Vol. xx, No. 4, pp. 373-84.

for its publication, rejoicing in the fact that the narrative cast an unfavorable light upon Congregationalism. While Weld may have regarded *A Short Story* as an admirable account of the efficiency with which heretics were dispatched in the Bay, 1644 was certainly not a propitious year in which to make public the difficulties which had developed under the Massachusetts system.

Thomas Hooker, writing to his son-in-law, Thomas Shepard, in 1646, said, "In the general, I easily see that the Scotch party do seriously set themselves to fortify their Presbyterian side, with the improvement of all means (I had almost said Jesuit-like) to weaken the proceedings and the persons of the contrary minded." To that end, he went on, "I cannot be persuaded but these men had a secret hand to provoke Mr. Welde to set forth his 'Short Story' touching occasions here in Mr. Vane his reign."[50]

Cotton's defense of his writings on polity, notably *The Way of Congregational Churches Cleared*, included also, of necessity, a clarification of his personal position toward Mrs. Hutchinson's opinions. Although he maintained a kinder attitude toward her than any of his colleagues, and continued to insist upon praising her good parts and blaming his sleepiness as well as deploring her utterances, the exigencies of the rhetorical situation, nevertheless, drove him to a reconciliation with his recent critics at home more quickly than would otherwise have been the case.

However, the pressures which hastened Cotton in his movement into a position close to that of his fellow elders were not exerted in England alone, nor were they supplied only by the conservative group in the Puritan party. Parliament's success had unleashed a variety of vehement radicals, and to deal with them Massachusetts had continuing need of its recently reconciled scholastic leader, John Cotton.

[50] Palfrey, *History of New England*, II, 173n.

CHAPTER SEVEN

THE MIDDLE PATH
(1645-1648)

THE AREA around Narragansett Bay in New England had become so fertile a breeding ground for zealots of extreme religious opinions that even Roger Williams, the staunch advocate of toleration, found his forbearance taxed. In the spring of 1642, he complained to Winthrop that "the tide is too strong against us, and I fear (if the framer of Hearts help not) it will force me to little Patience, a little Isle next to your Prudence." The immediate occasion of Williams's dismay was a group, headed by Samuel Gorton, holding a strange doctrine which combined a distortion of views on the supreme importance of the Spirit, such as Cotton held. Williams complained that Gorton: "having foully abused high and low at Aquidnick, is now bewitching and bemadding poor Providence, both with his unclean and foul censures of all the ministers of this country, (for which myself have in Christ's name withstood him), and also denying all visible and external Ordinances in depth of Familism."[1]

Two years later, Massachusetts proceeded severely against this same Samuel Gorton and his followers after receiving ample spiritual insult but dubious legal cause from them. Being brought to attend Cotton's sermon in October 1643, Gorton sought to confute it and when Cotton and others in turn cited further scriptural texts and interpreted them, Gorton's group refused to stand convinced. Winthrop noted with disdain that "They were all illiterate men, the ablest of them could not write true English,"[2] and the magistrates soon turned from any attempt to reason with them on matters of religion and prosecuted them for their dealings with the

---

[1] *Publications of the Narragansett Club*, First Series, VI, 141.
[2] Winthrop, *Journal*, II, 147.

Indians and their activities against Massachusetts, although there was more than a little doubt as to whether the Bay rulers could put forth the least legal claim to the Gortonists being under their jurisdiction.

John Cotton, however, was more concerned with the doctrines set forth by this group and by other enthusiasts whose numbers seemed to be increasing in the mid-1640's. He had never had the slightest doubt as to the justice of Protestant persecution of the Roman Catholics, indeed, had identified Elizabeth's anti-Catholic ordinance as a fulfillment of one stage of Christian history predicted in Revelation. While his theological basis for such severity followed his identification of Rome with antichrist and his belief that the Catholics sinned against their own consciences, his attitude was impelled by an Old Testament desire for revenge. God found it just that the Catholics were put to death, he was sure, for "they that have been so busie in putting to death innocents . . . should also be put to death." It was so in the Old Testament and "why should it be changed in the new?"[3] When he remembered scenes like that which the authorities had enacted in the Derby market place during his childhood, he did so with righteous fervor: "As she [Elizabeth] put those Popish Emissaries to the paine of High Treason, hanging, drawing, and quartering, and thus gave them bloud to drink; so . . . [the] Angel from out of the Altar saith *Even so*, he saith *Amen* to it."[4]

But the rapidly increasing number of Protestant "heretics" had never physically injured any of the true believers. They did not have their Mary, had never held any civil power whatsoever, and none in New England had been raised amidst tales of the horrors of persecution at the hands of such as they. Cotton, therefore, did not have the same literal revenge impelling his attack on such as Gorton; nor, for

[3] Cotton, *Seven Vialls*, "Third Viall," Sig. B4.
[4] *Ibid.*, Sig. A4.

the first time in his polemical career, was he opposing a group that spoke from entrenched strength.

Nevertheless, the American situation supplied him with a spiritual equivalent to the external reality of England in the post-Marian days. In England, the successful reformers were to buttress that country's defenses against Roman Catholicism in memory of what they took to be the primary earthly source of England's difficulty, and their destruction of the establishment was to result in a religious situation so fluid that there was no set oligarchy powerful enough to carry resentment against Protestant heresy to the point of systematic persecution. In America, however, no significant body of Roman Catholic settlers posed a threat to the New Englanders, and there was a system consolidating itself and anxious to reduce opposition to the theocracy, Catholic or not. Cotton, the most powerful of the ecclesiastical con-solidators, therefore, was quick to make the analogy between outright murder, such as the Puritans' persecutors in England had practiced, and "soul-murther." In the colony which had advanced more rapidly in reformation than the homeland, "soul-murther" was more visible, and the American oligarchy, Cotton hoped, was in a position to do something about it. He, therefore, counseled: "If any man had a conscience to turn men from God, he would have men of as much conscience to cut them off; if they make no conscience of the blaspheming the name of God, the Lord would have men make no con-science of cutting them off from breathing in the aire of God; If men make no conscience of murthering soules, or raising sedition, and tumult, and murthering men better then themselves, the Lord would have men make no conscience of paying every man in his owne kind."[5]

Anne Hutchinson was fresh in Cotton's mind as an example of the sleepiness of his stewardship in former times, and yet her errors were mild compared with the outright heresies

[5] *Ibid.*, Sig. C.

he now heard men like Gorton breaching in their confusion of Adam and Jesus, or Christ's redemptive act and mortal death. He was resolved to see them hounded, unto death if necessary, both in order to preserve a commonwealth which was now taking an ecclesiastical turn more to his liking as it solidified its position, and to preserve New England's good name in England where, he judged, news of such heresies would be woven into an argument fatal to Congregationalism.

The magistrates, following reasons similar to Cotton's, sought the death penalty for Gorton, but the deputies, less zealous for the *status quo* and more sympathetic to free expression, were reluctant to do so and agreed with the magistrates for a less severe but by no means light sentence.

Cotton's increased severity, as compared with his stand in the Hutchinson controversy, and his newly gained prominence in promoting Congregationalism, as compared with his Salem recantation of 1636, did not fail to call forth ironic notices of the turns in the path he had walked. While the magistrates now finally found him of tremendous value as an apologist, the deputies' distrust of his authoritarianism increased, and many of his fellow elders, like Thomas Shepard, who confided his thoughts apparently only to his notebook, were still in distrust of the sincerity of his differences from Anne Hutchinson. However, Nathaniel Ward, the hearty, outspoken wit who held the pulpit at Ipswich, was willing to mention what was on the mind of many so long as his auditors were not in responsible positions. One evening, he went to the window of the cell of one of Gorton's followers and discussed his plight with him in an endeavor to win him over to a recantation. Gorton reported: "Mr. *Ward* seemed to be much affected, being a man knows how to put himselfe into passion, desired the said *Richard* [one of the prisoners], that if he had done or said any thing that he could with good conscience renounce, he desired him to recant it, and he hoped the Court would be very mercifull; and saith he, it shal be no disparagement unto you, for here is our Reverend Elder, Mr. *Cotton* who ordinarily preacheth that publickly one year, that the next year he publickly repents of, and shews himselfe very sorrowful of it to the Congregation, so that (saith he) it will be no disgrace for you to recant in such a case."[6] The fifty-nine-year-old Cotton was paying the inevitable price for local eminence: his career was the topic of lampoon by his less prominent fellows. He had had to trim ship since coming to America and that trimming had been noticed.

Added to the difficulties caused by the extremists was a Presbyterian activity in Massachusetts, prompted by the success of that party in England. Thomas Parker[7] and James Noyes, pastor and teacher of the church at Newbury, had since their entrance into their offices in 1635 been reluctant to grant the right of consultation and assent in matters of discipline to their congregation. When the preponderantly Presbyterian Westminster Assembly gathered in England, therefore, they looked to it hopefully, eager to see Presbyterianism introduced in the Bay, at least to the extent of the elders receiving complete control of church government. Their attitude caused dissension in Newbury church, and since those holding similar views were also emboldened by events in England to state them publicly, a gathering of all the elders in the jurisdiction of Massachusetts was held at Cambridge in 1643 to meet the problems raised. The college provided accommodations for the group, who at the outset elected John Cotton and Thomas Hooker as moderators.

The result of the assembly was a disapproval of some features of Presbyterianism, but such disapproval was mild and not designed to chastise. While the role of the congrega-

---

[6] Samuel Gorton, *Simplicities Defence against Seven-Headed Policy* (London, 1646), p. 53n.

[7] Minister Parker gave a dramatic demonstration of his character in 1637 when he walked forty miles so that he could cast his vote against Vane.

tion in church matters was upheld, it was qualified severely by its being "at least by way of consent."[8] The Congregational insistence on all church members being professed believers was softened in a Presbyterian direction by the admission, against Cotton's inclination, that such believers might not be adept at a confession of faith and might, therefore, be approved in part if their outward behavior was decent. Synods meeting in a fairly regular fashion were not recognized as authoritative, but they were approved as "comfortable and necessary." On the whole, the conclusions reflected a church form markedly more conservative than had been the strict independence of Salem and Boston some ten years earlier, for the democratic elements were significantly weakened and superintendence over churches was all but a recognized fact.

Cotton, who was considerably more authoritarian in matters of polity than were the churches he found flourishing on his arrival in New England, had thus made headway in the synod in imposing greater restraints on the believers in each congregation. His personal success was not total—the meeting decided that behavior while not a substitute for a confession of faith could be taken as a good part of the evidence of a man's being a Christian—but, on the whole, matters were concluded as he wished. In *The Keyes*, his proximity to Presbyterianism manifested itself in the power with which he clothed synods once they had been convoked on just causes, the limited role he assigned to the members of the congregation in matters of church discipline, and his recognition of the wide spiritual obligations of the magistracy. By 1641, to his joy, set meetings to order church matters had become a fact in spite of the violence with which the simple idea of ministers meeting to discuss biblical texts had been greeted some eight years earlier. A critical observer in that year noted, "In *Boston*, they rule, most an-end, by unanimous consent, if they can, both in admissions, and censures, and

---

[8] *A Reply of the Two Brethren to A. S.* (London, 1644), p. 7.

other things. In *Salem*, they rule by the major part of the Church: You that are so minded hold up your hands; you that are otherwise minded, hold up yours."[9] The unanimity of Boston was achieved by the elders preparing matters and indicating the necessary steps, as Cotton, in *The Keyes*, had said they should. Salem's was the more democratic procedure but one which was less influential in 1643.

Although John Cotton reconciled himself to the fundamental independence of churches and the need for making an explicit covenant before one was a church member, he had never overcome his initial discomfort at the more democratic of the procedures he found within the church. He distrusted them as a potential source of divergence amounting to separatism, especially since they were reinforced by the rigorously maintained independence of congregations from one another. In the first wave of settlement his views were not popular, for his fellow settlers were reacting to a parish system which they had found much harsher than Cotton had, and his energies, at any rate, were soon turned to a defense of his doctrine. But with Puritan government an approaching reality in England and with the consequent need for a pronouncement on Massachusetts polity, Cotton was able to advance his version of polity because Massachusetts found itself opposing not only the Presbyterians but also the more radical sects. Greater authority was needed and Cotton's version kept that authority in the hands of a few. If his polity was not Presbyterian enough to win much approval at the Westminster Assembly, it was not so anti-Congregational that it failed to find powerful sympathizers among the members of the Bay oligarchy who were bent on entrenching themselves in the face of the twin threats of increasing democratic demonstrations at home and increasing Presbyterian control in England.

By the close of 1645, the Westminster Assembly had

[9] Lechford, *Plaine Dealing*, p. 14.

prepared a pattern of Presbyterian church government which soon thereafter received the substantial support of Parliament. As the intent of the Assembly became increasingly apparent in the Bay, measures such as the elders had taken in the assembly of 1643, mild as they were in their disapproval of Presbyterianism, were inadequate to check the many discontented who now saw allies both in church and state in England. Only 1,708 of the close to 20,000 residents of Massachusetts Bay had been admitted to citizenship, and those in favor of a wider extension of political privileges were able, as the parliamentary forces seemed bound for success in England, to gain allies in the supporters of Presbyterianism in the Bay. The pressure from this combined force was felt more oppressively by the authorities than had been any previous popular movement.

Seven prominent members of the Massachusetts community (Winthrop, their opponent, dignified them all with the title of "Mr.") climaxed one phase of such activity by preparing a petition to Parliament. In May 1646, they announced in Boston that unless their demands were heard, they would have recourse to England. Their complaint was clear: they, "being freeborn subjects of England," were, nevertheless, denied the liberty of subjects by being barred in church from the sacraments unless they entered a church covenant which was against their consciences, and by being required in the state to take a civil oath which was so opposed to the oath of allegiance in the homeland that they could not accept it. The result was their subjection to "an arbitrary government and extrajudicial proceedings."[10]

The magistrates prepared to do battle against the potent combination of democrats in civil matters and Presbyterians in church matters, both bound to find deep sympathy in Parliament, by readying Edward Winslow of Plymouth to act as an agent in London, and by attempting to halt the peti-

---

[10] Winthrop, *Journal*, II, 271.

tioners in New England and prevent their document from ever reaching the homeland. But the elders also had a role in the battle. Congregationalism could not afford to linger in infancy, but had to define itself more sharply than it previously had in the models which were written for the edification of persons thousands of miles across the ocean, or in the conclusions of unauthoritative gatherings of elders. In 1646, magistrates and ministers realized the time had come to crystallize an official position on church polity.

But whereas the power of the Presbyterians had, to a large extent, emphasized the need for a clear definition of New England polity, Congregationalism, by its very undefined nature, impeded the gathering of a synod. The deputies refused to join the magistrates in the calling of a synod on the grounds that if they called a gathering to draw up uniform practices this would seem "to give power either to the synod or the court to compel the churches to practise what should so be established."[11] With difficulty, the magistrates overcame this objection, and, at the May 1646 Court, a call for a synod was issued in which the Court emphasized that the matters which should be uppermost in the minds of those who met in synod were baptism and church membership, both of which were severely restricted. The exclusion of so many had been under heavy attacks from the Westminster Presbyterians and the Massachusetts petitioners.

When September 1646, the appointed time for the synod, arrived, however, Salem and Boston, the original church and the largest church, were not represented. A strong strain of the original independent spirit still remained in each of these churches, and fearing the superintending power of a synod— even though, in a sense, the synod had been called to erect defenses against an even more centralizing polity—the congregation of Salem would not give majority approval and the congregation of Boston was far from unanimous. Cotton

[11] *Ibid.*, II, 274.

and Wilson, united in their recognition of the need for a
synod, failed to carry their arguments unanimously when
they disputed with their flock and were forced, finally, to
inform their members that they were going to attend the
synod as invitees of the Court if not as representatives of
the congregation. They consequently received a majority
vote and set out for the synod on its strength, maintaining
that the exigency of the situation did not allow them to pause
and win over the dissenters. The agitations in Salem church
resulted, finally, in the elders' from that congregation also
attending the synod over the vehement objections of a sizeable
portion of their congregation. A synod called to define the
Congregational way in order to establish a more uniform
church polity and settle practical questions of great importance
was thus gathered over the protests of those who felt that
by the very gathering of the synod an important aspect of
Congregationalism was forfeited. But the elders felt that
Presbyterian opposition was too strong to be countered by
other than Presbyterian tactics.

John Cotton, however, went to the Cambridge Synod with
more than the threat of Presbyterianism to determine the
position he would take. Indeed, since 1640 he had been in
the fore of those actively engaged in promoting Congregationalism against Presbyterian objections in England and too
extensive Presbyterian modifications at home, and, as a result,
had become involved in an almost personal polemical war
as the counterattack turned *ad hominem*. But against this
background, an attack was made upon him in 1643-1644 from
quite a different source than he had anticipated.

In 1643, the letter Cotton had written to Roger Williams
immediately after the latter's banishment appeared in print
in London and although he disclaimed any connection with
its publication, Williams was conveniently located in London
with a press accessible to him at that time. Consequently, he
published, in 1644, *Mr. Cottons Letters Lately Printed*,

Examined and Answered. He followed in the same year with a publication of the tract on toleration which had been sent to Cotton for reply some ten years earlier, Cotton's answer to the tract, and his (Williams's) refutation of Cotton's answer, all under the title, *The Bloudy Tenent of Persecution.*

Thus, at a time when he was concerned with maintaining his view of the church body as a community of professed believers against powerful antagonists who were anxious to broaden the basis for church membership, Cotton also became engaged in a battle against one who opposed his polity as being too broad and insufficiently refined and separated from corruption. With his attention turned toward opposing so full a measure of church-state cooperation that the two became indistinguishable, Cotton had now to defend any role of the state in church matters. He agreed with Nye and Goodwin that his road was the "middle-way" between Presbyterianism and separatism. He did not believe that his support of what Williams opposed contradicted his attitude toward the Presbyterians, but, nevertheless, both pressures coming together so insistently made his task a difficult one. An overforceful defense against Williams at the back gate might leave the main entrance weakened for Presbyterian assault; a too vigorous foray against the Presbyterians might provide the opportunity Williams could use to undermine all.

In his address to the reader prefaced to his examination of Cotton's letter, Williams said that the wilderness pressed him too severely to afford him an immediate chance to answer Cotton. He now had time to devote to an answer, and, fortunately, Cotton's letter was now in print. Williams insisted, in his examination of Cotton's letter, that his banishment was not for civil disturbance but for opinions: that the right to the land did not come from the King but from the natives; that it was not lawful to administer an oath to an unregenerate person since such was a form of religious communion; that it was not lawful to listen to preaching in the parishes of England; and that the power of the civil authorities "extends only to the Bodies and Goods, and outward state of men."[21] He went on to justify these opinions, to insist once more that complete separation from the Church of England was the only true reformation, and to charge that the Bay churches were self-contradictory in stopping short of it.

Cotton was temperately answered in this examination of his letter. He was treated as a sincere godly person who was in error on certain details. But in *The Bloudy Tenent*, Williams's remarks took on a greater sting. After an epistle to Parliament in which he said he realized that he would be persecuted for his doctrine but that he could not stifle the truth (and indeed that body did subsequently order the book publicly burned, but also granted him a charter for his colony), Williams printed the toleration tract and Cotton's reply to it. Then, in a dialogue between Peace, who set up Cotton's contentions, and Truth, who battered them down, Williams painstakingly canvassed every argument in Cotton's reply. At times, he tediously accumulated scriptural citations and gave them what he thought to be their proper exposition; at times, he lashed out in vivid images against those who sought to maintain religion by the sword.

Williams's major argument was that the magistrates and ministers had separate offices which nowhere in the Bible were represented as binding upon one another. Israel's theocracy, Williams insisted, was a pattern ("type" was his term) not of the state but only of the church since when Christ came He brought Israel's antitype in the church which he established. If Israel were a type of the state as well as the church, Williams argued, then Christ's antitype would have included a Christian civil polity, but it did not. Therefore, insofar as the state is concerned, the church is just another

[12] Roger Williams, *Mr. Cottons Letter Lately Printed, Examined and Answered* (London, 1644), p. 5.

company within its jurisdiction. The state must see that the members of the church abide by the civil laws without in any way concerning itself with the doctrines or practices within the church so long as they cause no civil disorder.

Willing as he was to allow any religious opinion to exist in the state untroubled, Williams needed to supply protection from seduction for the true believer since this need was generally put forward as one of the chief reasons for magisterial concern with religion. Williams found this protection in predestination. Confident of the elect position of members of the true church, he saw no need for mortal interference to assure the elect of not falling since such falling was an eternal impossibility. Those who belonged to the church invisible would eventually enter the church triumphant, while those who did not belong to the church invisible would stray from the church militant. In either case, there was no need for civil measures.

If the magistrate kept order over the bodies of men, Williams maintained, the church could keep order over their souls through excommunication. In answer to Cotton's assertion that the tares in the parable were hypocrites and doctrines or practices near the truth, all of which must be allowed in the field of the visible church, Williams replied that the field referred to in the parable was not the church but the world, and that since civil magistrates ought not to let civil offenders alone, nor the church allow wrong doctrines to flourish, the tares must represent a third class composed of idolaters, false worshippers, and antichristians who were outside the church but peaceful in their civil behavior. These the magistrates should ignore because of their orderly conduct, and these the church should ignore as being outside of the company of true believers.

In addition to biblical interpretation, then, two basic principles supported Williams's advocacy of toleration. The first was that belief in the doctrine of predestination meant rejecting the possibility of the seduction of the elect away from the church or the compulsion of the elect into it. The second was that the church could refuse to tolerate any differences in doctrine in direct proportion to the state's willingness to tolerate them. Tolerance in the state was a corollary to the principle of intolerance in the church, which body, Williams insisted, could and must be kept pure.

Williams did not oppose Cotton's contention that the truth was so obvious that anyone with whom pains had been taken, if still unconvinced, could be regarded as sinning against his own conscience, but he questioned the consequences which should follow from this failure of conviction. The power of truth, however, was not at fault. Indeed, Williams held a higher opinion of the strength of truth than did Cotton and believed that it yielded a clear standard by which many matters which Cotton considered minor or indiscernible by man could be branded as false and vain. The difference was that Williams limited the enforcing of such truth to the church and would zealously drive all who were not pure from it, while Cotton believed that the truth was not so clearly discernible, that the range of human nature made it impossible for the church to be entirely pure, and that because of this murkiness the aid of the civil authorities was a necessity. Williams saw the power of truth as so great that unaided it would search out the pure and leave the others to their eternal punishment in hell. Cotton saw it as insufficient to convince human nature and maintain order in itself, and, therefore, was willing to solicit the sword to come to its aid. As the adopted land of both of these men developed, Williams's principle of toleration became one of its most cherished tenets, but, ironically, it did so not as the result of the acceptance of Williams's conviction that the pure were few in number and sure to be saved so that others might go to hell in their own fashion, but, rather, as the result of the reverse contention, that many roads led to heaven, if there was such a place, and a man should be left free to walk the one of his choosing. Cotton's principles, on the other hand, came to be held in abhorrence by those who recognized with him that human nature does not permit of any truth being voluntarily accepted by all. But political rather than religious truths came to be of prime importance and Cotton's principles were alienated to that realm.

Cotton prepared to answer Williams in the days immediately prior to the Cambridge Synod when the local Presbyterian threat was at its strongest. His reply was published in 1647 as *The Bloudy Tenent, Washed and Made White in the Bloud of the Lambe.*

In his prefatory remarks, Cotton rebuked Williams for publicly castigating him for what he had privately written as an office of Christian love. He devoted the body of his work to a detailed discussion of Williams's remarks on toleration, and to this appended a separate reply to Williams's examination of the letter he had written after Williams's banishment. In the reply to the examination, Cotton did not hesitate to use the same devices the Presbyterians were employing against him and he lumped Williams's followers with persons like Gorton in order to emphasize how radically erroneous were the consequences of Williams's beliefs. He continued to insist that Williams could not have been banished solely for the opinions he proclaimed because many who shared these opinions still lived peaceably in the Bay. The main ground of your banishment, he told Williams, was your "violent and tumultuous carriage against the Patent."[13]

With such remarks, of course, Cotton was talking through Williams to the believers in England as a whole, assuring them of Bay moderation and warning them of Williams's rebellious tendencies. He was able to demonstrate just how wrong the Presbyterians' confusion of Congregationalism with separatism

[13] John Cotton, *The Bloudy Tenent, Washed and Made White in the Bloud of the Lambe* (London, 1647), p. 27.

was also, for the Bay's sympathy with Plymouth's brand of Brownism could be overlooked in an emphasis of its difference from Williams's brand. So to Williams's insistence that the Bay had come only part way in its reformation and should complete it by cutting off all contact with the Church of England, Cotton responded: "Though there were no truely godly persons in a Church, yet if there be such as professe godlinesse (such as they call visible Saints) to meete together in a Congregation to worship the Lord, and to edifie one another in the administration of his holy Ordinances, I doe beleeve there is truth of Church estate."[14] To be sure, this was far from his whole mind on the point, for when he debated the same issue with Presbyterians he insisted on the extensive reforms necessary before members of the Church of England could expect to have communion with churches in the Bay, but the present context afforded him a fine opportunity to show a distinction between Congregationalism and separatism.

In discussing toleration, Cotton continued to insist upon a distinction between persecuting conscience, which should never be done, and persecuting one who sinned against his own conscience. "Conscience is Gods Vicegerent," he had once said in another writing, "set up in the throne of mans heart."[15] Maintaining this belief, he insisted that one who failed to obey the vicegerent, after the vicegerent had explained to him his orders from his chief, should be punished. For the vicegerent in each man had the same Regent and His instructions to each of His subordinates would not therefore be contradictory. Cotton added the practical argument, again with his eyes on the English audience, that those who were wrong according to conscience rather than in knowing disobedience of it were allowed to live in peace, and he pointed to the local Presbyterians and the benighted Indians as examples.

[14] *Ibid.*, p. 107.   [15] Cotton, *Commentary upon John*, p. 266.

As Cotton had earlier refused to agree with his own magistrates when they insisted upon church-state cooperation to the extent of what he believed to be identification, so he now refused to grant Williams that the two institutions should be kept completely apart from one another. His distinction in this area, however, had ceased to be an external reality ever since the Anne Hutchinson controversy and he was making a purely theoretical distinction when he traced the correct outline of a theocracy in response to Williams. His cherished ideal was never again to become a fact; indeed, the very situation which was yielding him his greatest influence to date—the need for consolidation—would also effectually tangle the ideal theocratic roles of church and state so that they would eventually be unknotted only by the knife which would completely separate them. In failing to share the theocratic ideal, Williams was ahead of his time although to his contemporaries he appeared singularly ignorant of the thrilling potential of his day.

Faced with Williams's principle that anyone who believed in the predestination of the elect did not need to look for earthly aids for the preservation of such an estate, Cotton was forced to rephrase certain of his basic views. In England, following Sibbes, his Christian doctrine had been ambiguously inconsistent on the matter of predestination, for while preaching the salvation of saints, absolute upon their election, he had also preached the reprobation of sinners, conditional upon their eternally foreseen misbehavior. When this doctrine was eventually attacked in print for its inconsistencies,[16] he had not troubled to defend it, for in America he was no longer faced with a mixed body of church believers, a considerable part of whom would find his preaching meaningless if he held their reprobation as absolute. He had, therefore, begun to preach the absolute covenant with his own powerfully

[16] William Twisse, *A Treatise of Mr. Cottons Clearing Certaine Doubts Concerning Predestination* (London, 1646).

emphatic insistence on man's utter inability to do anything without the Spirit, and he had maintained his right and intention to continue doing so through and after the Hutchinson controversy. Doctrine and polity, however, were not so clearly separate in practice as they were in theory, and, therefore, when, in the mid-1640's, the period of consolidation came to Massachusetts and his scholarly abilities were called forth in the practical matter of defining and defending Congregationalism, the exigencies of the time did not allow him to pursue a conservative policy in polity while maintaining his doctrine unchanged. A stand such as Williams's was unanswerable unless he yielded on one or the other, and the most pressing matter was to stand firmly for the New England establishment.

Consequently, Cotton became a reluctant and belated convert to the theory of federal grace, one which would allow a maintenance of the doctrine of predestination, and, at the same time, make it possible for the theocratic state to maintain its sway over the spiritual lives of all under its jurisdiction. The theory, one peculiarly necessary and appropriate in New England, was phrased by Cotton thus: "There is a double state of grace, one adherent, (which some not unfitly call federall grace) sanctifying to the purifying of the flesh, *Heb.* 9.13. another inherent, sanctifying of the inner man. And of this latter there be two sorts, one, wherein persons in Covenant are sanctified by common graces, which make them serviceable and useful in their callings, as *Saul, Jehu, Judas,* and *Demas,* and such like hypocrites. Another whereby persons in Covenant are sanctified unto union and communion with Christ and his members in a way of regeneration and salvation. . . . In respect of inherent common graces, *Saul* [and the others] . . . were sanctified of God to their severall callings for the service of his people, as Apostates may be, *Heb.* 10.29. Now there is no doubt but men may fall away from adherent federall grace, as also from inherent common graces; and yet without any prejudice to the perseverance of sincere believers, and without any countenance to the *Arminian* error of Apostasie from grace."[17] Here was yet another turnabout for such as Nathaniel Ward to snicker at, but it was an admirably practical doctrine and Cotton was following his usual cautious pattern in catching up with it. For if one could have grace so that he would be useful in his calling and be of service to God's people, and yet possibly have that grace only federally or adherently so that he might slip from it, God's people had to erect bulwarks against the useful members being seduced from them. All was not so simple as Roger Williams would have it; there were subtle shades of difference within the church and, Williams was told, although the elect shall be saved, yet if "Idolaters and Seducers" are tolerated they will subvert the servants of Christ and those who allowed them to do this by tolerating them would "stand guilty before God."[18]

Such a doctrine allowed Cotton to point up the weakness of Williams's interpretation of the wheat and the tares as applying to the state because there were no tares to tolerate in the church. Baptized children who had not yet made confession of faith and hypocrites, both groups partaking of federal grace but lacking inherent grace, he maintained, were in the church and were yet prone to seduction. Cotton's recognition of the existence of hypocrites in the church was an act of pure realism unmatched by any similar conviction of Williams's. They were in the church and yet could not well be rooted out because all men were not, as Williams thought, identifiably saints or sinners: "If the Church proceed

[17] John Cotton, *The Grounds and Ends of the Baptisme of the Children of the Faithful* (London, 1647), p. 43.

[18] Cotton, *The Tenent Washed*, p. 50. The core of this doctrine of grace is to be found in Calvin's *Institutes*, Book III, a study of which may modify the opinions of those who regard covenant theology as a peculiar product of New England. In this respect, see also: Everett H. Emerson, "Calvin and Covenant Theology," *Church History* (June 1956), Vol. XXV, No. 2, pp. 136-44.

against an Hypocrite, as such, meerely for his hypocrisie, for want of life and power of Godlinesse in his duties, they may soone roote out, sometime or other, the best wheate in Gods Field, and the sweetest Flowers in his Garden, who sometimes loose their fatnesse and sweetnesse for a season."[19] Man cannot always tell Jacob from Esau.

The implications of Williams's denial of Cotton's realistic view were an insistence that the visible church was as pure as its invisible counterpart and, therefore, Williams could not trust infant baptism and had to be extremely meticulous in appraising all whom he admitted into church fellowship with him. This, indeed, led Williams in his career into a spiral of experimentation which included rebaptism, separation in worship from even his wife, and denial of all formal church gatherings. He found none of these experiments satisfactory. If Cotton's doctrine led, finally, to a state which was intolerable as well as intolerant, Williams's doctrine tended to the destruction of any formal church gathering whatsoever. The latter was as hideous a situation for seventeenth-century America as the former is for the America of the twentieth century.

With his book against Williams fresh in his mind in 1646, Cotton was an influential member of the synod which began by defining the role of the civil magistrate in religion, a task which had been made necessary, for the most part, by the pressure of Presbyterian attitudes the very reverse of those of Williams. After asserting that the civil magistrate had power to command or forbid things "respecting the outward man, which are clearly commanded and forbidden in the word," the synod drew the following deductions: "he is not to mould up and impose what Erastian forme of Church polity he pleaseth . . . he is not to force all persons into the Church [as members, that is], . . . [he] may and ought to

[19] Cotton, *The Tenent Washed*, p. 48.

command and forbid such things so cleared in the word, albeit *de facto* oft-times he doe not."[20]

While this fence against Presbyterianism was abuilding, Roger Williams and the radical Puritans were not forgotten in the 1646 conclusions: "But this doth not hinder the Magistrate from that use of his coercive power, in matters commanded or forbidden in the first Table, no more then it doth hinder him from the like powers in matters of the second Table; none being ignorant what perplexing intricacies there are in these as well as in the former; as conscientious Magistrates finde by dayly experience."[21] Lest this walking between two supposed extremes be misapprehended, at the end of the synodical pronouncements on the religious role of the civil magistrate reference was made to the prevailing problem: "Will not this *Thesis* arme and stir up the Civill power in Old *England*, against godly Orthodox ones of the Congregationall way; or exasperate Civill power in *New England*, against godly, moderate, and Orthodox Presbyterians, if any such should desire their liberty here? we conceive no, except the civill disturbance of the more rigidly, unpeacably, and corruptly minded, be very great; yet betwixt men godly and moderately minded on both sides, the difference upon true and due search is found so small, by judicious, Orthodox, godly, and moderate Divines, as that they may both stand together in peace and love; if liberty should be desired by either sort here or there so exercising their liberty, as the publick peace be not infringed."[22] Here was a veritable invitation to Presbyterian factions (especially in Newbury and Hingham churches) to enjoy their own church way provided they did not lend support to the element which sought an extension of political privileges. The invitation also had attached to it a halfhearted attempt to protect the

[20] Williston Walker, *The Creeds and Platforms of Congregationalism* (New York, 1893), p. 190.

[21] *Ibid.*, pp. 190-91.

[22] *Ibid.*, p. 191.

Congregational brethren in the homeland, but in its recognition of their need for protection was an implicit concession that Congregationalists would not come to considerable power.

The above conclusions were reached in 1646, and the synod adjourned as winter set in. It reassembled in June 1647, only to disband quickly because of the development of an epidemic which, in its course, took the life of Thomas Hooker. The final session did not convene until August 1648, by which time the reasons for the original call had been altered. Edward Winslow, the colony's London agent, had been successful in defeating the petitioners and receiving assurance that the decisions of the Bay Court would not be tampered with by Parliament. The fact that his chief argument was implicitly accepted put an end, until the Restoration, to any fears (or hopes, as the case might be) that an alteration of civil conditions would be imposed from without the colony. Winslow succeeded, as American agents a century later were to fail to do, in convincing Parliament on the following point: "And for the matter of appeale from *New-England* hither, which is three thousand miles distant, it will bee found to bee destructive to them that there live: for no Countrey can subsist without government, or repaire so farre to it; nor will any wise man accept a place in Government where hee shall bee exposed to goe so farre to give account of his actions, though they bee never so just."[23]

In the interval between the first meeting of the synod and its last, in August 1648, another significant change had taken place. The Westminster Assembly had adopted and made public a confession of faith, one far less damaging to Massachusetts doctrines than the elders had originally feared. Consequently, in the closing sessions of the synod the questions about church membership and baptism which seemed so insistent two years before were again skirted and a platform

[23] Edward Winslow, *New Englands Salamander* (London, 1647), pp. 11-12.

of church discipline drawn up by Richard Mather from his and Cotton's works was adopted. The platform was prefaced by an explanation, written by Cotton, of certain features of New England practice, which was designed to refute the frequently made allegation that such practices were unsound.

Cotton, in the preface, asserted, "Wee believe & profess the same Doctrine of the trueth of the Gospell, which generally is received in all the reformed Churches of Christ in Europe," and maintained this tone by emphasizing the essential harmony of Congregationalism and Presbyterianism. He said that the confession of faith published by the Westminster Assembly expressed the judgment of the Massachusetts elders also and excepted only "some sections in the 25 30 & 31. Chapters."[24] The wording of the exception was designed to make it sound minor though he was referring to the issues of the autonomy of the local church, the character of a synod, and the authority from which a minister received his power over a particular congregation.

Cotton went on in his preface to discuss the three practical objections most frequently made to Congregationalism. The first, he said, was, "That by admitting none into the fellowship of our Church, but saints by calling, wee Rob many parish-churches of their best members, to make up one of our congregations."[25] This he answered at length, showing that churches had been gathered out of churches in the New Testament, that it was not proper for one to desert a Presbyterian church for a Congregational one because of minor defects in the former, and that even if some did so, such withdrawal certainly did not constitute schism.

The second objection was that Congregationalism provided no way of "calling in" the grossly erroneous and scandalous

[24] Walker in his *Creeds of Congregationalism* prints the complete preface but omits minor sentences from the platform. Cotton Mather, in Book v of his *Magnalia*, prints the entire platform but omits the preface. The quotation is from the former, p. 195.

[25] *Ibid.*, p. 196.

persons within a parish and therefore excluded them from the "wholsom remedy" of church discipline. In keeping with his belief in the infectiousness of error, Cotton pointed out that receiving such people into the churches would rather corrupt the well-disposed than heal the erroneous: "We . . . find it safer, to square rough & unhewen stones, before the[y] be layed into the building, rather then to hammer & hew them, when they lye unevenly in the building."[26] Cotton's distrust of the broad policy of church admission which the metaphor of the building stones revealed at one time led Roger Williams to hope for great things from the churches of the Bay; he was finally led to despair, however, by the consequences which Cotton derived from his principle, such as the state's requiring those who were not members to attend church services.

The third practical objection Cotton noted was that the seeds of division were sown by Congregationalism since a family could be broken up, some admitted to church membership, others not; or a master and servant could be so divided; or members of the same household could belong to different congregations.[27] He replied that all of these inconveniences, in point of fact, "do not fall out," or are "easily redressed," and again called upon a metaphor to support his contentions: "Bees may bring more hony, & wax into the hive, when they are not limited to one garden of flowers, but may fly abroad to many."[28]

Cotton concluded his preface by depreciating the differences between Congregationalism and Presbyterianism. He termed them mere stumbling blocks and no source of serious

[26] *Ibid.*, p. 200.

[27] For a discussion of the compensations church covenant provided for a disruption in traditional social relations, see: "The Social Bond of Church Covenant," *American Quarterly* (Winter 1958), Vol. X, No. 4, pp. 454-62, and Chapter VI in Edmund S. Morgan, *The Puritan Family* (Boston, 1944).

[28] Walker, *Creeds of Congregationalism*, p. 201.

impediment to a harmonious future for the church. The two disciplines could exist side by side; both were committed to extirpating the antichristian hierarchy of an episcopal system.

The platform which followed was a full description of the New England way, differing in no noteworthy manner from the texts which Mather had before him when he constructed it. Cotton's *The Keyes* and *The Way of the Churches of Christ in New-England* were not only followed, they were, in a great many places, paraphrased. Whereas the New England elders continued to insist upon local autonomy, membership restricted to visible saints, and elected elders, in ratifying the platform they had accepted also a more oligarchic and less independent system than that which had sprouted in the first decade of the Bay's brief history. Presbyterian control within the congregation was emphasized as Cotton had recommended in *The Keyes*; the liberty of the church member was, in practice, a liberty to assent to the propositions of the elders. Synods, "tho' not absolutely necessary to the being," were declared "necessary to the well-being of churches."[29] And while they had to be called in an orderly fashion and not for slight or routine matters, once called, a synod's directions, "so far as consonant to the word of God," were to be received by the autonomous churches with "reverence and submission."

In its spirit of cooperation with Presbyterianism; in its emphasis upon the power of the church official and its practical nullification of the power of the church members; in its theoretical hesitation but practical acceptance of the authority of synods; in short, in its oligarchic tone, the Cambridge Platform echoed the thinking of John Cotton more than that of any other person in the Bay. His writings composed the most considerable body of literature, both in quantity and quality, written prior to the platform and finding embodiment in it. While he had promoted the polity of the platform,

[29] Mather, *Magnalia*, II, 233.

however, Cotton had not originated its fundamental structure. This he had found shooting up when he arrived and this he had accepted reluctantly. What Cotton had succeeded in doing, however, was in imposing autocratic controls on what had been, basically, a democratic system. The contrast between the democratic structure and the autocratic controls necessary to insure its perpetuation was to tax the structure badly, and, in the days of Cotton's grandson, Cotton Mather, was to give rise to a full-scale battle in which those who wished to do as they pleased doctrinally, even to the denial of predestination, were to cite the old democratic Congregational formula as the basis of their right to proceed unhampered by other ministers or congregations, while those who sought to preserve the doctrinal spirit of the founders were increasingly inclined to Presbyterianism as the only possible polity. The circumstances of the Massachusetts church system's coming into being as a radical reaction to a conservative episcopalian system but crystallizing as a reaction to increased democratic pressures started in America two traditions with equal claims to antiquity and equal demands for respect.

John Cotton's influence was that of the primary mover of the antidemocratic provisions of Congregationalism. The new land had succeeded in imposing its either/or conditions upon him and his greatest public act was, finally, to abandon the middle path he had attempted to walk between the extremes of legalism and antinomianism and to throw in his lot with the former group. The final cause of his decision was concern for the perpetuation of the church, and in his admission of the side-by-side existence of Presbyterianism and Congregationalism he was conceding that talk of an absolutely true church, such talk as had settled the country and was still to vex the homeland, was, in effect, aimless. The chief task now was to suppress those who were absolutely wrong.

Massachusetts had invested close to two decades in pioneering and must now turn to holding what it had developed. The theory that America, at least the northeastern portion of it, was a haven for the persecuted had never been accepted by John Cotton. He and most of his colleagues held, rather, that it was the place in which the holy commonwealth was to be established although, coincidentally, those who wished to establish it had been, for the most part, persecuted. If that commonwealth was willing, in 1648, to grant that it was somewhat less than purely holy, it was also old enough to have acquired entrenched interests and a spirited determination on the part of those interests to resist any threats to the *status quo* raised by new or discontented settlers.

ᴀ CHAPTER EIGHT ᴈ

THE LATE HOWLING WILDERNESS
(1648-1652)

The Parliament's success in England had, to the dismay of John Cotton and his colleagues, opened the floodgates of religious opinion. Having helped to inundate the episcopacy, the Bay settlers were alarmed to find that they could not at a later date close the gates. The Cambridge Platform was intended as a dike against any further rising of the waters of opinion, but no sooner had it been finished than the waves began lapping over. New arrivals from England and constant visitors from the Narragansett Bay settlements brought horrifyingly erroneous opinions into the Bay colony, and, what was worse, these opinions were receiving sympathetic listeners.

A new generation growing up under the Massachusetts way was, understandably, less excited about its merits than were those who had established it in reaction to evils which they had experienced. Deprived of the idols which their fathers had smashed, they were prone to exercise their zeal on what they found ready to hand, and, therefore, were willing to listen to the new iconoclasts. Moreover, the rapid increase in population and the unchanged straitness of church admission had created a large number of people who chafed at their exclusion from church membership and were willing to lend their support to whatever represented a change.

The most attractive of the extreme doctrines was Anabaptism. To those outside of church membership whose children, therefore, remained unbaptized, this doctrine offered solace by plausibly arguing the erroneousness of baptizing children anyway, and to some of those bred to the zeal of the founders, Anabaptism seemed a logical extension of the work their elders had begun in Elizabeth's day, for by continuing their elders' scrupulous adherence to the Bible they thought they discovered that nowhere in the New Testament was there a clear word of command or a clear example for infant baptism. Maintenance of the sacrament for infants seemed to them a vestige of the old legal practices of the Israelites, one to be swept away by those living under the Gospel.

Cotton and the elders of the Bay, of course, regarded Anabaptism as a grievous heresy, and in keeping with the practical spirit which had accompanied the framing of the Cambridge Platform, they joined battle with it not only by publishing theoretical discourses deriving the grounds of the sacrament and by preaching biblical justifications of it, but also by considering a modification of the practices which seemed to force people to accept Anabaptism by reaction. In June 1649, Cotton, in correspondence, posed the hypothetical question of whether a pious man who was not a church member could have his children baptized after his death by giving them to a church member who had no children.[1] He answered his own question by saying that Wilson, Eliot, and he held for the affirmative. While the point was so academic as to seem inconsequential, it was, nevertheless, indicative of the fact that the elders were willing to tinker with their procedures in order to preserve the whole. The Bay polity, it appeared, would have to make its way in a wicked world and would be tinged by contact with wicked men for some time longer than had originally been anticipated.

In the same month, Thomas Shepard exhibited the same concerns as Cotton in a letter in which he said: "Children are members of the visible church, and their membership continues when adult, and the children of believers are to be accounted of the church until they positively reject the Gospel."[2] Previously, children had been accounted members of the church until they reached maturity, at which time a

---

[1] Felt, *Ecclesiastical History*, II, 12.   [2] *Ibid.*

confession of faith was necessary for them to continue in membership. Shepard, significantly, shifted the emphasis by allowing them to be members until they "positively reject the Gospel."

Yet a further step in the direction of broader church membership, brought about not only in response to Anabaptism but also in answer to increasing indifference, was indicated by Richard Mather. Writing to a friend in 1651, he said that he thought that the children of church members, having themselves been baptized, ought to be allowed to have their children baptized even though they themselves never made a further confession and therefore never came to be admitted to the sacrament of the last supper. "We have not yet thus practiced," Mather said, "but are now considering of the matter, and of sending to other churches for advice."[3] Mather was to encounter some difficulty in persuading his fellow ministers of the correctness of his idea, but within a decade of his first suggestion of the idea it became an accepted procedure and is recorded in the annals of Congregationalism as the Half-way Covenant.

These practical reactions of Cotton and his fellow elders to the question of baptism illustrated that the Cambridge Platform was regarded as less than sacred in detail. While the whole represented their viewpoint, any part could be tightened, loosened, or replaced as occasion demanded so that while the platform could be fairly characterized as the embodiment of orthodoxy, an orthodoxy which perpetuated itself well into the following century, no given plank in that platform was regarded as inviolable. Thus Richard Mather, the very penman of the platform, outstripped his fellows in modification of it.

In matters of doctrine, however, John Cotton was not inclined to be so flexible. The Anabaptist threat to church order might well be met by a reconsideration of the bases for

[3] *Ibid.*, II, 49.

church membership, but the Anabaptist doctrine of limiting the sacrament to professed (and therefore adult) believers was one to be vigorously condemned as heretical, and its exponents were to be held guilty of soul-murder. Satan, he said, having met with gigantic reverses in his attempt to advance Roman Catholicism and Arminianism, had now turned to fostering adult baptism because "he chooseth therefore, rather to play Small Game (as they say) then to lose all."[4]

The Anabaptists' key argument against the practice of infant baptism was that "it wanteth a word both of Commandment and Example from the Scripture," and Cotton realized that what he was faced with ultimately was an argument about biblical interpretation, which was complicated by his opponents' lack of university training and their consequent maddening insistence upon a literal reading of the scriptures. Although he could cite a number of texts in the New Testament which supported infant baptism, Cotton could not provide so literal an example or commandment as his opponents demanded, for the basis of his argument about baptism was the rite of circumcision in the Old Testament. This rite could not so facilely be cited to an untrained literalist, however, and, therefore, in arguing infant baptism Cotton also had to give an elementary lesson in how to read the Bible. When confronted by the son of a believer who argued Anabaptism, Cotton said, he had initially turned the arguments over to Benjamin Woodbridge, a young scholar who lodged with him, but the Anabaptist was unconvinced by Woodbridge's reply because it was "so full of Scholarship and termes of Art." Therefore, Cotton himself turned to answering the book which had misled his young friend, but he published his answer only because Anabaptism had grown to be a considerable threat and his colleagues had urged that he make his answers public even though they were "immethodicall" in reflection of the book to which they responded. The Anabaptists seemed to

---

[4] Cotton, *Grounds of Baptisme*, p. 3.

him incapable of following a more orderly and elegant argument.

Cotton explained to the Anabaptists that "It is a Tempting of God, even limiting of the Holy one of *Israel*, to put upon him to deliver his will onely by Commandment or Example, or not at all; As if God might not deliver his will, by promise or threatning, by Proportion, or deduction, by consequence, as well as by expresse Commandment, or Example. What Commandment or Example is their for women to partake of the Lords Supper? yet the Proportion of the Lords Supper with the Passeover, and Deduction from such Scriptures as put no difference between male and female, make it to be received as the will and Ordinance of Christ."[5] Once his respondent would grant that deductions and proportions were to be used in reading the Bible, then Cotton could turn to the rite of circumcision as clear support by proportion for infant baptism.

A further lesson in interpretation which Cotton felt it necessary to teach the Anabaptists was that "if one Proposition in a Syllogisme be found in the Word of God, and the other Proposition be found certaine and evident by sense or reason, the conclusion is a conclusion of faith. As for example, it is a proposition in Scripture."[6] The Puritan party had, more than a half-century earlier, based its objections to episcopal government on so close a reading of the scriptures that Richard Hooker was forced in his reply to them to ask that they grant him the premise that in church matters the "Law of Reason" could be cited. He told the Puritans that reason was so frequently the basis of the laws in the Bible that it could safely be cited directly without the arbitrary machinery of scriptural deduction intervening. In another day, in another ruling ecclesiastical class, John Cotton, the protégé of Hooker's opponents, had to defend the role of reason, at least in the minor proposition, in order to check what he considered to be an ignorant literalism.

[5] *Ibid.*, p. 4.   [6] *Ibid.*, p. 167.

More than proof of the validity of certain ordinances was at stake in Cotton's arguing against the Anabaptists, then, for he saw their uneducated rage for reform as detached from and ignorant of Christian history. As a result, they destroyed the meaningfulness of the church with such actions as their attack on infant baptism since, eventually, this stemmed from their inability to perceive whence the true church had come, and, consequently, where it was to go.

The reading of "proportions" in the Old Testament was valid and necessary, Cotton believed, because that part of the Bible was not simply the record of God's relations with men prior to Christ's appearance and the new dispensation. Rather, it was the story of the operation of the Trinity on earth and of the two dispensations, the old and the new, developing side by side until Christ, by His taking upon Him the flesh of man, offered the new dispensation to more men than just the Jews. The literalist who believed that the new dispensation began only with the birth of Christ tended, eventually, consciously or not, to destroy any validity whatsoever which the Old Testament might have. In clarifying his view, Cotton said that when the scriptures themselves referred to the Old and the New Testament, sometimes reference was being made to the very books of the Bible but sometimes the terms were used for the covenants of the law and of grace. The two covenants, however, did not correspond to the two parts of the Bible, because the institution of the covenant of grace was God's selection of Abraham and his seed which was the New Testament (in the sense of grace) occurring in the Old (in the sense of a book). The Old Testament (in the sense of law) also was instituted in the Old Testament (in the sense of book) when God covenanted with the Israelites at Sinai. These two covenants, therefore, existed side by side in the Old Testament as they continued to do throughout the New to the present day. In the oldest days, none who was not of the seed of Abraham could hope

[235]

for salvation because the covenant of the law was impossible to fulfill, but Christ's coming brought salvation to other than the literal seed of Abraham. Nevertheless, they were thus saved by the very same covenant of grace which Abraham had enjoyed rather than by another instituted by Christ. The Son of God, rather than bringing a new covenant, had, through His sacrifice, applied the covenant of grace to a different group of people. It followed, therefore, that "the substance of the New Testament, and the circumstances of [its ordinances] . . . which are changed in the books of the New Testament, they are not changed by way of abrogation or diminution, but by way of accomplishment and enlargement."[7]

This comprehension of Christian history made the full resources of the Bible available to Cotton and his fellow New Englanders and allowed them to draw strength from the examples of the Israelites in the wilderness. Their travail was thus made meaningful, linked as it was to both the past and the future. Any theory which would ignore proportional reading of the Bible and deny the link with the past through asserting that Christ's appearance broke history in half and started the world anew in the year 1 would tend in its logic also to destroy the continuity with the future and eventually to deny the meaningfulness of the eschatological expectation. Although such literalists were, in fact, the most vociferous anticipators of Christ's immediate arrival on His second visit, in holding this belief they provided Cotton with further proof of their ignorance. For having disposed of the operation of grace in the Old Testament, they were, in effect, denying the presuppositions on which their expectation was based. They viewed the past as a series of unconnected catastrophes —creation, the flood, Christ's birth—and their sense of the present was, therefore, one of a dark night pierced at unpredictable intervals by flashes of lightning. They confidently expected the final and enduring flash to come soon,

[7] *Ibid.*, p. 159.

[236]

but the expectation was isolated from any consistent view of God's purpose throughout history and was, therefore, meaninglessly enthusiastic.

Christian history was continuous; this Cotton felt as a reality. He said: "A great part of the New Testament, or Covenant is expresly delivered in the bookes of the Old Testament. *Paul* professeth publickly, he taught nothing but what *Moses* and the Prophets did say should come, *Acts* 26.22. And the greatest part of the bookes of the Old Testament hold forth the Doctrine, Worship, Order and Government of the New Testament, to such who have not a vaile laid over their hearts in the reading of the Old Testament."[8] His conviction of the validity of his pronouncement sustained him throughout his life in New England and integrated his inner self and his outer self, his doctrine and his polity. For whatever discrepancies might at times occur between what he believed and what he had to modify in practice, he was certain that the matters which appeared separate from one another on the surface and which were often disengaged for the sake of rational discourse and efficient practice were, nevertheless, fundamentally united in the same whole—though man might be blind to the complete union—and that the whole in which they were united was God's consistent disposition of man on earth. As time passed, the links between seeming discrepancies would become more and more evident so that at Christ's coming His kingdom would appear not catastrophically but organically from what had been previously developed. The Bay theocracy which he envisioned was to be close to that kingdom, and if after the Cambridge Synod he had to tinker with an already compromised platform, it was only because Christian history had not moved so far toward its goal as he had hoped, not because his view of history was unsound.

As zealous an opponent of the new radicals as he was,

[8] *Ibid.*

however, John Cotton assiduously avoided the related civil controversies which raged about the new opinions. In 1647, he had written Roger Williams that he was "as seldome present at any Civill Court, (if not more seldome) then any man of our calling,"[9] and even after his prominent role in the synod, his scholarly habits and his theocratic ideal led him into his study and away from civil matters. John Norton, who was to succeed him at Boston, marvelled that in spite of his great learning he was "above other men [in] declining irregular and unnecessary interesting of himself in the actions of the Magistrate."[10] The death of John Winthrop in 1649 tended to reinforce Cotton's retiring inclination for although the Hutchinson controversy had opposed him to the late governor, the two, nevertheless, were able to settle their differences harmoniously and commanded mutual respect. Now, however, leadership was descending into the hands of John Endicott and Thomas Dudley, men with whom Cotton not only had had his differences but with whom he had never succeeded in fully sympathizing. Dudley had distrusted Cotton's loyalty to Anne Hutchinson and had wanted the teacher prosecuted also, failing to appreciate in the least his scholarly habit of qualification and hesitation. Endicott was a man of impulsive action who, earlier in his career, had rashly leaped to the defense of Roger Williams and had destroyed the cross in the ensign. Now that he had changed his mind and was in agreement with his fellow magistrates, he tended to advance the ideas of the oligarchy in just as rash a fashion. His habits, then, were also antipathetic to Cotton's.

Moreover, in the years after the Cambridge Synod, the civil authorities tended to concentrate more actively on supervising the manners of the community. Massachusetts Bay had always enforced seemly behavior on the part of its inhabitants as a necessary quality in a holy commonwealth. But as

[9] Cotton, *Bloudy Tenent, Washed*, p. 25.
[10] Norton, *Abel Being Dead*, p. 39.

various forms of doctrinal and political dissension bubbled to the surface after the synod, the enforcement of regulations over proper manners became a disjointed outlet for the disappointed magistrates' rage for uniformity, and grew severer as the dissension increased. The remedy for the pot's boiling was to screw the lid down tighter rather than to adjust the temperature through the addition of colder water or through the reduction of the flame.

In October 1648, the severity of the law against drunkenness was increased because it was found that the drinking habits of Massachusetts tended to "the dishonor of God, the discredit of the Gospel, to the shame of the country."[11] In 1649, Governor Endicott led the authorities in a related public pronouncement: "Forasmuch as the wearing of long-hair after the manner of Ruffians and barbarous Indians, has begun to invade New-England contrary to the rule of God's word. . . . We doe therefore earnestly entreat all elders to manifest their zeal against it in their public ministrations."[12] The sixty-three-year-old John Cotton who spent so much time in his study that he knew nothing of the problems of church discipline within his own congregation except for what the ruling elders told him was even less concerned with taking a part in civil discipline.

This did not mean, however, that Cotton was not in agreement with continued civil action against those holding the worst of the dissenting religious positions. When, in July 1651, the Court ordered the severe whipping, fining, and imprisonment of the Anabaptists John Clark, Obadiah Holmes, and John Crandal, opposition to the action was widespread. Cotton, nevertheless, preached against the heinousness of the prisoners' opinions. Whatever age and experience in Massachusetts had taught him, the lesson did not include toleration of soul-murderers and he was in

[11] *Records of Massachusetts*, II, 257.
[12] Hutchinson, *History of Massachusetts-Bay*, I, 130n.

agreement with Endicott's severe measures although that magistrate's severity was also the result of Clark's role in procuring Rhode Island a charter from the Parliament.

In the following year, Roger Williams published another treatise in the persecution controversy, one which Cotton did not live to read, and appended to it a letter to Endicott urging his former ally to a greater moderation in his dealings with religious dissenters. Williams reminded Endicott of the fleeting nature of life on earth and the eternity in which he was to be judged, including in his appeal one of the nautical images at which he was masterly: "Every gray haire now on both our heads, is . . . a warning piece to prepare us, for the waighing of our last *Anchors*, and to be gone from hence, as if we had never been."[13] But the authority of the Bay called Massachusetts, unlike his colleague at the one called Narragansett, believed himself to be doing the work of eternity on earth and did not heed the message. In 1652, however, Roger Williams's book was not burned in England. It was read.

As news of the Bay persecutions reached England, the friends of the colony added their private reproaches to the public protests of men like Williams. Hearing of the punishment of Clark, Sir Richard Saltonstall wrote to Cotton and Wilson in 1652 about the reputation their practices were gaining in England. Saltonstall had been friendly with Cotton during his Lincolnshire ministry and had lived for a while in Boston. His letter, therefore, was a rebuke from a sympathizer and served to indicate the turn which reform had taken in England. He said in his letter: "It doth not a little grieve my spirit to heare what sadd things are reported dayly of your tyranny and persecutions in New-England as that you fyne, whip and imprison men for their consciences. First you compel such to come into your assemblies as you

[13] Roger Williams, *The Bloody Tenent Yet More Bloody* (London, 1652), pp. 312-13.

know will not joyne with you in your worship, and when they shew their dislike thereof or witness against it, then you styrre up your magistrates to punish them for such (as you conceyve) their publick affronts."[14] He warned that "these rigid wayes have layed you very lowe in the hearts of the saynts," and went on to declare that some congregations in England remembered Massachusetts in their prayers by asking the Lord to grant the colonists meek and humble spirits. At the outbreak of the war, Saltonstall said, he had been in Holland and had communicated with Dudley about the possibility of certain exiled groups (Anabaptists, Seekers, Antinomians) settling in New England. He was shocked to learn that those who differed in opinion would not be tolerated although they held "the same foundation in religion." When he asked Dudley for his explanation, he said, he was referred to the written debates between the Presbyterians and the Independents, but "if that had been sufficient, I needed not have sent soe farre to understand the reasons of your practice." Saltonstall concluded by hoping that all might be of one accord in the Lord even if they did not speak and think the same things.

Cotton's answer to Saltonstall was concerned mainly with justifying the particular procedures against Clark, Holmes, and Crandal rather than with restating his theory of toleration. Saltonstall in his letter, however, had reminded Cotton that he, too, had once fled from persecution and should therefore be wary of practicing it, and this rebuke, coming from a friend rather than an acknowledged opponent, spurred Cotton to a jot more heat than was his wont. He said in his letter to Saltonstall: "We believe there is a vast difference between men's inventions and God's institutions. Wee fled from men's inventions, to which wee else should have been compelled. Wee compell none to men's inventions."[15] The

[14] *Collections of the Massachusetts Historical Society* (Boston, 1816), Second Series, IV, 171.   [15] Felt, *Ecclesiastical History*, II, 63.

trouble with the path reformation was taking in the homeland, Cotton believed, was that his brethren failed to distinguish between means and ends. Persecution had not been that which he had opposed and from which he had fled; rather, it was the doctrines which the persecutors held. He had come to practice his own preachings in America, to be, as Saltonstall himself put it, "eyes to God's people" in England. After accomplishing so much, however, he was turning around to find that those for whom he thought he was acting as eyes had quite lost the point of the Massachusetts theocracy and were abandoning sound hopes of establishing God's common-wealth on earth in favor of a *laissez faire* reformation which tolerated all who would agree loosely on fundamentals, including Anabaptists and Seekers.[16] He was, therefore, moved to point out: "If our wayes (rigid wayes as you call them) have layd us low in the hearts of God's people, yea, and of the saints (as you stile them), wee do not believe it is any part of their saintship."

He closed his argument on a more gentle note: "We are far from arrogating infallibility of judgment to ourselves or affecting uniformity. Uniformity God never required, infallibility, he never granted us." But the examples of toleration which Cotton gave Saltonstall were insufficient to remove the sting from his remarks on the sainthood of the English brethren. If the English observers saw nothing but paradox in the New Englanders' being persecutors after having been persecuted—a paradox which has successfully generated itself through time as the most convenient descrip-tion of New England practice—Cotton responded in puzzle-ment at a reformation which with such good prospects had, in effect, ceased trying, even though he and others had come some three thousand miles and met with more than a little

[16] This is an important feature of the central problem in the study of John Winthrop by Edmund S. Morgan: *The Puritan Dilemma* (Boston, 1958).

success in their attempt to construct a model to be followed.

Two years earlier, Cotton had greeted the news of the purging of Parliament and the execution of the King with statements of loyalty to his English allies, and on a thanksgiving day had preached in justification of the army's proceedings.[17] Fearing a difference in the fundamentals of doctrine more than one in polity, he had, in the same sermon, urged a closer alliance between Presbyterians and Congregationalists, explaining to his hearers: "As for Presbyterie and independency, it was no great difficulty to provide for toleration of both for present. It is certain the body of the nation of England is not capable of fellowship in Independent churches. There will be a necessity therefore of giving way to the other way of government." In the phrase, "giving way," Cotton's rhetoric created the impression that the Congregationalists in England were as much in power as those in Massachusetts. He realized, however, that so far was this from the actual case that his English allies were welcoming the support of the more radical sects in their struggle against Presbyterianism. In Massachusetts, however, the Congregationalists were the entrenched group and the radicals tended to combine with the Presbyterians in their activities against the *status quo*. Acutely conscious of the American situation and profoundly committed to the supreme importance of man's inner condition, Cotton was willing to compromise, if compromise he must, by cooperating with Presbyterians rather than with groups, such as the Anabaptists, whom he regarded as heretical. Speaking from relative strength, then, he argued for a peaceful coexistence with Presbyterianism and a vigorous opposition to unorthodox doctrines. Meanwhile, his allies in England were opposing entrenched strength and replied by urging him to wider tolera-

[17] This sermon, in manuscript, is in the possession of the Massachusetts Historical Society and is identified as a sermon of John Cotton's delivered on the 10th day of the 11th month, 1650. Both the spelling and the punctuation of the quotation from it have been modernized.

tion of unorthodoxy. The very success of the Massachusetts Congregationalists had alienated them from the interests of their party in the homeland, as Cotton's correspondence with Saltonstall illustrated.

So John Cotton, after the Cambridge Synod as before it, continued in his polemical works addressed either to radical or Presbyterian to be conscious of the other group, and was, therefore, wary of statements so broad that they would tend to obscure his distinction from both sides. His tone toward the Presbyterians, however, was milder than ever, and he actively sought the conditions for a truce.

To a tract answering the Presbyterian polemicists Robert Baillie and Samuel Rutherford, in 1650,[18] he prefaced an epistle: "To My Honored, Worshipfull, and worthy Friends, the Major, and Justices, the *Aldermen* and *Common Councell*, together with the whole Congregation and Church at Boston." These Lincolnshire friends of his had continued to contribute to his support after his exile and had on several occasions since the success of the Puritan arms invited him to return to England and resume his ministry over them. He now publicly declined the invitation, citing his duties to his Massachusetts congregation and his advanced age and uncertain health. He added, moreover, that the current practice of St. Botolph's in admitting more than professed saints to the ordinances, and the government of that church being subject to an "extrinsecall Ecclesiasticall power" would be a "perpetuall scruple and torment to my conscience." He did not wish to misjudge them, he said, but "every man is to be fully perswaded in his owne minde, and I must live by my own faith." The succeeding treatise, he hoped, would point the way for the communion of their church with other Congregational churches.

In the epistle, Cotton made reference to New England in a much used phrase, but he introduced a qualification. He

[18] John Cotton, *Of the Holinesse of Church-members* (London, 1650).

called the colony "this (late) howling wildernesse," and the parenthetical adverb told more eloquently than any of his other remarks why in his sixty-fourth year he would remain where he was and write against extremists and for a compromise with but separateness from Presbyterianism. The howling wilderness no longer raged, so far as he was concerned; it had been tamed. He was far from regarding its domestication as perfect, but taken all in all it seemed the holiest commonwealth on earth, one in which an old Christian could take justifiable comfort. It was this tone that informed his treatise. He did not claim an absolute superiority for the Massachusetts polity, but as he viewed the other reformed polities established throughout Europe and, he told the Presbyterians, considered their church form, then, relatively at least, Massachusetts still showed the way. Said Cotton: "He that in shooting aimeth at the top of a mountain, though he do not alwayes reach it, yet he shall shoot higher, then he that aimeth at a molehil: so they that aime at receiving no members into the Church, but such as in judgement of charity are Saints, and faithfull brethren; they shall keep their Churches more pure, then they that indifferently accept carnall persons, and grosse hipocrites, if so be they will ordinarily hear the word, and receive the Sacraments."[19] Cotton had admitted to Roger Williams that hypocrites were bound to creep into the visible church, but this did not lead logically to what seemed to be the Presbyterian conclusion that all should therefore be admitted to membership, any more than it did to Williams's conclusion that the church must use a super-refined process in screening its tentative members. He admitted that Massachusetts had not hit the top of the mountain, but certainly it had come closer than the molehill aimers.

Cotton's continuing debate with the Presbyterians was also concerned with scriptural interpretation as had been his

[19] *Ibid.*, p. 44.

writing against the Anabaptists. "Scotch Baillie" was hardly the man to be given a university lesson by his respondent and Cotton could make much more sophisticated distinctions when talking to such as he, but they did disagree on one large point. The Presbyterians claimed that many of Cotton's arguments were based solely upon parables, contrary to the axiom of Thomas Aquinas, *"Theologica Symbolica non est Argumentativa."* Cotton, however, recognized the justice of Aquinas's proposition only as an apt injunction to the medieval Catholic scholars who had strained their wits in fanciful interpretations of parables and equally ingenious conversion of "plain" scriptures into parables. He stated that "Commandements in Parables are not alwayes given as an injunction of what ought to be done by way of Ordinance, but as a Prediction of what will be done by way of providence."[20] Therefore, first and foremost, he insisted upon his right to read parables in an "historicall way." He argued, in addition, "Why should Christ (as well as some Prophets before him, and *John* the Apostle after him) delight so much in Symbols and Parables, if they were not Doctrinall and Argumentative? . . . He would never have so much accustomed himselfe to Symbols and Parables, if so much of them were to be pared off (as husks and shels) . . . or if Parables were not effectually Argumentative to all those ends of Ministery, for which any other word of Doctrin might serve?"[21] More than most, even of his New England colleagues, Cotton was confident of his ability to gain the whole meaning of scriptures through careful study and comparison, and, he insisted, "I never yet observed any part of a Scripture Parable, but without carnall affectation, or straining of wit; it might holily be applyed both with power, and profit, and delight to an honest heart." His tendency in the late wilderness was toward a more historical reading of the Bible and a more comprehensive use of it in argumentation than any member of the other Puritan

[20] *Ibid.*, p. 64.   [21] *Ibid.*, p. 69.

groups, Presbyterian or radical, indulged themselves in. Partly this was the result of his very profound commitment to scholarship, but it stemmed also from the facts of his situation as promoter of a specific theocracy which friends and enemies alike regarded with distrust at the least.

Earlier in his career, while he was a young preacher in Lincolnshire, Cotton had opposed the separatists by querying, "If it be lawful to read Psalmes, why is it not lawful to read Prayers?"[22] Like the majority of the New England elders, he now thought he knew the answer to this question and did himself insist upon the lawfulness of psalm-singing while he opposed the use of set forms of prayer. Tracts on these subjects emerged from his study in his later years. Characteristically, the treatise against set forms of prayer was addressed to the Presbyterians who retained them, and the work in favor of psalm-singing assumed an audience of extremists who would carry reformation to an irresponsible stripping of the ordinances of the church.

Cotton's objections to set prayers stemmed directly from his confidence in the action of the Spirit in making over a believer into a new man so that he had the gift to address the Lord spontaneously. Set prayers were human inventions which came between man and what he wished to say, for times changed and the members of the church would never have exactly the same thing to say to the Deity on two separate occasions. Reliance on a prepared prayer, therefore, was reliance upon a vain idol; the analogy which suggested itself was that of the *memento mori*: "A man passing through a burying place may see a dead mans scalpe cast up, and thereby take occasion from the present object to meditate (for the present) on his mortallity, and to prepare for like change: but if he shall take up, and keepe that dead mans scalpe in his Closet, or Bed-chamber, to be an ordinary helpe to him to put him in minde dayly of his mortality: Now in so doing

[22] Cotton, *Commentary upon John*, p. 157.

he maketh an Image of it, to himselfe, by setting it a part to be an helpe to him in Gods worship; which . . . now becomes a sinne to him against the second Commandement."[23] Another analogy which suggested itself consistently in his argument was that between the true believer's gift of spontaneous prayer and the minister's gift of preaching. With his unceasingly abundant faith in the power of grace, Cotton refused to admit that the minister could read even his own sermon without sin, and insisted that "I have knowne a Minister to edifie the people more by silence in the pulpit through strength of temptation, then ever I knew any doe by reading a Homily upon the Booke."[24] As he was to point out to his English allies, reliance on such human inventions, rather than persecution per se, had been the practice which had driven him from England, and his debates in his London hiding place centered around the applicability of the second commandment to ordinances such as set forms of prayer. In now insisting upon a Presbyterian change of attitude, he was not deserting the reformation, he was being deserted by it.

Singing of psalms, however, was a far different matter, for the type was included in the Old Testament not only as a ceremony but as a moral obligation. The saint's joy in God's mercy to him, the overflowing of his heart, could not better be expressed than in making a joyful noise unto the Lord. Not only did David write psalms to be sung, but "any private Christian, who hath a gift to frame a spirituall Song, may both frame it, and sing it."[25] Moreover, the use of musical instruments to accompany psalm-singing was legal so long as attention to the instrument did not distract the heart from the song. Since God had left words but no music, it was permissible to sing the psalms to any grave and solemn tunes

[23] John Cotton, *A Modest and Cleare Answer to Mr. Balls Discourse of Set Formes of Prayer* (London, 1642), p. 20.

[24] *Ibid.*, p. 28.

[25] John Cotton, *Singing of Psalmes A Gospel-Ordinance* (London, 1650), p. 15.

which could be constructed, and, of course, the psalms themselves should be translated into an English which would
make them most fit for singing. Cotton had done such
translating for the *Bay Psalm Book* and it was to him that the
Puritan poet Francis Quarles dispatched translations of the
psalms for comment and for publication in the New England
volume.[26]

In supplying non-biblical precedents to support his case
for psalm-singing, Cotton did not hesitate to draw upon
the Anglican church which he had condemned for human
inventions in his other treatises, for the period on which he
drew was that glorious reign of Elizabeth, and his specific
allusion was to the childhood experience which had made
so profound an impression on all who had lived through it.
Psalms were songs of joy to be sung to the Lord by the
grateful faithful: "As the like did fall out in the yeare 88.
Rome being spirituall *Aegypt, Rev.* 11.8. And the Pope with
his Prelates resembling *Pharaoh* with his Task-masters, and
the *Spanish Armado* marching forth with like pride and
fury, to bring us backe to the Aegyptian bondage; and the
Redemption from them all being alike miraculous: upon
which miraculous deliverance, not onely the matter of *Moses*
Song, but the very words also were then fitly used, and still
may be for a spirituall Song of thankesgiving unto the Lord."[27]
Those were stirring times for a very young boy, but they
were only the beginning of a life of such remarkable events
and John Cotton sixty years later still believed himself part
of the great cavalcade of Christian history. The color of
Elizabethan England had been muted in Puritan New
England but the predictable pattern of God's will continued
unfolding itself there with greater clarity than ever it had
before.

[26] John Josselyn, *An Account of Two Voyages to New-England* (London,
1674), p. 20.
[27] Cotton, *Singing of Psalmes*, p. 27.

Although his defense of psalm-singing and his assertions about the use of parables were more remote from the world of public affairs than had been his writings on polity, they were much more his labors of love because in them he was not merely responding to an opponent, he was drawing upon his scholarship and teaching. The attacks upon his polemical works continued past the time of his death, but with the establishment of the Cambridge Platform and the liberal turn English thought had taken, his heart did not yearn for a continuation of such battles. In 1651, Daniel Cawdrey, sometime preacher at Martin's-in-the-Fields and a member of the Westminster Assembly, attacked Cotton and Thomas Hooker in *The Inconsistency of the Independent Way with the Scripture and Itself*. Writing with Cotton's principal publications on Congregationalism together with Hooker's *Survey of the Summe of Church-discipline* before him, Cawdrey magnified all discrepancies found among these works. The principal contradiction he exploited was that between Cotton's agreement with Hooker, in *The Way of the Churches of Christ in New-England*, that the church could excommunicate its presbytery and his denial of this power in *The Keyes*. Cawdrey also made much of the qualifications with which the English Independents, Goodwin and Nye, received the New England way. Cotton, in his last year of life, prepared again to enter into published debate but his death, in December 1652, came before he could complete his answer. His unfinished treatise was published with an expanded defence written by John Owen, as *A Defence of Mr. John Cotton from the Imputation of Selfe Contradiction Charged on Him by Mr. Dan: Cavvdrey* (Oxford, 1658). Cotton argued that he had changed his mind about the excommunication of the presbytery, as he was entitled to do, and that he wished his opinion in *The Keyes* to stand as final. As for differences with other Independent spokesmen, he said that he "Discerned no Dissent at all between them and me."[28] On the whole, Cotton belittled the differences and evidenced a willingness to allow his work to be qualified by his Independent brethren if it so pleased them. He was a man who was only too willing to dispense with any further controversy on matters of polity and who, therefore, found a more Presbyterian, or authoritarian, interpretation of his writings to be acceptable. In the same year that he started his answer to Cawdrey, Cotton was being reattacked by Roger Williams, but Cotton was dead by the time the book reached New England.

In his final years, as in the first years of his ministry, John Cotton believed that the single most efficacious ordinance of Christ was the preaching of the word. He regarded himself primarily as a preacher and the greatest part of his daily scholarly efforts went toward the construction of his sermons and lessons. During his career in the church of Boston, he, in an expository way, went over the Old Testament once, and a second time as far as the thirtieth chapter of Isaiah; the whole New Testament once and a second time as far as the eleventh chapter of Hebrews; and in his sermons and lectures on Sundays and Thursdays of each week he preached on each verse of the Acts of the Apostles, the prophecies of Haggai and Zechariah, the books of Ezra, the Revelation, Ecclesiastes, Canticles, second and third Epistles of John, Epistle to Titus, the Epistle to the Romans, and both Epistles to Timothy; in addition to which he preached a great many times on special occasions when his text was chosen for its appropriateness to the occasion.[29] In spite of the Hutchinson controversy and the increased legalism of his polity, to his death he remained New England's most prominent preacher because his constant refrain was an insistence upon the power of grace and the passivity of the believer. His urgings to

[28] John Cotton, *A Defence of Mr. John Cotton from the Imputation of Selfe Contradiction Charged on Him by Mr. Dan: Cavvdrey* (Oxford, 1658), p. 26.
[29] Mather, *Magnalia*, I, 285.

await Christ at night, to take heart from the trickling of grace much more than from the flood, to continue wading deeper and deeper into Christ, to feel the divinity welling up inside one, found a more enthralled audience and resulted in more remarkable attestations of faith than the words of any of his colleagues. From his ordination as teacher of Boston church in 1634 to his death in 1652, 1,034 children were baptized in the church and 652 adults were admitted to membership. Over that period, only seventeen persons were admonished publicly, and of those, only five were eventually excommunicated.[30] The increase, of course, was in large part to be accounted for by the tremendous rate of immigration during the first decades of the colony's history and the commercial importance of the town of Boston. Even after this acknowledgment, however, Cotton's parishioners and colleagues realized that a great part of the success of Boston church was the result of his preaching, and, indeed, that to a considerable extent the town itself was indebted to him for its size because so many people wanted to live within easy distance of his lectures. During his career in Boston, Cotton saw his congregation move to enlarged quarters twice and while he assiduously avoided any interference in the affairs of the magistrate, he was a constant source of authority and arbitration in church matters though, unlike Wilson, he was not primarily concerned with discipline and was relatively unaware of what occurred in the lives of his parishioners unless the problems were brought directly to him. At ninety pounds a year, his salary was the highest of any minister in the Bay.

Although New England did not provide the same quantity of scholars as did the homeland, Cotton, nevertheless, retained a keen interest in the educating of young men. He boarded scholars with him, and the first graduate of Harvard,

---

[30] William Emerson, *An Historical Sketch of the First Church of Boston* (Boston, 1812), pp. 81-82.

Benjamin Woodbridge, was one of his lodgers and disciples although in later years Woodbridge, ironically, employed his talents in preaching against Antinomianism and in succeeding to the pulpit of William Twisse, the man who corrected Cotton's Calvinism and who presided over the Westminster Assembly. Cotton's sons, Seaborn and John, were also among his scholars and he saw Seaborn graduate from Harvard in 1651, in the same class which included Michael Wigglesworth, the budding poet laureate of the New England ministry. Seaborn's taste for music and poetry, inherited from his father, led him to the transcription of ballads into his notebook, and when he married in 1654, his bride was the daughter of Anne Bradstreet, New England's most famous poet.

Two of John Cotton's children, his oldest daughter Sarah and his youngest son Rowland, gave him another reminder of the role of poetry, for they both died in the smallpox epidemic of 1649. Cotton responded on that occasion with three sets of verses, one set each for the boy and the girl, and a third for them together, but he emphasized the private and consolatory nature of the poem by writing it in Greek characters although the words thus recorded were English. In his verse on Sarah, he wrote:

> "Pray, my dear father, let me now go home!"
> Were the last words thou spak'st to me alone.
> Go then, sweet Sara, take thy *sabbath rest*,
> With thy great Lord, and all in heaven blest.

In his stanza, *"In Utrumque,"* he remembered Christ's commandment to suffer the little ones to come unto Him, and added, "We do not only *suffer* them, / But *offer* them to thee."[31]

Cotton's concern for the welfare of young scholars, one which had sustained him through various offices when he was a fellow at Emmanuel College and which caused him

[31] Mather, *Magnalia*, I, 285.

to take them under his roof and into his tutelage, led him in the winter of his sixty-eighth year to cross the Charles River in order to preach to the students of Harvard on the text, "Thy children shall all be taught of the Lord." He took ill as a result of the exposure on the river and it was evident to all in November 1652, including himself, that he was a dying man. Accordingly, he apologized to his congregation for preaching over so much so rapidly, but since he wanted to finish his course of lectures on the second Epistle to Timothy, he increased the number of verses dealt with in each sermon. He did manage to conclude that book and to go on to preach one more sermon, this final one on a text from John: "And the word was made flesh and dwelt among us, (and we beheld his Glory, as of the only begotten Son of the Father,) full of grace and Peace." A contemporary noted that of all the matter in his last sermons, "he chiefly insisted upon those Words, *Grace be with you all.*"[32]

No longer able to leave his bed in December, Cotton was visited by a host of colleagues and parishioners, many of whom added to their sincere mournfulness a desire to partake of the last words of a great saint. The crush of people finally led him to ask his attendants to bar all from his room so that he might prepare himself in peace. As he lay abed, a comet was noted falling in the New England sky, and the connection was inevitable for most of the colonists. Asked about the phenomenon by the curious, the dying teacher would only say that it portended great changes, but more particular application than this was made by most of the faithful.[33]

[32] Norton, *Abel Being Dead*, p. 43.

[33] Joshua Scottow, for example, remembered the phenomenon thus: "The Venerable *Cotton*, our New-Englands greatest Apostle; who as in his Life, Light, and Learning was the brightest and most shining Star in our Firmament; so in his Sickness and Death he was wonderfully remarkable by a *Satelles* to the *Pleiades*, or an attendant to the seven Stars, which continued visible all that while, and until his buryal, which was six days after his death, and then disappeared." *Old Mens Tears for Their Own Declensions* (London, 1691), p. 16.

John Cotton died on 23 December 1652. The town gossips said that his last words were spoken in response to his colleague John Wilson's prayer that God would lift up the light of His countenance upon the dying man and shed love into his soul. They were, "He hath done it already, Brother."[34]

His heirs discovered his autobiography among the papers left in his study. It consists of five sentences, one each devoted to his birth, physical condition, youth, ministry, and spiritual condition; each expanded into a four-line stanza. The title he gave the autobiography is "A Thankful Acknowledgment of God's Providence":

In mothers womb thy fingers did me make,
    And from the womb thou didst me safely take:
From breast thou hast me nurst my life throughout,
    That I may say I never wanted ought.

In all my meals my table thou hast spread,
    In all my lodgings thou hast made my bed:
Thou hast me clad with changes of array,
    And chang'd my house for better far away.

In youthful wandrings thou didst stay my slide,
    In all my journies thou hast been my Guide:
Thou hast me sav'd from many-an-unknown danger,
    And shew'd me favour, even where I was a stranger.

In both my Callings thou hast heard my voice,
    In both my matches thou hast made my choice:
Thou gav'st me sons, and daughters, them to peer,
    And giv'st me hope thou'lt learn them thee to fear.

Oft have I seen thee look with Mercy's face,
    And through thy Christ have felt thy saving-grace,
This is the Heav'n on Earth, if any be:
    For this, and all, my soul doth worship Thee.[35]

[34] Norton, *Abel Being Dead*, p. 45.
[35] *Ibid.*, pp. 28-29.

John Cotton's version of his life breathes symmetry and contentment, and its expression in verse, even this rough verse, heightens its effect of balance. The Lord never allowed him to want physically and this mercy was matched by a divine care of his spiritual estate. His English ministry had lasted for a little more than twenty years and was matched by a nearly equal amount of time spent in his New England calling. He had two wives and his life with each corresponded roughly to his time in each of his two pulpits. He had six children, three boys and three girls to match ("peer") them. When death came to a son, within the month it came also to a daughter. For John Cotton the conclusion of such an autobiography could only be that life on earth, marred as it was by the corruptions of the flesh, did, nevertheless, present a recognizable counterpart to life in the kingdom of heaven, that, indeed, "Heav'n on Earth" when used by him to describe his own career was an intensely felt reality, not an automatic formula.

John Cotton's version of his life was, of course, a prayer of thanksgiving and was severely selective. He, doubtless, in his later years, felt keenly the vicissitudes through which he had passed and looked with some distress at the turns he had to take, the setbacks he had experienced, the public foes he had made. Nevertheless, when preparing his hymn of thanksgiving to the Lord, the version of his career which was most meaningful to him was not that of the pilgrim at the end of the twisting road, the ship come safely to harbor at last, or the warrior snatched from the clutches of his pursuers; it was, rather, of the beautiful symmetry of all that was worth recording, of the graceful balance of his inner with his outer estate, his new English with his old English life; so that, finally, he viewed his becoming as a being and his progress through life as the attainment of equipoise.

THE ORDERLINESS of life on earth which discovered itself
to John Cotton was to be missing from the perceptions of
their careers which his successors had. Cotton's belief in a
divine plan which linked every occurrence in human history
organically so that the years appeared to be ripening toward
a harvest which the Lord would come to pluck was not
equalled by that of Increase Mather, his son-in-law, who
actively entered civil as well as ecclesiastical politics in order
to preserve what he took to be his inheritance. By the time
Cotton Mather, who gave his grandfather his literary apothe-
osis, had come of age, John Cotton's vision was a distinct
anachronism and it appeared eccentric in the mind of Cotton
Mather not as the result of Mather's being an eccentric
person who tended to exaggerate and distort his beliefs but
because only an eccentric person would now be attracted by
such ideals. In his incessant swaying from an intense concern
with physical matters, even the involuntary bodily functions,
as mysteries by which God discovered his will, to mystic
ecstasies which transcended the bounds of Christian piety,
the grandson provided a towering example of how impossible
it was to reconcile the inner demands of salvation with the
outer demands of church and civil polity in his day. The
times had passed Cotton Mather by; he had talents which
fitted him for success in a society structured as that of his
grandfather had been; occurrences took place which destroyed
his grandfather's organic view of history. Either he had to
revise all the assumptions of Christian history so as to account
for what was occurring in his day, or he had to abandon
that view altogether. The former alternative would have
been artificial since the theory of history would then have
become just that, a theory, rather than an everyday perception
of reality, as it had been for John Cotton. The latter alternative
would have meant, as it did for the great Americans to come,

the acceptance of new realities. Cotton Mather elected neither and in pursuing his magnificent and lonely course bore living testimony to the obsolescence of his grandfather's vision.

John Cotton's death had come at a propitious time for his immediate reputation for unlike some of his contemporaries he had not been forced to become a living anachronism. The sincerity of his words and deeds had been challenged by events, and like the Elizabethan he was he had bent and yet held fast at the roots. But the new winds which were blowing in 1652 soon combined to produce a powerful storm which defied fixity and stripped of verdure all who chose to remain rather than move with it. The gathering storm which was not strong enough to affect the roots of John Cotton's life has long since affected his philosophy. An America in search of a past has gone to Roger Williams as a true parent and has remembered John Cotton chiefly as a monolithic foe of enlightenment. Such memories of John Cotton, phrased as they are in the rhetoric of progress and the secular state, are suitable only in a world which refuses to relinquish the perfectibility of man.

It is clear, however, that John Cotton perceived another world, no less real for all the debates which can be held as to whether it ever did exist or should have existed. His reality was based upon his experience of the presence of the Deity within him and his perception that the power which had discovered itself within his soul could and would discover itself in man's institutions. This led him to accept the organic nature of history, to strive for the embodiment of the theocratic ideal, and to encourage the suppression of those who would murder a man's chance to share in the divine experience. No judgment of the validity or invalidity, goodness or badness, truth or error of any one of Cotton's tenets, however well supported, affects the reality itself and how he acted once he had located himself in terms of it.

The same license which students of American culture use

[258]

in applying the term "American Renaissance" to the period of Hawthorne and Emerson can be invoked in terming that of John Cotton to be American Medieval. The pattern of this American medievalism has been effectively shattered and while any piece would have been of little value to John Cotton without the others, for the value of the whole was its symmetry, nevertheless, modern America is affected by the fragments of its medieval period. What Cotton Mather failed to puzzle together we no longer wish to unite, and we experience the simultaneous existence of a yearning for the socially scientific state and a vaguer but persistent dedication to the theocratic ideal, to a commonwealth in which the laws of God and the laws of man are to be one. In conjunction with the literary impulse operates an ambiguous distrust of the creative product merely for the sake of the experience it contains or the beauty it achieves. The Saviour is not expected tomorrow and yet we shall live to see one or another millennium; we shall have our rendezvous with destiny. The future science holds out is extended to us in the terminology of the promised land as if our present existence were a wandering in a wilderness.

The pattern John Cotton pieced together on the shores of Massachusetts Bay and into which he placed elements of the England of Elizabeth as well as those of the Israel of Moses never had a physical embodiment, a concrete life, and, for that reason if for no other, has never had a death. Although the pattern is no longer whole, its fragments are strewn throughout the course which the American people run.

⟨ BIBLIOGRAPHICAL NOTE ⟩

I

THERE is ample evidence that the majority of John Cotton's works reached the press within a year of their composition although during the most productive years of his literary life he was thousands of miles from a printing press. This evidence exists in the form of explicit mention of the date of composition by the writer of the preface, subject matter in pointed response to known polemical writings, and dated references in the body of the work.

The New England clergy had many friends in England who were happy to see their works through the press, and a proof sheet rarely made the trip across the Atlantic to its author and back again to the press before the work was published. Indeed, to this fact we may attribute the remark frequently made in second printings of Cotton's works, "more exactly corrected." The various printings of all of the known works of John Cotton are expertly described in Julius H. Tuttle's "Writings of Rev. John Cotton," *Bibliographical Essays: A Tribute to Wilberforce Eames* (Cambridge, 1924), pp. 363-380; among other things, these printings testify that the first edition was often Cotton's proof sheet.

There is good reason to believe, however, that the dates of the first editions of some of Cotton's works do not reflect the dates of their composition. The reason for the lag between composition and publication differs from work to work, but tends to belong to one of the following categories: (1) the work was a compilation of sermons set aside in favor of polemical writing and then, in a tranquil period, polished for the press; (2) the work was a compilation of sermons recorded in shorthand by an auditor and then, at the copyer's discretion, sent to the press with or without the preacher's consent; (3) the work was intended for "private edification" but was made public without Cotton's consent, most often, of course, posthumously.

Since the chief sources of this work are Cotton's writings, and since I assume that certain of Cotton's works were composed in a period other than that immediately preceding their publication and reconstruct parts of his career on these assumptions, I here give, in brief, some indication of how I arrived at the dating of such works. I shall discuss the works in question in the order of what I take to be their period of composition although with the first group, works composed in England, I do not argue that the order within the group is chronological, such precision being beyond my reach. I include also a chronology of the composition of the works in the Roger Williams-John Cotton controversies. Finally, on this point of dating the composition of John Cotton's works, I must claim some validity for my general judgment, based on my working with these writings over a period of years.

I. *A Brief Exposition* . . . *upon the Whole Book of Ecclesiastes,* 1654.

The assumed date of composition of this work is Cotton's English ministry, i.e., between 1612 and 1632.

The positive evidence for this assumption consists only of Norton's statement in his *Memoir of Cotton,* pp. 37-38, that during his English ministry, Cotton, on Sundays, "preached over . . . the whole book of Ecclesiastes." Since Cotton would have needed the equivalent of his *Brief Exposition* as a basis for these sermons, and since there is nothing in the *Brief Exposition* to indicate its composition after 1633, it is a reasonable assumption that it was composed prior to 1633. It must be remembered that this exposition contains "uses" which admit of being highly temporal so that the argument from the absence of specific American allusions is stronger than the usual argument from omission.

II. *A Brief Exposition of the Whole Book of Canticles,* 1642.

The assumed date of composition of this work is Cotton's English ministry, i.e., between 1612 and 1632.

The argument for this assumption is the same as that which has been offered for the exposition of Ecclesiastes. Norton says, p. 38, that Cotton, in England, on his lecture days "preached through . . . the whole book of *Solomons Song.*"

III. *Christ the Fountaine of Life,* 1651.

The assumed date of composition of this work is Cotton's English ministry, i.e., between 1612 and 1632.

These are sermons on I John 5: 12-17, and Norton says, p. 38, that Cotton on his lecture days in England "preached through the whole first and second Epistle of *John.*" The argument here and in connection with Canticles is perhaps stronger than that in connection with Ecclesiastes since Norton's remark is about sermons and still there is no internal evidence of an American audience.

IV. *Some Treasure Fetched Out of Rubbish,* 1660.

The assumed date of composition of this work is Cotton's English ministry, i.e., between 1612 and 1632.

The preface tells us that "these ensuing Treatises were found laid by the Walls, and covered with dust, in the study of an old Non-Conformist [in England]." They are published at this time, the year of the restoration of monarchy, "for the preventing of the imposition and practice of sapless superstitious Ceremonies." The quoted treatise is one debating the right of church governors to command "indifferent decent things." This issue was of paramount importance for Cotton when he served in an episcopal system, and such a consideration, coupled with the fact that the work was discovered in England after his death, constitutes the evidence for its composition prior to 1633.

V. *A Treatise I. of Faith. II. Twelve Fundamental Articles of Christian Religion. III. A Doctrinal Conclusion. IV. Questions and Answers upon Church-government,* 1713.

The assumption is that the twelve articles were an explicit part of Cotton's teaching as early as 1635.

Although the circumstances of the publishing of these papers in 1713 are not known, the possibility that they were located and published together because they were written in the same period exists. This means that the remarks on the chapter heading of the questions and answers, "Begun 25 11m. 1634," may be significant for the twelve articles also if other evidence corroborates or does not contradict such a contention.

Thomas Lechford in his *Plaine Dealing* (1642) wrote, "There was a sermon lately made by Master *Cotton* in *October, Anno* 1640. upon 1 *Cor.* 11. 19, ... called the sermon of the twelve articles of Religion." He then went on to enumerate these articles; they are the same as those of Cotton's treatise. This, then, establishes 1640 as the latest possible date for the formulation of the articles.

In establishing the earliest possible date I contend that the twelve articles provide the basis for defining Cotton's position as opposed to that of his fellow ministers. Since his difference was known publicly by 1636 I believe these articles may be legitimately used to amplify and explicate material stemming from that period. They contain the seed of the Antinomian dispute and, in the face of the conference to which Cotton was called and the known questions and answers which ensued, it is difficult to assert that they were not formulated until after the controversy. The sermon Lechford cites was, of course, preached after the controversy and since we find him thus far from his colleagues at the date, I believe it more reasonable to assume that, if anything, his twelve articles were more rather than less radical in 1634 and legitimately serve the exposition to which I have put them. I think it safe, therefore, to conjecture that the date of 1634 assigned to the questions and answers also applies to the articles.

VI. *A Treatise of the Covenant of Grace*, 1659.

The assumption is that this work is illustrative of Cotton's teachings in 1636.

This is the third title under which this work appeared. It was corrected successively at each appearance. In 1654 it appeared as *The New Covenant* and in 1655 it appeared as part of *The Covenant of Grace* (to be distinguished from *The Covenant of Gods Free Grace*, 1645). *The New Covenant* is described on the title-page as "being the substance of sundry sermons preached by Mr. Cotton ... some years since." As to how long since, the answer would seem to be not long before or after the Antinomian controversy. Cotton shows himself to be wary of Antinomianism in these sermons with such remarks as, "If any therefore shall accuse the Doctrine of the Covenant of free Grace as Antinomianism. . . ." I therefore use the sermons as being illustrative of Cotton's teachings prior to the controversy since the point being made is that of the peculiarity of Cotton's doctrine; if the sermons, indeed, were preached after the controversy, with all their evidence of Cotton's peculiarity even after that uniformity-enforcing event, they strengthen rather than weaken the use to which I put them.

VII. *Sixteene Questions of Seriovs and Necessary Consequences Propounded unto Mr John Cotton . . . together with his Answers*, 1644.

The assumed date of composition of this work is 1636.

Winthrop says in the 10 December 1636 entry in his *Journal*: "The ministers had met, a little before, and had drawn into heads all the points, wherein they suspected Mr. Cotton did differ from them, and had propounded to him, and pressed him to a direct answer, affirmative or negative, to every one; which he had promised and taken time for."

The heading of the first page of the *Sixteene Questions* tells us they were "propounded by sundry of the teaching elders in the Bay." There can be no doubt that these are the points referred to by Winthrop when their contents are compared with the issues at stake in 1636.

VIII. *The True Constitution of a Particular Visible Church Proved by Scripture*, 1642.

The assumed date of composition of this work is 1634-1635.

The contents of this work are practically identical with the questions and answers which made up part four of *A Treatise I. of Faith*. As noted in the discussion of that publication, they bear the note "Begun 25 11m. 1634."

IX. *An Exposition upon the Thirteenth Chapter of the Revelation*, 1655.

The assumed date of composition of these sermons is 1639-1640.

Thomas Allen says in the prefatory remarks to the reader: "I do here declare and testifie unto the world that . . . these Sermons . . . were published by . . . Mr. John Cotton, about the 11. and 12. monaths (if I mistake not) of the year, 1639, and the first and second of the yeare 1640, upon his weekly Lecture at Boston."

X. The Roger Williams-John Cotton Controversies

1. About 1634 Cotton composed a reply to a treatise arguing the question of toleration of all religious opinions in the state.

In chapter one of *The Bloudy Tenent Washed and Made White in the Bloud of the Lambe* (1647), Cotton says, "Mr. *Williams* sent me about a dozen years ago (as I remember) a letter, penned (as he wrote) by a Prisoner in *Newgate*, touching persecution for Conscience sake: and entreated my judgment of it for the satisfaction of his friend." Williams, in his *The Bloody Tenent Yet More Bloody* (1652), denied that he was the sender of the prisoner's treatise and claimed, "One Master Hall of Roxbury, presented the prisoners Arguments against persecution to Master Cotton, who gave this present controverted Answer." Subsequent scholarship (e.g., Samuel Caldwell in Volume Three of *Publications of the Narragansett Club*) upholds Williams in his claim that he was not the sender. At any rate, this treatise and Cotton's answer first appear in print as the first and second parts of *The Bloudy Tenent of Persecution* (1644) by Roger Williams.

2. A letter was sent from Cotton to Williams on the subject of the latter's banishment shortly after it occurred in 1635.

This letter first appeared in print as *A Letter of Mr. John Cottons . . . to Mr. Williams* (1643). In his *The Bloudy Tenent Washed,* Cotton admitted his authorship but claimed the printing was unauthorized.

3. Williams, in 1643, composed an answer to Cotton's letter after it had appeared in print.

This was published as *Mr. Cottons Letter . . . Examined and Answered* (1644), and in it Williams stated that although he was not responsible for the publication of the Cotton letter in the previous year, he was taking the occasion of its publication to make a public reply.

4. During 1643-1644 Williams finished an answer to Cotton's reply to the prisoner's treatise.

This was published as *The Bloudy Tenent of Persecution* (1644), and included, as has been noted, the first publication of the prisoner's treatise and Cotton's reply to it. In 1646, the prisoner's treatise and Cotton's reply appeared again, minus Williams's attack on Cotton's position, as *The Controversie Concerning Liberty of Conscience in Matters of Religion* by John Cotton.

5. During 1645-1646 Cotton composed an answer to Williams's examination of the letter Cotton sent to Williams after the latter's banishment.

This was published as *A Reply to Mr. Williams His Examination* and was bound with *The Bloudy Tenent Washed* (1647), but is separate from it in content and in pagination.

6. During 1645-1646 Cotton composed an answer to Williams's criticism of his answer to the prisoner's treatise.

This appeared as *The Bloudy Tenent Washed and Made White in the Bloud of the Lambe* (1647).

7. Between 1648 and 1652 Williams composed a reply to Cotton's *The Bloudy Tenent Washed.*

This appeared as *The Bloody Tenent Yet More Bloody* (1652).

Roger Williams and John Cotton, then, carried on two overlapping but, nevertheless, distinct debates: one on liberty of conscience and another on the particular reasons for Williams's banishment from Massachusetts Bay. The two have often been confused with consequent damage to a right understanding of the arguments of the participants and the underlying issues at stake.

II

John Cotton is the subject of four unpublished dissertations which I have consulted, one for the degree of M.A., the other three for the Ph.D. The master's dissertation is "John Cotton: Covenant Theologian" by Wayne H. Christy (Duke University, 1952). The doctoral dissertations are Donald R. Come, "John Cotton, Guide of the Chosen People" (Princeton University, 1949), Judith B. Welles, "John Cotton, 1584-1652, Churchman and Theologian" (University of Edinburgh, 1948), and Harry A. Poole, "The Unsettled Mr. Cotton" (University of Illinois, 1956). Miss Welles's dissertation was of especial value to me because of her intelligent use of the English sources for a reconstruction of Cotton's career.

In spite of the recent important work on the intellectual trends and the Cambridge of Cotton's day, I have drawn more directly on earlier studies such as those of Mullinger, Fuller, Heywood and Wright, and Masson, cited in the notes to Chapter One, because my particular concern was the theological-political milieu in which Cotton found himself and recent scholarship is of a more specialized nature. For example, with regard to the important point of Cotton's contact with such influential Cambridge figures as William Perkins and Laurence Chaderton, Mark H. Curtis says, "Little can be added to Mullinger's account of their combined influence over academic generation after academic generation."[1]

In addition to the works which I cite in the notes, the most influential primary works which have contributed to the study of Cotton's English career are the published sermons, tracts, and treatises of members of all shades of religious opinion in his day. When one compares the teachings of a William Perkins with those of a Richard Sibbes within the Puritan movement, or those of a John Preston with a Robert Sanderson within the broader confines of the Church of England, he is, finally, feeling the very pulse of the times.

For a secondary study of the Puritans in England the work of William Haller, both as editor, *Tracts on Liberty in the Puritan Revolution, 1638-1647* (New York, 1934), *The Leveller Tracts, 1647-1656* (New York, 1944, with Godfrey Davies), and as author, *The Rise of Puritanism* (New York, 1938), and *Liberty and Reformation in the Puritan Revolution* (New York, 1955), is invaluable. In this category also are M. M. Knappen, *Tudor Puritanism* (Chicago, 1935), a work which causes one to deplore the absence of complementary volumes on the Stuart and American phases of the Puritan movement executed with the same simple precision, and A. S. P. Woodhouse, "Introduction" to *Puritanism and Liberty* (Chicago, 1951). A crucial phase in the history of Puritanism is examined in Raymond P. Stearns, *Congregationalism in the Dutch Netherlands* (Chicago, 1940), a work

[1] *Oxford and Cambridge in Transition* (Oxford, 1959), p. 204.

[269]

which has served as the basis for identifying the American Puritans as laboratory workers with a blueprint before them although its material by no means points that way unambiguously; as Professor Stearns shows, Hugh Peter, considered a conservative influence in Salem, was a radical in Rotterdam, and Thomas Hooker in Holland professed abhorrence of ideas which were already in practice in New England.

For Cotton's American career, the most valuable sources, other than those cited in the chapter notes, are the manuscripts in the Prince Collection of the Boston Public Library and those in the possession of the Massachusetts Historical Society. The publications of the historical clubs were invaluable to me, especially those of the Massachusetts Historical Society, the Colonial Society of Massachusetts, the Prince Society, and the Narragansett Club. As with Cotton's English career so with his American: the very pulse of the times is best appreciated in the works of his contemporaries, an excellent representative list of which appears in the bibliography of Perry Miller and Thomas H. Johnson (eds.), *The Puritans* (New York, 1938).

Our knowledge of the period has unquestionably been improved with the emergence of historians who dared to be critical of the orthodoxy, e.g., C. F. Adams, James T. Adams, and Vernon Parrington, but a serious student of the period must rely on the documentation of Herbert L. Osgood, C. M. Andrews, and the "clerical" historians of the nineteenth century, especially John G. Palfrey, Williston Walker, Joseph Felt, and Henry M. Dexter.

The greatest modern contribution to an understanding of American Puritanism is pre-eminently that of Perry Miller: *Orthodoxy in Massachusetts* (Cambridge, 1933); *The New England Mind: The Seventeenth Century* (New York, 1939); *The New England Mind: From Colony to Province* (Cambridge, 1953), *Roger Williams* (New York, 1953); and *Errand Into the Wilderness* (Cambridge, 1956). Since my findings within the relatively narrow bounds of a study of

John Cotton tend to contradict several of Professor Miller's contentions, I must emphasize my over-all indebtedness to his masterful reconstruction of the intellectual content of Puritanism.

The works of Samuel Eliot Morison, especially *Builders of the Bay Colony* (Boston, 1930), *The Puritan Pronaos* (New York, 1936), and *The Founding of Harvard College* (Cambridge, 1935), have been of great interest to me in connection with this study, as well as that of Kenneth B. Murdock, *Literature and Theology in Colonial New England* (Cambridge, 1949). In my opinion, Professor Murdock's challenge to students to present the influence of Puritanism on American literature has thus far gone without a substantial answer, and I must close this note with an admission that although I regard Chapter Five of this book as a contribution toward that goal, for the most part the task remains to be done.

INDEX

man, 154-55; writings as literature, 157-65; view of special providence, 166-69; eschatology, 171-73; reaction to Puritan Rebellion, 173-79; answers to English queries on New England practices, 184-89; *The Keyes of the Kingdom of Heaven*, 191-96; attacked for writing and conduct, 197-98, 201; and separatism, 199; defense of his writings, 202; attacked by Roger Williams, 212-17; answer to Williams, 217-22; and Congregationalism, 225-28; attitude toward Anabaptism, 231-32; and biblical interpretation, 233-34; theory of Christian history, 234-37; attitude toward civil matters, 238-40; rebuked by Saltonstall, 241-42; debate with Presbyterians, 244-47; view of psalmsinging, 247-49; belief in preaching of the word, 251-52; final illness, 254; version of his life, 255-56

Publications: *The Bloudy Tenent, Washed and Made White in the Bloud of the Lambe*, 217-18, 221-22, 238; *A Brief Exposition of the Whole Book of Canticles*, 48, 83; *A Briefe Exposition with Practicall Observations upon the Whole Book of Ecclesiastes*, 13, 14, 151, 163, 175; *Christ the Fountaine of Life*, 80, 108, 110; *The Churches Resurrection*, 151, 153, 174, 177; *A Coppy of a Letter of Mr. Cotton of Boston*, 185, 187; *A Defence of Mr. John Cotton from the Imputation of Selfe Contradiction Charged on Him by Mr. Dan: Cavvdrey*, 251; *Discourse about Civil Government in a New Plantation Whose Design Is Religion*, 97-98; *An Exposition upon the Thirteenth Chapter of the Revelation*, 174, 175, 176-

77; *God's Promise to His Plantation*, 60-62; *The Grounds and Ends of the Baptisme of the Children of the Faithful*, 221, 233-37; *The Keyes of the Kingdom of Heaven*, 191, 192-96, 199; *A Letter of Mr. John Cottons to Mr. Williams*, 92; *A Modest and Cleare Answer to Mr. Balls Discourse of Set Formes of Prayer*, 186, 248; *Moses His Judicials*, 104-105; *The New Covenant*, 109-10; *Of the Holinesse of Church-members*, 82, 244-46; *The Powring Out of the Seven Vialls*, 158, 163-64; 172-73; 178; 204, 205; *A Practical Commentary or an Exposition . . . upon the First Epistle Generall of John*, 157, 161, 162, 247; *A Sermon Preached by the Reverend Mr. John Cotton Deliver'd at Salem, 1636*, 96, 97; *Singing of Psalmes A Gospel-Ordinance*, 248-49; *Sixteene Questions of Seriovs and Necessary Consequences Propounded unto Mr. John Cotton together with His Answers*, 119-20; *Some Treasure Fetched Out of Rubbish*, 48, 49; *Spiritual Milk for Boston Babes in Either England*, 183n; *A Treatise of the Covenant of Grace*, 111; *The True Constitution of A Particular Visible Church Proved by Scripture*, 185, 187; *The Way of Congregational Churches Cleared*, 47, 49, 53, 116-17, 127, 130, 132, 134, 146, 199, 200; *The Way of Life*, 151, 152, 154-55, 157; *The Way of the Churches of Christ in New-england*, 191

Cotton, John (son), 169, 253
Cotton, Mariah (daughter), 169
Cotton, Mary (sister), 4
Cotton, Roland (father), 4, 22; (brother), 4